THE MOSCOW
CORRESPONDENTS

THE MOSCOW CORRESPONDENTS

Reporting on Russia from
the Revolution to Glasnost

Whitman Bassow

William Morrow and Company, Inc.   New York

Library of Congress Cataloging-in-Publication Data

Bassow, Whitman.
The Moscow correspondents: Reporting on Russia from the Revolution to
Glasnost/Whitman Bassow.
p.   cm.
ISBN 0–688–04392–5
1. Foreign news—United States.   2. Soviet Union—Foreign opinion,
American.   3. Foreign correspondents—United States—Biography.
4. Foreign correspondents—Soviet Union—Biography.   5. Moscow
(R.S.F.S.R.)—Intellectual life.   I. Title.
PN4888.F69B37   1988
070.4'33'0922—dc19
[B]

Printed in the United States of America

First Edition

1 2 3 4 5 6 7 8 9 10

BOOK DESIGN BY SUSAN HOOD

TO MY WIFE

Foreword

I was listening to Walter Cronkite reminisce about his years in Moscow as a United Press correspondent. He was one of the five correspondents and four former U.S. envoys to the Soviet Union who spoke at the Overseas Press Club's reunion of journalists who had reported from Russia over the past four decades. The dining room of the Seventh Regiment Armory in New York City was filled with Moscow "graduates" and brimming with nostalgia. The vodka flowed like vodka.

I remember the date well: January 14, 1983. The idea for the reunion was mine, and with pride of authorship went the privilege of serving as toastmaster. When the audience roared with laughter at another of Cronkite's stories, I turned to my wife and exclaimed, "This is history! Somebody should write about it. Otherwise it will be gone forever."

"Why don't you do it?" Mimi asked. My immediate and unthinking response: "Why not?"

This book is about the most exclusive club in American journalism. Since 1921, when the Russians opened their borders to U.S. news organizations, only some three hundred Americans were permitted to enter as resident correspondents. Yet, this minuscule group helped shape perceptions of the Soviet Union held by generations of Americans, from the man in the street to the man in the White House. In all those years, no one has scrutinized these reporters, how they lived, the changing conditions under which they labored, nor examined the frustrations, the pressures, the rivalries, the excitement of covering that special place, which Pulitzer Prize

winner Harrison E. Salisbury has called the "cruelest assignment." Nor has anyone set that assignment within the framework of Soviet history and the relationship between the
reporters and the society about which they were writing. This
is what I have sought to do and, at the same time, to tell the
story about a small band of dedicated professionals trying to
do their job under the most difficult and challenging conditions.

Without knowing it, I had been preparing to write this book
ever since I received a doctorate in Russian history from the
Sorbonne. My dissertation was on a subject dear to the hearts
of the Soviets, a history of the pre-Revolutionary *Pravda* to
which V. I. Lenin, founder of the world's first Communist
state, was a frequent contributor. My preparation was advanced by three years as a United Press correspondent in
Moscow, then two years as *Newsweek*'s first bureau chief until,
in 1962, the Soviets expelled me for violating unspecified
regulations. My career in Moscow had ended abruptly, but my
interest in Russia and the Russians has never flagged. One
result is now in your hands.

This book is intended for the general reader, and I beg
forgiveness from the specialists who seek footnotes and doc-
umentation. They are available on request, and there is a
bibliography. The principal sources for the book are the
former correspondents who agreed to be interviewed, all on
the record except for one. From over thirty-five hundred
pages of transcriptions, I have culled the best material and the
most relevant. The earlier chapters dealing with the period
prior to World War II are based to a large extent on already
published materials. The thread that pulls everything together
is my five years as a reporter covering some of the most
momentous Soviet developments of the postwar years.

To simplify the customary problems with Russian names
and transliterations, I have used "Russia" and the Soviet
Union interchangeably, although Russia (or the Russian Republic) is only one of the fifteen Soviet republics, albeit the
largest and most populous. For the same reason, I have not
adopted the transliteration system of the Library of Congress

but have freely used names already well known in English, although they do not conform to the system. For example, *Izvestiya,* the government newspaper, remains *Izvestia.*

I alone bear responsibility for the facts and the judgments presented here, not only to my colleagues but to my Russian friends who also are part of this book.

Acknowledgments

This book was made possible by 76 colleagues who generously shared their experience and insights as correspondents in Moscow. They provided the material that brings my four-year effort to life:

Erik Amfiteatrov (*Time*), Raymond Anderson (*The New York Times*), Anthony Astrakhan (*Washington Post*), Frank Bourgholtzer (NBC), Louise Branson (UPI), Henry Cassidy (AP), John Chancellor (NBC), Mathis Chazanov (AP), Fred Coleman (UPI, *Newsweek*), Ernest Conine (McGraw-Hill), Walter Cronkite (UP), Robert B. Cullen (*Newsweek*), B. J. Cutler (*New York Herald Tribune*), Clifton Daniel (*The New York Times*), Nicholas Daniloff (UPI, *U.S. News & World Report*), Dusko Doder (*Washington Post*), Harry Dunphy (AP), Reinhold G. Ensz (AP), Roxinne Ervasti (AP), Farnsworth Fowle (CBS), Alfred Friendly, Jr. (*Newsweek*), Murray Fromson (CBS), James P. Gallegher (*Chicago Tribune*), Ann L. Garrels (ABC), Robert Gibson (McGraw-Hill), Peter Grose (*The New York Times*), Richard H. Growald (UPI), James O. Jackson (UPI, *Chicago Tribune*), Sam Jaffe (ABC), Robert G. Kaiser (*Washington Post*), Marvin Kalb (CBS), Robin Kinkead (*The New York Times*), Charles Klensch (INS), Robert J. Korengold (UPI, *Newsweek*), Axel Krause (McGraw-Hill), George A. Krimsky (AP), Tom Lambert (*New York Herald Tribune*), Larry Lesueur (CBS), Irving R. Levine (NBC), Stuart Loory (*New York Herald Tribune*, Cable News Network), Joseph Michaels (NBC), Drew Middleton (*The New York Times*), Aline Mosby (UPI), Seth Mydans (AP, *The New York Times*), Andrew Nagorski (*Newsweek*), Angelo Natale (AP), Joseph Newman (*New*

York Herald Tribune), Christopher Ogden (UPI), Peter Osnos (*Washington Post*), Stewart W. Ramsey (McGraw-Hill), Jack Raymond (*The New York Times*), Jack Redden (UPI), Bernard S. Redmont (CBS), Charlotte Saikowski (*The Christian Science Monitor*), Harrison E. Salisbury (UP, *The New York Times*), Serge Schmemann (UPI, *The New York Times*), Daniel Schorr (CBS), George Seldes (*Chicago Tribune*), Theodore Shabad (*The New York Times*), Henry Shapiro (UPI), Alison Smale (AP), Hedrick Smith (*The New York Times*), Howard Sochurek (*Life*), Edmund Stevens (*The Christian Science Monitor, Time*), William H. Stoneman (*Chicago Daily News*), Emil Sveilis (UPI), Seymour Topping (*The New York Times*), Robert Toth (*Los Angeles Times*), Harry J. Trimborn (*Los Angeles Times*), Howard Tyner (UPI, *Chicago Tribune*), George Vicas (NBC), George Watson (ABC), Craig R. Whitney (*The New York Times*), Thomas Whitney (AP), Carol Williams (AP), and James Yuenger (*Chicago Tribune*). (The news organization refers to the reporter's affiliation during the Moscow assignment.)

Dr. Lawrence F. Silverman, professor of history at the University of Colorado, Boulder, read the manuscript and offered comments with erudition and humor.

To three mentors who, at critical points in my professional career, advanced me toward my journalistic goal—the Moscow post—and consequently this book, I express my gratitude. They are deceased, but for the record, I want to convey my profound appreciation to Dr. Philip E. Moseley, my political science professor at Columbia University's Russian Institute; Professor Pierre Pascal of the University of Paris, who helped me uncover the world of Russian history and culture and who supervised my doctoral dissertation; and Earl J. Johnson, vice president of the United Press, who had the imagination and courage to hire a neophyte for the Moscow assignment.

Every writer needs a quiet place to work. Raymond Vulliez, my dear friend since Paris student days, generously provided an oasis of tranquillity in his New York town house, where a good part of this book was written.

I am indebted to my colleagues at the World Environment Center who patiently endured the diversion of my time and energy from my real work: protecting and enhancing environmental quality worldwide.

I am grateful to the New York Public Library for use of the Frederick Allen Room, where some of my initial research was conducted. To the staff of the Guilford Free Library, my thanks for assistance in obtaining hard-to-find books and references.

Sibby Christiansen of the AP and Howard Tyner of the *Chicago Tribune* provided rare photos that put faces with the names. Howard Sochurek took the jacket photo, for which I thank him.

To my wife, I owe so much that I cannot begin to describe the moral and intellectual support she provided during the long gestation period of this opus.

And for Harvey Ginsberg, my editor, who provided rigorous on-the-job training for the author of a first book: *Bolshoe spasibo!* Many thanks!

—W.B.
Guilford, CT
June 1987

Contents

1

John Reed: Reporting a Revolution

No matter what one thinks of Bolshevism, it is undeniable that the Russian Revolution is one of the great events of human history, and the rise of the Bolsheviki a phenomenon of world-wide importance. Just as the historians search the records for the minutest details of the story of the Paris Commune, so they will want to know what happened in Petrograd in November, 1917, the spirit which animated the people, and how the leaders looked, talked and acted. It is with this in view that I have written this book.

In the struggle my sympathies were not neutral. But in telling the story of those great days I have tried to see events with the eye of a conscientious reporter, interested in setting down the truth.

John Reed
Ten Days That Shook the World
1919

"Welcome to Leningrad!" exclaimed Alexander Osipov. "Welcome to the successor to John Reed!"

The correspondent of the Soviet news agency TASS offered his hand to Emil Sveilis, just arrived in Leningrad to open a United Press International bureau, the first American reporter in the USSR ever to be based outside Moscow. The UPI hailed the event as a breakthrough in providing its thousands of newspaper, radio, and TV clients around the world with exclusive news and features. For the Russians, the arrival of thirty-three-year-old Sveilis in 1976 provided an opportunity to recall his predecessor from Portland, Oregon, the legendary reporter John Reed, whose brilliant eyewitness account of the Bolshevik Revolution endeared him to the leaders of the new Communist state and enshrined him in the pantheon of Soviet idols. The American earned his special niche, for if in the

history of international reporting there was one instance when
the cliché about the right man in the right place at the right
time could go unchallenged, the time was November 1917; the
place was Petrograd, capital of the former Russian empire;
and the man was John Reed, Harvard '10, revolutionary
romantic and classmate of Walter Lippmann and T. S. Eliot.

Russia in 1917 was in turmoil. The three-hundred-year-old
House of Romanov had collapsed with the abdication of Tsar
Nicholas II in March. (All dates in this chapter are stated in
the modern Gregorian calendar instead of the Julian
calendar still used in 1917, which was thirteen days behind.)
Russian armies were fighting and losing a bloody and
demoralizing war against Germany. Soldiers were deserting
their units by the hundreds of thousands. Hunger ravaged
the countryside and food was short in the cities. Peasants
demanded the breakup of the large estates and immediate
redistribution of the land. This chaos was presided over by a
weak and divided Provisional Government awaiting with
trepidation the convocation of a Constituent Assembly, an
elected body that would determine the future of the country.
Elections were scheduled for the end of November, but in
Petrograd, a bewildering array of parties and factions were
already sniping at the government from the left. They bore
such cryptic names as Right Socialist Revolutionaries; Left
Socialist Revolutionaries; Popular Socialists; and the Russian
Social Democratic Labor Party and its two wings, the
Mensheviks and the Bolsheviks. The country was a bomb
with a short fuse already sputtering.

Into this scene walked thirty-year-old John Reed, notebook
in hand, ready to cover one of the most significant events of
modern times: the birth of the world's first Communist state.
He knew no Russian. He knew little of the struggles that had
led to the March Revolution and even less of its leaders and
the political parties vying for power, but he had superb
reporting tools: a quick and inquisitive mind, sharp eyes, good
ears, boundless energy, and strong legs. Out of Reed's encounter with revolution came a masterpiece of reporting, *Ten
Days That Shook the World*, the most vivid description we have of

the events that led to the Bolshevik seizure of power and the men who shaped them.

Published in 1919 in New York, *Ten Days* was an instant success. Not only was it the first comprehensive eyewitness account of what occurred, but also the ultimate inside story, a coup unique in the history of journalism. No other reporter before or since has had the opportunity to cover an event of such magnitude from such a privileged position, unless it was William L. Laurence, science editor of *The New York Times*, who was requested by the U.S. government in May 1945 to become the official, and only, chronicler of the secret development of the atom bomb. There was one difference, however: William Laurence was invited; John Reed elbowed his way into the story. He vividly portrayed the sights and sounds of revolution: the tramp of boots as Red Guards marched off to battle the forces of the Provisional Government, the crack of rifles echoing across the vast squares of the former imperial capital, the endless meetings and angry debates in the Petrograd Soviet, a council of workers' and soldiers' deputies elected from all parts of Russia. Reed was able to tie the human beings to the events so that a coherent picture emerged. He brought to life the main actors in the drama: Vladimir Ilyich Lenin, the cool, ruthless strategist of the Bolshevik victory; one of his closest collaborators, Leon Trotsky, the charismatic orator who dreamed of a world Communist revolution; and the loser, Premier Alexander Kerensky, who fled Petrograd by a car to join his troops at the front, never to return.

Within seven months of publication, the book went into four printings. One reason for its astonishing success was that during those fateful ten days, neither John Reed nor any of the other correspondents on the scene could transmit detailed reports on what had occurred. Bolshevik Red Guards were trying to capture the Central Telephone Exchange and its telegraph facilities. When the building was finally taken, the clerks refused to work with the censors appointed by the Petrograd Soviet, making transmission of the correspondents' dispatches impossible. Not until November 15 did the new

Bolshevik censor permit Reed to telegraph his story to the New York *Call*, the Socialist weekly to which he was accredited. A week later, the full report finally appeared in print, but only to the limited audience of the *Call*.

For a decade, *Ten Days* was obligatory reading for American correspondents sent to Moscow as the best introduction then available to the new Soviet Russia, its politics and leaders. If the book is now read mainly by students of Russian history and in schools of journalism, in its time *Ten Days* was a powerful and positive influence on the thinking of many Americans about the Russian Revolution and the "Soviet experiment." When it was published in Moscow at the end of 1923, Lenin's wife, Nadezhda Krupskaya, did the translation and he himself wrote an introduction to the 1922 edition published in New York, praising its "truthful and most vivid exposition of the events so significant to the comprehension of what really is the Proletarian Revolution and the Dictatorship of the Proletariat." Yet for almost thirty years after Lenin's death in 1924, *Ten Days* was banned by Joseph Stalin because it factually reported the leading role played by his archrival Leon Trotsky. The book reappeared in Moscow's stores after Stalin's death in 1953, snatched up by new generations of Russians who had heard about *Ten Days* but had never been permitted to read it.

John Reed was born in Portland, Oregon, on October 22, 1887. His father, Charles J. Reed, was a United States marshal and a Republican progressive in the style of Theodore Roosevelt. At nineteen, young Reed went off to Harvard, where he studied under Professor Charles Townsend Copeland, the most prominent teacher of writing at the college. A student with broad interests and talents, Reed wrote for the *Lampoon*, the humor magazine, helped edit the *Literary Monthly* with his brilliant Socialist friend and classmate Walter Lippmann, and also found time to captain the water polo team, sing in the glee club, and write lyrics for the Hasty Pudding show. After he received his degree in 1910, Reed traveled in Europe, then returned to New York to write for *American Magazine*, a muckraking, mass-circulation publication. He lived in Greenwich Village, mixing with avant-garde writers, poets, and artists who were to have a profound influence on his intellectual and professional development. Among them were Socialist writer Max Eastman; sculptor Jo Davidson; poet Edward Arlington Robinson; and Margaret Sanger, founder of the family planning movement. When *Masses,* a radical New York magazine, was founded in 1911, John Reed joined the staff. As a reporter, he wrote articles on social problems, including a brilliant and moving account of the strike of twenty thousand textile workers in Paterson, New Jersey, one of the largest walkouts in U.S. history. Stirred by the defiance and anger he saw on the picket lines, he wrote and staged a pageant about the strike in Madison Square Garden.

John Reed's emotional involvement with the workers and his natural sympathy for the underdog strengthened his interest in radical movements. He began to believe that only fundamental changes could bring social equality and a better life for American workers, goals to be achieved, if need be, through revolution. That idea was further reinforced when *Metropolitan Magazine* sent him to Mexico in late 1913 to report on Pancho Villa's desperate peasant rebellion against dictator Victoriano Huerta. After tracking Villa down in the mountains of Chihuahua, Reed joined the rebels and fought alongside them. His vivid, detailed reporting, replete with dialogue, read like fiction. As the articles appeared in the magazine, Walter Lippmann, already recognized as a thinker of originality and force, wrote Reed:

> It's kind of embarrassing to tell a fellow you know he's a genius. I can't begin to tell you how good the articles are. . . . If all history had been reported as you are doing this, Lord—I say that with Jack Reed reporting begins.

In 1914, after his return from Mexico, John Reed's reputation as a journalist was further enhanced by his report in *Metropolitan Magazine* about a miners' strike against the Rockefeller-owned Colorado Fuel and Iron Company. The strike became known as the "Ludlow Massacre" when state militia and company thugs set fire to a tent city housing strikers, their wives, and their children, resulting in twenty-five deaths. The hardships endured by the strikers, the callousness of the company, and the brutality of the soldiers pushed Reed further toward Socialist thinking.

When war began in Europe in August 1914, *Metropolitan* sent John Reed to the Western Front and then on to the Eastern Front, where the armies of the tsar were said to be suffering immense losses. Traveling with Boardman Robinson, a noted illustrator and distinguished artist, Reed crossed the Balkans into Russia and was able to reach Petrograd. Because of his Socialist views, he received a cold official reception and was barred from the front. Reed and Robinson immediately returned to New York. The brief stay in Russia, however, aroused Reed's curiosity about the huge country, with its many different nationalities, millions of land-hungry peasants freed from serfdom only fifty years earlier, its all-embracing church and all-powerful ruler. He sensed that the forces unleashed by the war against Germany were shaking the autocracy. For John Reed, the Socialist, the sweet smell of revolution was in the air.

In New York, Reed resumed his literary and journalistic activities, publishing poetry and helping establish the Provincetown Players, the company that first produced the plays of Eugene O'Neill. As Reed's articles became increasingly critical of the war in Europe and America's imminent involvement, the market for his work in the popular magazines shrank. By early 1917, John Reed was writing mainly for the radical press but had not broken entirely with his upper-class Harvard friends. They still remembered him as the tall, charming, quick-witted Jack who laughed at tradition—and got away with it. He even voted for Woodrow Wilson in 1916, probably confounding many of his Socialist comrades. At the same time, he flirted with the Industrial Workers of the World, the "Wobblies," an organization whose anticapitalist militancy and "one big union" ideology placed it at the extreme left of the American political spectrum. For the edification of his fellow alumni and perhaps to annoy them, at the end of his class report for 1917, Reed wrote: "Member: Harvard Club, IWW."

During a trip to Portland in 1916 to visit his family, John Reed met Louise Bryant, a dentist's wife who quickly became enamored of the handsome, glamorous man about whom she had heard so much, and decided to follow him to New York. She fit easily into the bohemian life of Greenwich Village and the intellectual and artistic circles frequented by Reed. Louise Bryant became his wife in November 1916. Four years later, she was his widow.

In March 1917, revolution engulfed Russia, and Tsar Nicholas the Second became Tsar Nicholas the Last. With his abdication, the most autocratic regime in Europe, if not the world, came to a dismal end. A loose alliance of leaders representing the educated classes, landowners, industrialists, conservatives, and advocates of a constitutional republic organized a Provisional Government. For John Reed, this was the Big Story, bigger than writing poetry or plays, bigger than Socialist politics, bigger even than the war. He decided that he must go to Russia—as he had felt he had to go to Mexico—to see for himself. Not until August was Reed able to raise money for the trip, contributed by supporters of *Masses*. Together with Bryant, he sailed to Stockholm and from there to Petrograd to cover the story, accredited to *Masses* and the Socialist weekly the New York *Call*. She held credentials from the Bell Syndicate, one of the largest American news agencies, and from *Metropolitan Magazine*. By mid-September, John Reed was on the scene, ready to watch the drama unfold.

How does a reporter cover a revolution in a strange country whose language he does not speak, whose leaders he does not know, whose customs and politics are unlike anything he has ever experienced?

John Reed solved the language problem by finding émigré radicals from the United States who spoke Russian and who offered to serve as interpreters for interviews and meetings. Through them he met the leaders of different political groups with whom he could converse in English, German, and French. His radical friends also tutored him in the complexities of Petrograd politics, explaining who was doing what to whom and why. Because he was accredited to Socialist publications, Reed was treated differently from the other foreign reporters. Regarded as a "comrade," he was given access to closed meetings of the Bolsheviks, who were plotting to oust the Provisional Government.

Reed kept a daily diary of the events he witnessed, taking detailed notes on his interviews and assiduously collecting every piece of printed matter he could lay his hands on, including official documents, posters, leaflets, and decrees that were the press releases of the Revolution. He even obtained the scribblings of A. I. Konovalov, a minister of the Provisional Government, arrested by Red Guards at a cabinet meeting in the tsar's Winter Palace.

Day in, day out, week after week, John Reed tirelessly tracked the action. Early in the morning, after sleeping in overcoats, he and Louise would leave their sparsely furnished unheated room and return late at night or the next day. Joining them as they plodded through the streets were Albert Rhys Williams, a Congregational minister from Boston with strong Socialist convictions, transformed into a reporter for the *New York Evening Post;* and Bessie Beattie, correspondent of the *San Francisco Bulletin.* Each day, Reed's notebooks grew in number, containing descriptions of everything from a meeting at the Putilov factory where forty thousand workers gathered to listen to the speeches of Social Democrats, Socialist Revolutionaries, and anarchists, to a national convention of Russian Orthodox priests, while including the details that brought a story to life: a red flag in the hand of Catherine the Great's statue that stood outside the Alexandrinski Theater; the old bureaucrats leaving their offices at five o'clock, still wearing the uniform prescribed by the Imperial Court; and Salvation Army posters announcing gospel meetings that bewildered and amused the Russians. Everything was grist for his reporting.

On November 5, Reed was taking notes in the crowded,

smoke-filled Great Hall at Smolny Institute, formerly a fashionable girls' school, where a thousand delegates to the Petrograd Soviet had been meeting day and night. He heard its chairman, Leon Trotsky, shout from the rostrum that the life of the Provisional Government was destined to end as it "awaits the broom of history." Two days later, Trotsky's prediction came true. At Vladimir Lenin's relentless urging, the Bolsheviks, through control of the Military Revolutionary Committee of the Petrograd Soviet, sent Red Guards into the streets to occupy railroad stations, bridges, the State Bank, and the Central Telephone Exchange, encountering little resistance from troops loyal to the government. On the grand Nevsky Prospekt, the city's major thoroughfare, trams were running, stores were open, and the entire population seemed to be taking the traditional evening stroll. Even the theaters were crowded. Reed had tickets for the Marinsky Theater, a favorite of the tsars, but he decided that there was going to be more drama in the streets than on the stage.

After dinner, John Reed returned to Smolny, which was ablaze with lights. Armored cars and machine guns were guarding the entrance. Flashing his credentials, he entered the building and almost ran into Lev Kamenev, one of the senior Bolshevik leaders, who was waving a communiqué. The Petrograd Soviet, controlled by the Bolsheviks, had just passed a resolution "saluting the victorious Revolution of the Petrograd proletariat and garrison. . . ." A "Workers' and Peasants' Government" would be established to transfer the land to the peasants and industry to the workers, ending the "miseries and horrors of war." The Revolution had been launched with a sheet of paper and a show of hands.

The following day, John Reed was back at Smolny. The long-awaited Second All-Russian Congress of Soviets, now also dominated by the Bolsheviks, was in session. Reed sat at a press table with other reporters in the crowded chamber, awaiting the entrance of the Congress officials who had been meeting for seven hours elsewhere in the building. They finally entered and strode onto the platform, Lenin among them, to "a thundering wave of cheers." It was the Bolshevik leader's first public appearance in Petrograd since he had fled arrest in July. John Reed caught his first glimpse of the future ruler of the Soviet state:

"A short, stocky figure with a big head set down on his shoulders, bald and bulging. Little eyes, snubbish nose, wide, generous mouth and heavy chin; clean-shaven now, but already beginning to bristle with the well-known beard of his past and future. Dressed in shabby clothes, his trousers much too long for him. Unimpressive to be the idol of the mob, loved and revered as perhaps few leaders in history have been. A strange leader—a leader truly by virtue of his intellect; colorless, humorless, uncompromising and detached, without picturesque idiosyncrasies—but with the power of explaining profound ideas in simple terms, of analyzing a concrete situation. And combined with shrewdness, the greatest intellectual audacity."

Reed's portrait of Lenin may have been the first provided to the American public, a year after the event. By all accounts, it was accurate. Oscar Cesare, a cartoonist for *The New York Times*, sketched Lenin from life in 1922 and caught the same look: the small beady eyes, the bulging forehead, the wide mouth. By then, the heavy chin was covered with a pointed beard. Cesare's portrait was published on January 22, 1924, with a front-page dispatch from Moscow reporting Lenin's death. He had succumbed to a stroke the day before.

In the late hours of November 8, 1917, however, Vladimir Ilyich Lenin was alive and well. On the platform inside Smolny, he gripped the edge of the lectern, surveyed the hundreds of uplifted faces oblivious to the ovation that thundered through the chamber, and made the historic announcement "We shall now proceed to the construction of the Socialist order."

Later that morning, the Congress approved the formation of a Provisional Workers' and Peasants' Government headed by a Council of People's Commissars, with Lenin as chairman. Leon Trotsky was named commissar for foreign affairs, and the relatively unknown Joseph Stalin was appointed chairman for nationalities. Prominent Bolsheviks filled most of the other posts. Lenin's triumph was complete.

Ten Days contained the entire story; the other correspondents in Petrograd had it only in parts. Charles Stephenson (A. P. Charlie) Smith, the Associated Press bureau chief, and his staff reporters, Walter C. Whiffen and H. L. Rennick, roamed the streets observing the fighting, the crowds, and the confusion. They filed dispatches, but John Reed alone knew and had talked with the principal players, had mastered the complex politics of the numerous factions and understood the relations among them. During his brief stay, he had learned a great deal about Russia and Russians, adding up to what many foreign correspondents seek but few achieve: instant expertise. With the same access, he could have covered any other big, complicated story, be it the Communist triumph in China or Hitler's seizure of power in Germany.

John Reed, however, had become more than just a reporter. He was so enthusiastic about his experience that he was converted to the Bolshevik cause. While in Petrograd, he and Albert Rhys Williams edited *The Russian Revolution in Pictures,* a weekly propaganda magazine distributed to German and Austrian troops fighting on the Eastern Front. When Reed left for New York in January 1918, he immediately ran into difficulties because of his Communist affiliations. Temporarily barred from returning to America by U.S. authorities, he had remained in Christiana (Oslo), Norway, where he wrote *Ten Days*. After Reed was finally permitted to enter the United States, he abandoned journalism and threw himself into left-wing politics, helping to establish the Communist Labor Party, which was competing with the American Communist Party for recognition by the Soviet-sponsored Communist International (Comintern) as the only and legitimate representative of the American working class.

In the fall of 1919, using a false passport, John Reed returned to Russia, where he was welcomed as the heroic author of the acclaimed book on the Great October Revolution, the new official name for the Bolshevik coup. Reed was a disappointed hero, however. When the Comintern decided to back the American Communist Party instead of his Communist Labor Party, Reed found himself without a party and without a cause.

Some of his friends said that at this point he broke with the Bolsheviks. When he tried to leave Russia via Helsinki, he was arrested by Finnish police and returned to Moscow.

In 1920, John Reed agreed to address a Soviet-sponsored Congress of the Toilers of the East in Baku on the Caspian Sea, where he contracted typhus. He died in Moscow on October 17, 1920, five days before his thirty-third birthday, Louise at his side.

One week later, Reed's ashes were buried at the foot of the Kremlin wall facing Red Square, an honor accorded few Russians and even fewer foreigners. Above the mourners, who included a weeping Louise Bryant and senior Soviet and Comintern officials, fluttered a huge red banner proclaiming in letters of gold, LEADERS DIE, BUT THE CAUSE LIVES ON. After World War II, Reed's ashes were reinterred with those of Inessa Armand, a beautiful, vivacious Russian of French origin who was one of Lenin's most trusted lieutenants and reputedly his mistress. She also died in 1920. In the 1960s, Reed's grave was moved to a new site behind Lenin's mausoleum where "fallen heroes" of the Revolution are buried. He still shares the headstone with Armand.

Three years after John Reed's death, Louise Bryant married the future and first U.S. ambassador to the Soviet Union, William C. Bullitt. They had met in Washington in 1916 and were to meet again in Paris in 1922. The mix of Philadelphia socialite and Greenwich Village bohemian did not succeed, however, and they were divorced in 1930. Apparently unable to cope with Reed's death, Bryant began drinking and taking drugs. In 1935, at the age of forty-nine, she died alone and penniless in a shabby Paris hotel room. Bullitt, however, was not one to forget the past. In 1933, a few months before he was to be appointed ambassador by President Franklin D. Roosevelt, he made a private visit to Moscow. When he arrived, Eugene Lyons, the United Press correspondent, drove him to Red Square, where he laid a wreath at the grave of John Reed. Bullitt bowed his head in front of the Kremlin wall for several minutes. When he returned to the waiting car, tears were streaming down his face.

Despite his brief but brilliant career as a reporter in Russia, John Reed served as neither model nor inspiration for most of the Americans who followed. He was like a flash of lightning that illuminated earth and sky and disappeared. His successors were of a different mold, largely apolitical, more experienced professionals, and for the most part, less gifted. Their challenge was vastly different, to report in an intelligible way not the drama of a revolution but significant changes in a country that was to be transformed in less than thirty years from a peasant society to a world power.

John Reed is still revered in the Soviet Union, and his halo even hovered briefly over his "successor" Emil Sveilis. After the UPI correspondent began to file his stories, however, the glow diminished and then disappeared. Eighteen months after Sveilis arrived in Leningrad, agents of the Committee for State Security (KGB) tried to kill him.

2

Riga:
Waiting for the
Train

By January 1921, after almost seven years of war, revolution, civil war, and Allied military intervention costing millions of lives, Soviet Russia was at peace. The young Red Army had vanquished the anti-Bolshevik forces, driving their generals and troops out of the country. Except for Japanese contingents in the Far East, all Allied troops had also departed, accompanied by the last remaining foreign correspondents, including a few Americans, on Russian soil.

Headed by Vladimir Lenin and Leon Trotsky, the new rulers began trying to put a shattered nation together while building a society based on Marxist principles. At the same time, they were fomenting international revolution, calling on the workers of the world to throw off the chains of their capitalist oppressors. The Communists, to avoid prying eyes while attempting to achieve these goals—especially reporters for the "bourgeois" press, whom they regarded as intelligence agents—had barred all foreign journalists from the country. The Bolsheviks had seen these correspondents cover civil war battles from the anti-Soviet side, from the headquarters of former tsarist generals fighting the new Red Army, and marching with the Allied troops against the Bolsheviks in support of the White Russian armies. One result of this experience: Soviet leaders viewed reporters as enemies of the Revolution, as spies to be denied information about people and events. The suspicion and hostility, compounded by traditional Russian xenophobia, have remained a formidable obstacle to the present day for foreign journalists working in the Soviet Union.

Aware of the momentous events occurring in Russia and with no correspondents on the scene to cover them, American editors were forced to rely almost entirely on rumors, gossip, and thirdhand reports emanating from foreign capitals such as Berlin, Paris, Tokyo, and Warsaw. To pick up scraps of news, as did their French and British counterparts, they sent correspondents to Riga, some three hundred miles from Petrograd, transforming the Latvian capital into a major listening post for Russia, in the same way that Hong Kong served for Communist China in the 1950s and 1960s when Peking had no relations with the West. In Hong Kong, however, China's radio broadcasts and press could be monitored and defectors interviewed. Unfortunately for American newspaper readers, information available in Riga came from former tsarist officials and generals, deposed politicians hawking private causes, diplomats who claimed direct access to Lenin and Trotsky, and tipsters who would produce rumors for cash. The reporting was so confused, inaccurate, and hostile to the Bolsheviks that no one really understood what was happening inside Russia, let alone why.

Among the Riga reporters was Walter Duranty, Paris correspondent of *The New York Times,* who had been trying in vain to obtain a visa for Russia since 1919, when he met Maxim Litvinov in Dorpat, Estonia. He failed to convince the deputy commissar for foreign affairs that reporters based inside Russia could report developments more accurately than from the rumor mills of Riga and Warsaw. Litvinov's curt reply was *"Nyet!"*

The *Times* then sent Duranty to Riga, where he wrote dispatches similar to those of other correspondents eager to portray the Bolsheviks as international bomb-throwers seeking to sweep capitalist countries from the face of the earth. Typical was an exclusive story about the Latvian police intercepting a Soviet courier headed for New York carrying "seditious documents" and money and letters for American Communists. Under such headlines as REDS SEEK WAR WITH AMERICA, Duranty made the front page of the *Times* for almost a week with lurid articles about the captured courier who had a "gorilla jaw and receding forehead." He reported:

> The document seized on the Red courier . . . can be taken to establish the fact that whether or not we believe ourselves at war with the Bolsheviki, the Bolsheviki are certainly at war with ourselves.

The courier incident held an important lesson for America, according to Duranty:

> First and foremost, this Bolshevist gang at Moscow cannot be trusted. . . . At the very time when this conspiracy was under way the Bolshevik representatives at Dorpat and Copenhagen were trumpeting their desires to have peace and to be friends with all the world.

Fifteen years later, Walter Duranty conceded that the infamous document "was silly inflammatory stuff, telling American Communists to work on American troops as they came home from France and induce them to kill their officers," but when he wrote the story, his perspective was different. The editors of the *Times* liked the articles so much, they gave Duranty a bonus—the only one he ever received from the newspaper.

The flavor of Duranty's reporting from Riga was captured in a dispatch he wrote in January 1920 while covering a combined Polish/Latvian invasion of Red-held territory. An interrogation of Red prisoners reveals the Bolshevik system in its true light as one of the most damnable tyrannies in history. It is a pity some of the zealous advocates of Bolshevist theories were not present to learn how Bolshevism works in practice. Actually it is a compound of force, terror and espionage, utterly ruthless in conception and execution.

As foreshadowing Soviet policy under Stalin, these lines were prophetic, but in 1920 they reflected only the wild exaggeration and hyperbole that competing journalists produced in Riga.

The sensational, distorted, and unverifiable stories that came out of Riga and other European capitals prompted Walter Lippmann and Charles Merz to undertake their famous study, published in the *New Republic,* documenting in embarrassing detail the ineptness of *The New York Times* coverage of developments in Russia. They found, for example, that between November 1917 and November 1919 the newspaper reported:

- The Bolshevik government had fallen or was about to fall: ninety-one times.
- Lenin and Trotsky were preparing to flee: four times.
- Lenin and Trotsky had fled Russia: three times.
- Lenin had been imprisoned: three times.
- Lenin had been killed: once.

Unfortunately for a newspaper that proudly proclaimed its dedication "to give the news impartially, without fear or favor regardless of any party, sect or interest involved," none of these reports was true.

The *Times* coverage was so slanted, so anti-Soviet, and so eager to portray the Bolsheviks as eventual losers that the effect was to convince readers that the new regime would soon perish. "In large," the study stated, "the news about Russia is a case of seeing not what was, but what men wanted to see."

Taking direct aim at the Riga rumor mill and probably at Walter Duranty himself, Charles Merz and Walter Lippmann concluded that "even so rich and commanding a newspaper as the *Times* does not take seriously enough the equipment of the correspondent. For extraordinarily difficult posts in extraordinary times something more than routine correspondents are required. . . . It is habit rather than preference which makes readers accept news from correspondents whose usefulness is about that of an astrologer or an alchemist."

This criticism was not taken lightly at the *Times,* where publisher Adolph S. Ochs was determined to make the newspaper the best, the most influential, and the most profitable daily in the world. By then, Walter Duranty had returned to Paris and was probably wondering how the Lippmann/Merz report would affect his own future, which he began to see as linked with Russia. Since the *Times* was looking for someone to open a Moscow bureau and Duranty was lobbying for a field reporting assignment, he was told that he would get the job if and when the Soviets agreed to admit "bourgeois" journalists. That seemed like a dim prospect at the end of 1920, but within a few months an ominous development forced the Bolsheviks to reverse their policy and open their borders to American correspondents.

As a result of wartime dislocation and destruction, the normally fertile and productive wheat-growing regions of the Ukraine and the Volga basin were barren. Thirty million people, one fourth of the country's population, were facing famine. With no Russian grain to feed them, the Bolsheviks were obliged to plead for help—even from erstwhile enemies. Maxim Gorky, the writer and probably Russia's most internationally respected figure, appealed to the world for food and medical supplies. Faithful to its humanitarian traditions, the United States responded quickly and generously, offering grain, complete field hospitals, ambulances, and medical supplies. There were, however, several provisos. Among them: All imprisoned American citizens had to be freed, and American correspondents must be permitted to enter Russia and travel freely to report on distribution of the food.

In early August 1921, Lenin dispatched Maxim Litvinov to Riga to negotiate an agreement with Walter Lyman Brown, representing Herbert Hoover, head of the American Relief Administration (ARA). As word of the talks reached newsrooms in the United States, editors sent even more reporters to Riga to wait for the Russians to open the door. One quick response came from Colonel Robert R. McCormick, the conservative publisher of the *Chicago Tribune*. An ardent and vociferous anti-Bolshevik, he still could recognize a good news story when he saw it and cabled his foreign news director, Floyd Gibbons, in Paris, to send a man to Riga. Gibbons ordered thirty-one-year-old George Seldes, a Berlin-based reporter, to take the first train to the Latvian capital. On arrival, Seldes checked into a hotel and immediately went to the headquarters of the Litvinov mission to fill out a visa application. Like all the other American correspondents, he waited and waited, usually at the hotel bar. Among those keeping him company were James Howe of the Associated Press, Percy Noel of the *Philadelphia Ledger*, Francis McCullough of the *New York Herald Tribune*, Sam and Bella Spewack of the *New York World*, and Walter Duranty.

Toward mid-August, while the Litvinov-Brown negotiations were edging to a conclusion, a small German aircraft landed at the Riga airport, and out jumped Floyd Gibbons himself. A tough, resourceful reporter of the Chicago school, he had made his reputation as a war correspondent. In February 1917 he was aboard the Cunard liner *Laconia* when it was torpedoed by a German submarine in the Atlantic. His dramatic account of the sinking and the subsequent rescue of the passengers influenced President Wilson's decision to enter the war. Later, Gibbons lost his left eye at the French front during the Battle of Belleau Wood and proudly wore his black eye patch as a medal of honor. Many of his peers, including Seldes, regarded him as the best reporter of his generation.

Old Bolshevik Maxim Litvinov, who later outfoxed President Franklin Roosevelt over terms of U.S. recognition of the Soviet Union, was to meet his match in Floyd Gibbons. Plotting with Seldes, the reporter set a trap for the commissar that might just give Gibbons what he sought: a visa to Moscow ahead of the other Americans. The bait was that German airplane. Instead of rushing to the Soviet mission to fill out an application, Gibbons ordered his pilot to refuel the plane, stock food and other provisions, obtain maps of Russia, and prepare to take off immediately. In the meantime, he checked into the most expensive hotel in Riga and embarked on a leisurely sightseeing tour of the city. News of Gibbons' arrival and imminent departure for parts unknown quickly reached Litvinov. The following day, a Soviet military attaché called on the reporter at his hotel and invited him to meet the commissar.

"Play it close to the vest," Seldes advised.

Maxim Litvinov received Gibbons in his office, peering at him through pince-nez spectacles.

"I asked you to call, Mr. Gibbons, because I wanted to ask you frankly what your intentions are."

"Mr. Ambassador, my instructions are to proceed to Moscow immediately."

"I assume you have made the customary application," said Litvinov, well aware that Gibbons had not done so.

Gibbons admitted that he had not but stated that he was determined to go to Moscow, with or without a visa.

"Let me tell you what is on your mind, if you won't tell me yourself," announced Litvinov triumphantly, "I know that you have an airplane here and you propose to fly to Moscow without permission of the Soviet government. If you do, Soviet artillery will shoot you down and, furthermore, you'll be arrested when you land."

Floyd Gibbons narrowed his one good eye at the commissar and reminded him that under terms of the relief agreement, the Soviet government had promised to free all American prisoners. Shooting him down and putting him in prison would not only jeopardize the agreement but also would anger the American government. If you want the food, you would have to release me anyway, Gibbons argued, so why go to all this trouble?

The message was clear, and Maxim Litvinov, a tough negotiator, realized that he had no bargaining position. He looked steadily at Gibbons, suddenly smiled, and offered him a Russian cigarette.

"My government would prefer that you do not enter the country by airplane," he said. "It would excite people to see a foreign plane, and we don't want them excited. Will you come to Moscow with me by train tonight?"

Floyd Gibbons smiled and accepted the offer. His bluff, for indeed it was a bluff, had worked. He later told Walter Duranty that he would have gladly flown and even landed in Red Square, but he had promised the German pilot that under no circumstances would they enter Soviet air space. (In May 1987, Mathias Rust, a nineteen-year-old West German, proved that such a landing was feasible, to the consternation of the Soviet military establishment.)

"As it was," chortled Gibbons, "I had to put up a bond of five thousand dollars before he would fly to Riga."

That night, the *Chicago Tribune* correspondent took the train to Moscow. A few days later, George Seldes, Walter Duranty, James Howe, Francis McCullough, Percy Noel, and the Spewacks followed. Sam Spewack, who in collaboration with Bella would later become a successful Broadway play-wright with such hits as *Boy Meets Girl* and *Kiss Me Kate,* added a touch of class to the contingent. Along with his portable typewriter, he had brought his violin.

After a jolting five-day journey, the small band of Americans arrived at their destination. They knew little about the hard-ships, the frustrations, and the arduous living conditions they were to encounter, nor about the surveillance, censorship, and barriers to obtaining and transmitting news. The reporters were cheerful and excited at the prospect of seeing Soviet life for themselves, of being able to cover a big story not from the bars of Riga but from the towns and villages of Russia. After an absence of almost three years, the MOSCOW dateline would once again appear in the newspapers of America.

3

Moscow—at Last

I went to Russia as an enemy of the Communist regime and I returned perhaps as a greater enemy, but a more enlightened one.

George Seldes
The Chicago Tribune
1921–23

Whaddya gonna believe, me or your own eyes?

Marx (Groucho)

The handful of American reporters who made the trip from Riga to Moscow arrived at the start of a tumultuous and fast-changing period in Soviet history. Economic devastation resulting from war, revolution, and civil war and the collapse of the economy had all but destroyed the productive capacity of the country. In addition to the great famine, serious unrest and armed peasant uprisings in Tambov in central Russia alarmed the Communist leadership, forcing V. I. Lenin, chairman of the Council of People's Commissars since November 1917, to rescind the harsh economic policies of the War Communism period and total state control of production and distribution. He launched the New Economic Policy (NEP) in March 1921, which restored some of the elements of a market economy in industry and agriculture. Private enterprise was permitted in trade, and foreign concerns were invited to restart operations. Peasants were allowed to till their lands and sell their products on the open market. By 1928, when revival of the economy was achieved and most of the ravages of the

wars and revolution were healed, Joseph Stalin, Lenin's successor, launched the country on the first of a series of Five
Year Plans that would transform Russia into an industrial
power. At the same time, he embarked on a costly and bloody
campaign to seize the private holdings of millions of peasants
and convert them into collective farms. Paralleling these
developments was Stalin's rapid ascent to the pinnacle of
power in the Communist Party after Lenin's death in January
1924. On his way to the top, Stalin used temporary allies to
isolate and eliminate his opposition, and when the goal was
achieved, he formed new alliances, which again proved to be
opportunistic and fleeting. In January 1925 Stalin was able to
dismiss his chief rival, Leon Trotsky, from his post as war
commissar, the first step in the downfall of one of Lenin's
closest collaborators. Within four years, not only would
Trotsky be expelled from the party he had helped lead to
power, but he would also be exiled from the Soviet Union.
Other members of the opposition were less fortunate. In the
great purge trials of the 1930s, most of them were found
guilty of treason and shot. Trotsky himself was assassinated in
Mexico in 1940 by a presumed agent of Stalin.

Carrying a canvas bathtub, an electric hot plate, a flashlight, a
portable typewriter, and a bulging suitcase, George Seldes
descended from the Petrograd train at Moscow's Nikolaevski
Station. The other reporters, most of them experienced war
correspondents, had taken no chances, either. They were
equipped with bedrolls, blankets, and crates of canned food.
Although Soviet officials in Riga had promised that they
would be met at the station, no one from Narkomindel, the
People's Commissariat for Foreign Affairs, was waiting. A
CHEKA security officer explained that no one ever met trains
in Moscow, because no one knew if and when they would
arrive. Since neither porters nor taxis were available, Narkomindel dispatched an open truck to transport the Americans
and their baggage to its shabby headquarters on Petrovka
Street in downtown Moscow. An official speaking fluent
English with a New York accent welcomed them, then read

aloud the list of names, pausing when he came to Walter Duranty.

"Oh, yes, Mr. Duranty, I know you; they nearly put me in jail in New York two years ago on account of the cables you sent from Riga."

"Well, now you will have a chance to turn the tables," retorted Duranty.

"In Soviet Russia," replied the annoyed bureaucrat, "we do not put *innocent* men in prison!"

Somewhat reassured, the correspondents were informed that accommodations were reserved for them at the Savoy Hotel on nearby Rozhdestvenka Street. Furthermore, there would be no charge for the rooms, since they were guests of the Soviet government, a gracious gesture, indeed, thought the Americans—until they saw the hotel! It bore no resemblance to its luxurious London namesake. Run down and rat-infested, the Savoy's filthy rooms contained beds but no mattresses or linen. Electricity was erratic and available for a few evening hours only. Worst of all, there was no running water, just a daily kettleful per person from the kitchen boiler to be used for tea or washing.

The Savoy also had a manager without a sense of humor. One convivial evening, after the Americans had been partying in one of the correspondents' rooms and were walking down the corridor, a rat scurried across their path. Without thinking, Sam Spewack bashed it with his violin case. He pinned it by the tail to a notice in the dank hallway that warned hotel guests against keeping animals in their rooms. Deeply offended, Comrade Podolsky scolded the Americans for being unappreciative of Soviet hospitality.

When the correspondents stepped out of the Savoy into the street, they saw a city that was just beginning to recover from the ravages of war and civil war. The capital, with a population of about 1.2 million, spanned both banks of the winding Moscow River. At its heart lay the ancient Kremlin, with its gold-domed churches and palaces ringed by crenelated red brick walls. Electric tramcars crossed the city on broad avenues and boulevards. Two-story houses with inner courtyards lined winding streets, mingling with the mansions built by wealthy merchants. Traditionally a city of traders, shopkeepers, merchants of wood and grain, bankers, and entrepreneurs, its shops had offered Chinese silks, woolens from English mills, exquisite rugs from Persia, and fine French furniture and leather goods. Now the stores were closed and empty; windows were boarded up or gaping where the boards had been ripped off and used for fuel. On his first day in Moscow, Walter Duranty saw only three kinds of shops open for business, and few of those: barbershops and beauty parlors with grinning wax dummies in the windows; dingy little stalls selling wizened pears and apples; and strangely enough, stores displaying scientific equipment such as sextants and microscopes. Most of the residential buildings were in total disrepair with no water—and without water, there could be no steam heat in a city where the temperature in winter often dropped to thirty degrees below zero. In desperation, Muscovites built brick stoves in their rooms, often occupied by three or four people, and burned nearly every scrap of wood they could find, stripping bare the gardens and arbors of the famed circular boulevards and the birch forests surrounding the city.

While the Americans were settling into the Savoy, Floyd Gibbons, thanks to the head start obtained from Maxim Litvinov, had departed for Samara on the Volga. After a forty-hour train trip from Moscow, he arrived in the heart of the famine-stricken region. An experienced correspondent, Gibbons had thoroughly prepared for his journey. As the train slowly entered the station, he slipped off to avoid the crowds he knew would be on the platforms. Covering his nose and mouth with a towel soaked in a strong disinfectant to ward off typhus and cholera, he crossed the tracks to the street behind the station. This is what he saw:

> Opposite the railroad station was a cemetery with long rows of freshly dug graves. I saw groups carrying dead into the cemetery. One man preceded each group carrying a coffin cover on his head while the rest followed with an open box in which

reposed a horrible shrunken figure—matted hair and beard, yellow fangs, greenish skin. I saw two weeping women carrying a small wooden cradle between them with a baby's body lying on some rags.

A boy of twelve with a face of sixty was carrying a six-month-old infant wrapped in a filthy bundle of furs. He deposited the baby under a freight car, crawled after him and drew from a pocket some dried fishheads, which he chewed ravenously and then, bringing the baby's lips to his, he transferred the sticky white paste of half-masticated fish scales and bones to the infant's mouth as a mother bird feeds her young.

Floyd Gibbons witnessed death and devastation of an incomprehensible magnitude, but he had covered disasters before. The object of his trip was not to observe but to report, to get his story back to the *Chicago Tribune* over five thousand miles away. He knew that somewhere in Samara there was a post office and, maybe, even a telegrapher. Stepping over the dead and the dying, Gibbons made his way back to the railroad station. En route he found what he was looking for: a post office where an emaciated telegrapher was still on duty. Gibbons typed his story, changing each Latin character to its closest Cyrillic equivalent, and handed it to the old man. The telegrapher tapped the copy out on the keyboard to Moscow, where George Seldes was waiting to forward it to London. The Russian had sent off thousands of words without understanding a single syllable.

Floyd Gibbons' dispatch, the first eyewitness account of the famine, horrified the world. As he traveled through the afflicted region, he continued to file stories, scoring one of the biggest reporting triumphs of the early 1920s. Back in Moscow, however, the other American reporters were in a rage of fury and frustration. They pleaded with the Narkomindel to permit them to join Gibbons, while their editors were bombarding them with angry cables ordering them to match his enterprise. All in vain. The bureaucrats replied in words that were to be heard again and again over the next decades: "We are making the necessary arrangements. . . ."

Seldes, however, was delighted with Gibbons' triumph and still chuckles when he talks about it. "That man," he told me, "was terrific."

Eventually, all the American correspondents were allowed to visit the famine areas, where an ample supply of misery remained for many other reports. Soon, however, there was good news: Food and medical supplies shipped by the American Relief Administration were arriving; American officials were setting up headquarters in Moscow to administer the relief program, and distribution centers were established in the Volga region and the Ukraine. Millions of Russians were being fed, and millions of lives were being saved. Soon the excitement over the famine subsided, Floyd Gibbons departed for Paris, and the correspondents turned to reporting on the new world around them.

For Walter Duranty, thirty-seven, the Moscow assignment was an extraordinary opportunity that he parlayed into a career, becoming one of the most influential if controversial correspondents in the history of *The New York Times*. During his fourteen years in Russia he covered every major development, striking up friendships with many senior Communist Party officials as well as writers, artists, and intellectuals. Distinguished visitors from abroad sought him out for his opinions on Soviet politics. Stalin favored him with two interviews, an achievement unmatched by any other foreign correspondent. Duranty's longevity imparted an aura of authority to everything he wrote, making him the world's best-known foreign correspondent. Even though he added luster to the *Times*, he was attacked by conservatives as an apologist for the Kremlin and by liberals and Communists as anti-Soviet.

A native of Liverpool, Walter Duranty graduated from Cambridge in 1907 with honors in classics. For the next six years he drifted on the fringes of journalism in London, New York, and Paris. In 1913 Wythe Williams, the Paris correspondent of *The New York Times*, hired Duranty as an assistant to read the French press and do the legwork in the bureau. When World War I erupted a year later, Duranty continued to leaf through the French newspapers for snippets of information that were used by the senior reporters in their stories. Despite his frequent requests to cover the fighting, he did not get to the front as a war correspondent until July 1918, a few months before the Armistice. Although he covered the Versailles Conference with distinction, his future at the *Times* appeared bleak. The newspaper was thinning out its European staff, and Charles E. Selden, the new Paris bureau chief, regarded him as "most unreliable and tricky" and refused to work with him. One reason for Selden's antipathy toward Walter Duranty may have been the stories circulating in Paris about the Englishman's private life and his alleged association with Aleister Crowley, a compatriot who attracted a following with his black arts and pseudo-religious homosexual rituals. Perhaps to ease Duranty out of Paris, the *Times* sent him to the Baltic states in October 1919 to try to fathom what was going on in Russia. During the next two years he filed many of the Riga rumors that were so appreciated by his editors, and eventually he was offered the Moscow assignment. Apparently no one in the New York office, least of all publisher Adolph Ochs, knew about Duranty's presumed extracurricular activities in Paris, hardly the sort of background for a reporter on an august newspaper like *The New York Times*.

George Seldes was more typical of the first correspondents stationed in Moscow. Born in Vineland, New Jersey, of immigrant Russian parents, he began his journalism career as a copy boy on the *Pittsburgh Leader* in 1909. Seldes made his mark at the newspaper when an outraged William Jennings Bryan refused to answer a question about his presidential aspirations and shoved the young man out the hotel room door. The following day, the *Leader* carried a banner headline:

BRYAN ASSAULTS LEADER REPORTER

For that story, the aspiring journalist achieved instant fame and a salary increase from $3.50 to $8.00 per week.

Over the next five years, George Seldes covered local news

and politics, the police beat, and church sermons—the best training for a young reporter—and then moved on to the *Pittsburgh Post*. When the war began in Europe, he joined the United Press in London and in 1917 became the youngest correspondent accredited to the headquarters of General John J. Pershing, commander of the American Expeditionary Force. After the war ended, publisher McCormick launched the Chicago Tribune Foreign News Service, headed by Floyd Gibbons, who staffed the new agency with reporters he knew, among them George Seldes.

Life in Moscow for the American correspondents was at first a challenge to survival. The Savoy was as dilapidated and uncomfortable as a Bowery flophouse, but the reporters had all fared worse in the trenches of the Western Front. With their own imported food as a modest supply base, the correspondents were able to live better than their Russian neighbors. They quickly found the only private restaurant in Moscow, whose proprietor spoke English and French and proved to be a resourceful provider of decent meals. Centrally located in the Arbat district, the restaurant soon became the American press hangout. Within weeks after Lenin's decree, however, the impact of his New Economic Policy could be seen in the city, materially changing the lives of the correspondents. Shops were reopened, repaired, and rapidly filled with goods that had been hoarded or lost in the red tape of bureaucracy. Restaurants with elaborate menus sprang up overnight, offering French champagnes and wines. Horse-drawn hansom cabs (*droshkies*) appeared on newly paved streets, a convenient alternative to the overcrowded trams. Gambling establishments and nightclubs were opened by enterprising businessmen catering to the *nouveau riche*, while prostitutes walked the sidewalks in a red-light district near Trubny Square. Most important, for the first time in years, peasants came from the countryside and set up sidewalk stands to sell fresh fruit and vegetables. The metropolis was returning to normal.

Walter Duranty was the first to escape from the Savoy by taking advantage of a new municipal law granting any person who renovated an apartment the right to occupy it rent-free for three years. Joining with his friend Herbert Pulitzer, owner and roving correspondent of the *New York World,* Duranty found a street-level restaurant that had fallen into ruin and transformed it into one of the most comfortable apartments in Moscow, down to an English-style fireplace in the living room. With an excellent cook and access to the well-stocked canteen of the American Relief Administration, the *Times* correspondent began to entertain frequently and lavishly. He quickly became the social leader in the small foreign colony, giving the best and most sumptuous parties in Moscow and attracting Russians equally eager to meet foreigners and to eat and drink well. A brilliant and captivating raconteur, Walter Duranty was always the center of attention. Jane Gunther, wife of journalist and author John Gunther, recalled that he "had a kind of magic. . . . An evening with him was like an evening with no one else." Among the Russians Duranty met was the beautiful Katya, whom he hired as a secretary and who later became his mistress and mother of his child, Michael. After Herbert Pulitzer returned to New York, she moved into the apartment and became his housekeeper as well. Over the years, Katya had to fend off a succession of rivals, foreign and Russian, who also found Walter Duranty's charms irresistible.

From their "press center" in the Savoy, the American correspondents faced a formidable task. Covering Moscow, as they were quick to learn, was unlike reporting from Paris, London, or Berlin. It was more like covering a war, with the military controlling every movement, deciding what could and what could not be seen, what could or could not be filed, all executed with a Russian kind of bumbling inefficiency that leavened the harsh working conditions. In addition, correspondents were handicapped because almost without exception, they did not know the language, the history, the politics, or very much about the men who shaped the visible events. Among the inhabitants of the Savoy Hotel there were no Soviet experts, nor even as British journalist Paul Winterton, later put it, people with "varying degrees of ignorance." What little they knew about Soviet Russia they probably learned from John Reed and their own newspapers.

Working in their hotel rooms, which served as bedrooms and news bureaus, the reporters quickly established a routine that set the pattern for almost every Moscow correspondent in the years ahead: Hire a secretary and have him or her read the newspapers and magazines aloud in English while you scribble or type notes. When an item appeared newsworthy, the secretary went into greater detail or translated it. The reporter wrote his story, delivered it or dispatched it to the censor, then transmitted it via telegraph to the home office. With few variations that was how the correspondents started their working day.

Like John Reed, George Seldes knew no Russian but followed his predecessor's example by teaming up with someone who did, not a Russian-speaking radical émigré from the United States but his friend and colleague Sam Spewack, the only American who spoke the language. Born in Russia and taken to America as a child, Spewack retained sufficient fluency to make his way around Moscow. The two men worked together in the city and whenever they could, traveled together around the country, repressing the normal competitive instincts of reporters, which seemed irrelevant under the circumstances.

Seldes' secretary/interpreter was a Comrade Kheikin, whom he dubbed his "CHEKA spy" and who undoubtedly, as did all employees of foreigners, reported to the security police. Every morning Comrade Kheikin would arrive at the Savoy to read Seldes the Communist Party organ *Pravda* (Truth), the government newspaper *Izvestia* (News), and other publications, the principal sources of official information. Sixty-five years later, the Soviet press is still the source for a large percentage of the stories reported by foreign correspondents.

Walter Duranty's solution to the language problem was different from his colleagues', probably reflecting his academic training and intellectual curiosity. He plunged into an enthusiastic study of Russian. The results, however, were barely sufficient to enable him to read newspapers with the aid of a translator. As for his spoken Russian, it was far from fluent, although he could eventually carry on an ungrammatical conversation and make himself understood without difficulty.

The *New York Times* bureau was located in Walter Duranty's apartment, where he worked within reach of his bar and Katya. He followed the same daily routine as Seldes, reviewing the press, making a few phone calls to the other correspondents, perhaps checking with American Relief Administration officials to find out if there were any new developments. Making a special point of cultivating the diplomats of the ten countries that had relations with the Soviets, Duranty paid regular calls on the ambassadors and ministers. He developed a cordial relationship with the German ambassador, Count Ulrich von Brockdorff-Rantzau, whom he had met at the treaty-signing ceremony at Versailles and who was one of the best-informed foreigners in Moscow. Their common language was French.

When the correspondents reported to the Press Department to receive their identity cards, they were informed about filing procedures. Every story they wrote would have to be submitted to a Narkomindel official for approval before it could be transmitted. The system originated in the Russia of the tsars and was immediately adopted by the Bolsheviks when they seized power in November 1917. John Reed's first dispatch, for example, was cleared for transmittal by Felix Dzerzhinsky, member of the Military Revolutionary Committee of the Petrograd Soviet and future chief of the CHEKA. Not surprisingly, however, the Bolsheviks refused to call censorship by its real name, avoiding the word *tsenzura*, which carried overtones of evil, since it was used by imperial Russia to stifle unorthodox thought, including Lenin's own writings. Maxim Litvinov himself often declared to reporters that there was no censorship in the Soviet Union, even as Konstantin Oumansky, the chief censor in Narkomindel, stood at his side. When Oumansky was named ambassador to the United States in 1939, he insisted that a dispatch "was never changed against the will of a correspondent."

A half-dozen censors worked in the foreign affairs commissariat in 1921, mainly party officials who had lived in Europe or the United States as Bolshevik exiles. Usually they had such a good command of English that correspondents could rarely slip anything past them. During this period, the censor had a name and a face and received the copy directly from the person who wrote it, making it possible for the reporter to argue over a lead, an interpretation, or the facts. Sometimes persuasion worked; most of the time it did not. George Seldes' *bête noire* was Comrade Kogan, who was smart enough never to use a blue pencil to cross out banned copy; instead he snipped it out with a scissors. Seldes was "mad as hell," but there was little he could do at first other than take his see-through copy to the telegraph for transmittal to London, holes and all.

The Americans soon discovered that they could evade the literary services of Narkomindel by smuggling stories out of the country through the diplomatic pouch of the American Relief Administration, which was protected by protocol. Barely disguised as personal letters, the dispatches were addressed to editors in the United States or news bureaus in Europe to be forwarded by telegraph. George Seldes often wrote to John Steele in the *Tribune*'s London office, usually beginning with a few paragraphs of a personal nature. He recalled one in particular that would never have passed the censor:

> Dear John: How are Mrs. Steele and the children? I'm having an interesting time. Last week I was on a trip to the Ukraine. I found the beginnings of a revolutionary movement. I found peasants who were secretly hoarding arms—rifles. . . .

Filing this way was risky for the Americans, as they would soon discover, but it was the only means to get the story to their newspapers. And they were willing to take the risk. To protect himself, Seldes instructed his editors never to use a Moscow dateline on the uncensored stories and never to publish the story under *any* dateline in the Paris edition of the *Tribune,* the only one received by Narkomindel in Moscow.

"We got a lot of stuff out that way," Seldes recalled with a grin.

One of George Seldes' biggest problems was not the censorship but his publisher, Colonel McCormick, whom he could evade less easily than the Russians. An artillery officer in World War I, McCormick ran his newspaper like a military organization, dispatching orders to his troops through daily cables. He bombarded his foreign correspondents with instructions and demands for exclusive coverage and interviews. Accustomed as he was to instant responses, he found Moscow a constant source of frustration and annoyance. The colonel finally decided that he'd had enough from the Reds.

In 1923 George Seldes was summoned to the foreign affairs headquarters and ushered into the presence of Georgi Vasilyevich Chicherin, the commissar himself. Comrade Chicherin, an erudite intellectual who had spent many years in London exile, was undiplomatically angry. He waved a cable at Seldes and threw it on the desk for him to read:

SELDES HOTEL SAVOY MOSCOW. INFORM CHICHERIN TRIBUNE WILL WITHDRAW CORRESPONDENT AND GET OTHER PAPERS TO DO LIKEWISE UNLESS CENSORSHIP IS STOPPED. MCCORMICK

"Who is your McCormick?" shouted Chicherin. "Is he a nation? Is he a foreign office? Is he a government?

"What is this? He sends ME an ultimatum? He addresses ME as an equal power? You can cable your McCormick that until he can prove to me that he is a foreign office, I cannot accept an ultimatum from him."

Seldes calmly explained that he had never seen the cable and that, if the commissar had not intercepted it, he would have advised Colonel McCormick that no government could accept a communication from a mere publisher, a message he promised to transmit to Chicago.

Colonel McCormick's cable, of course, was an empty threat, although he could undoubtedly have recalled George Seldes from Moscow. Whether any of the other newspapers, after waiting so many years to get into Russia, would also have withdrawn their correspondents because of the censorship is dubious. And in the early 1920s, the censor's blue pencil was used less frequently and less harshly than at almost any other time in Soviet history.

Besides the press, Seldes' news sources were limited to what he could observe and occasional interviews with government and Communist Party officials. He wrote about the people in the streets, how they lived, what they ate, and how they dressed. What he saw in the stores, the price of food and clothes, made good features. His daily routine also included a stop at ARA headquarters, the only place where he could talk to American officials in contact with the Soviet government on a continuing basis. Sometimes he would pick up a shred of information or leads for stories.

Like other American reporters, George Seldes could travel anywhere in Russia on the trains that were carrying relief supplies. He and Sam Spewack would often go to a railroad station, inquire about the destination of the next train and, if it suited them, they could catch a ride, usually in a comfortable sleeper. When they arrived at the end of the journey, they could write about anything they saw: life in the countryside, in the towns, conversations with ordinary people, and interviews with officials and the local angles that made these more interesting than similar stories written in Moscow.

Every correspondent sought to interview Lenin, Trotsky, and other Communist leaders. Lenin, still recovering from a stroke suffered in April 1922, was inaccessible and rarely appeared in public, while Trotsky, now the commissar for war, spent most of his time traveling around the country on military affairs. Finally, during a November 7 parade in Red Square, George Seldes got close enough to Trotsky to take pictures, but just as he was aiming his camera, he was elbowed by a Russian who announced that only he had the right to take photos. Seldes, speaking in German, complained to Trotsky that the Bolsheviks were supposed to have ended monopolies on *everything*! The commissar laughed and ordered the Russian to leave the American alone. Seldes got his pictures. He was equally persistent in obtaining interviews with Soviet officials, even arranging a meeting with Y. A. Peters, one of the three men who headed the CHEKA, at the headquarters of the security police on Lubyanka Square. Before the Revolution, the building housed one of Russia's largest insurance companies, and as he entered the lobby, Seldes was astonished to see that the old advertisements were still on the walls. Either they were retained by someone with a morbid sense of humor, or the new landlords just did not care. One of the signs urged visitors, who often arrived under armed guard and were headed for prison or worse, to:

INSURE YOUR LIFE NOW! PROTECT YOUR WIFE AND
CHILDREN WHEN YOU ARE GONE!

After passing through several checkpoints, Seldes was ushered into Peters' office, where he showed the CHEKA official a copy of *The Times* of London reporting that the Bolsheviks had killed 1.7 million "counterrevolutionaries" during the Red Terror, including seventy-two thousand professors. Seldes asked Peters to confirm the figures.

Peters replied with a laugh, "There aren't even seven thousand professors in all of Russia. It's a joke."

Seldes pressed for the total number of victims.

"Two thousand?"

"No, more than that."

"A hundred thousand?"

"Much less than that!"

"Split the difference? Fifty thousand?"

"That's about right," conceded Peters. "A few thousand more or less. In wartime, mind you . . . traitors, spies, enemies of the Communist revolution!"

George Seldes got the story he was looking for: the first official confirmation of the number of "counterrevolutionaries" executed, and probably on the low end of the scale. The censor passed the dispatch without delay.

The American correspondents were finally able to meet Lenin in November 1922, at a meeting to mark the fifth anniversary of the Revolution. In the grand chamber of the Kremlin Palace where the tsars of Russia once held court, hundreds of Communists and their sympathizers from all over the world gathered to listen to the Bolshevik leaders recall the glorious days of 1917. The reporters, George Seldes and Walter Duranty among them, sat at a press table near one of the entrances. At each door, a soldier was stationed with a wooden board on which were pinned seven or eight colored cards. Everyone who entered—delegates, Soviet officials, journalists—had their admission cards checked against those on the board.

"Then I saw a little man, I didn't recognize him, I hadn't seen him before," recalled Seldes. "He was trying to get in and arguing in a low voice. He was causing trouble because I could see that the soldier was getting angry.

"Apparently someone on the platform looked over and recognized Lenin. He was about five feet five, I think, because when I was talking to him later, I put my hand on his shoulder. You're liable to do that when you're talking to a smaller man.

"He walked from the door to the platform on tiptoes. There was no carpet on the floor and he didn't want to disturb the speaker—Zinoviev. He walked past the press table and went up the three steps leading to the platform. Of course, when he got to the top, all hell broke loose and he said, 'No! No! Comrade Zinoviev has to finish!' "

Speaking in German, which George Seldes understood, Lenin spoke briefly, occasionally turning to someone on the platform to ask in Russian for a word in German. He was physically unimpressive and unassuming, Seldes found, "not hard, certainly not cruel-looking as cartoons and many frowning pictures made him out to be. He had a schoolteacher way with his audience, presenting unimpassioned facts and statements, reasoning things out, putting them plainly for his young students." Both George Seldes and John Reed were struck by Lenin's didactic style when he explained complicated political issues. He even had a low-keyed sense of humor. Sounding like an American president, Lenin complained that despite his efforts to reduce the number of bureaucrats, "after four years . . . we have an increase of twelve thousand."

Lenin spoke with a slur, a thick, throaty, wet voice, evidence that he had not fully recovered from a paralytic stroke that had incapacitated him for half a year. Walter Duranty, who had spent all too much time in front-line hospitals during the war, immediately caught the medical implications of the slurred speech but was prevented by the censor from filing his conclusions.

After his address, Lenin was escorted by bodyguards to an adjacent room, followed by reporters trying to ask questions. Seldes recalled with annoyance that "there is always some damn fool in any group of newspapermen who asks a dumb question. So somebody asked, 'Mr. Lenin, do you speak English?' instead of a serious question about Russian policy.

"So, Lenin replied, 'I speaking in the English language not so very good.' And by then we couldn't really ask him anything important. He was on the way out of the room, but he suddenly stopped and said in English, 'I cannot understand you, Americans especially, because you hate the word BOLSHEVISM—so you make BOLSHEVISM the most hated word. After all, there are many interpretations of Karl Marx and BOLSHEVISM is one of them. We have merely changed the name, but we adopted the American interpretation, the one that Daniel DeLeon started in the Socialist Labor Party.' "

George Seldes almost cried out, "That's my father's friend you're talking about!" And indeed, DeLeon and Seldes' father had met in Vineland, New Jersey, in the 1880s and as friends had worked together in the nascent Socialist movement in the United States.

That was the last time Seldes saw Lenin alive. Forty-four years later, on his second trip to Moscow, Seldes visited the mausoleum on Red Square where Lenin's body lies under a glass case. Despite rumors that the figure is a wax dummy, Seldes is convinced it was Lenin.

"They may have embalmed him or stuffed him or waxed him, but it's Lenin's body, I'm sure."

The Kremlin meeting was to be one of the last big public events that Seldes covered in Moscow. In 1923, CHEKA agents accidentally discovered the misuse of the ARA diplomatic pouch by several American correspondents. Responding to rumors that ARA employees were illegally trading food for diamonds and jewelry that they were smuggling out of the country, the police arrested a Relief Administration courier on the train to Riga in violation of the Litvinov-Brown agreement and brought him back to Moscow. He was taken to Lubyanka where the pouch, actually a leather bag, was slashed open. No diamonds were found, but it did contain "letters" of four American correspondents, including those of George Seldes. Commissar Chicherin was furious, ordering the Americans to leave the country, the first of the many who were to be expelled over the next six decades. In addition to Seldes, Francis McCullough of the *New York Herald Tribune*, Percy Noel of the *Philadelphia Ledger*, and Bella and Sam Spewack of the *New York World* were also banished—all members of the group that arrived in August 1921.

A few days later, the correspondents packed their bags and bade farewell to the Savoy Hotel and to Moscow. Their departure was not joyful. Despite the difficulties and the discomforts that went with the assignment, Seldes, looking back thirty years later, recalled:

"Each of us realized that we were at the vital center, the focus of a new world. We were writing and talking about a new force which all, friends and enemies, agreed would change the course of history.

"It impressed everyone. Even the most stupid, careless, and irresponsible correspondent in Russia in those early days realized that it was not just another assignment, like being transferred from a democratic republic to an absolute monarchy for a year or so. We were present at the making of a new system of government which was fundamentally different. Its pattern had not yet been set and the men who were setting it,

Lenin and Trotsky, whether victorious or defeated, we knew were already men of history. It was this sense of being part of an historical event of first importance, which affected almost everyone there, which made everyone think, for once, about the meaning of things in a changing world."

George Seldes' appraisal was remarkably correct. Almost every American correspondent who has served in Moscow since those early days has had the same sense of being in a different and important place where history was being made by leaders whose decisions would have a profound impact on the rest of the world.

After he was expelled from Russia, George Seldes continued to report for the *Tribune* as chief European correspondent, but when Colonel McCormick began to censor his copy, he quit to write books exposing the seamy side of the newspaper business, especially how news was suppressed and distorted by powerful publishers and editors. *You Can't Print That,* published in 1929, was one of the first serious, well-documented critical studies of the American press. Seldes broke new ground with a four-page newsletter called *In Fact,* which for ten years served as an influential gadfly for the U.S. news media by printing muckraking stories that were too hot for the establishment newspapers to handle.

Seldes never retired from his profession. In 1960, at the age of seventy, he published *The Great Quotations,* a compendium of his own voracious readings that sold over a million copies. Twenty-seven years later, his 490-page autobiography *Witness to a Century* appeared, bestowing on Seldes at ninety-six the distinction of being America's oldest living publishing author, an achievement that gave him particular pleasure.

In mid-1987 George Seldes, a widower, lived alone with a white cat in a comfortable brick house on a dirt road outside Hartland Four Corners, a hamlet in Vermont, the only survivor of the little band of Americans who first reported from Soviet Russia, the original Moscow correspondents.

Walter Duranty served longer in Moscow than Seldes and, indeed, all the others who arrived on the train from Riga, to become one of the best informed and most influential foreign correspondents of the 1920s. He covered Lenin's funeral in January 1924 and said it was the high point of a journalistic career that included the day war was declared in Paris when a "frenzied mob" surged down the grand boulevards singing the *Marseillaise* and shouting "On to Berlin!" and the delirious Armistice night four years later. He tracked the ideological and personal struggle between Joseph Stalin and Leon Trotsky for Lenin's place, although the conflict was obscured by secrecy, half hints, and cautious whispers. As early as January 1923, however, Duranty had already tabbed Stalin as a man to watch. In a dispatch to the *Times* describing the five men who ruled Russia as Lenin lay disabled by a stroke, he wrote:

> Finally there is the Georgian Stalin, little known abroad but one of the most remarkable men in Russia today. Stalin is officially head of the ministry for the nations that constitute the Soviet Union, and more important still is the general secretary of the Communist Party, but his influence is not measured by his official position. . . . During the last year Stalin has shown judgment and analytical power not unworthy of Lenin.

Walter Duranty has admitted that he missed some valuable clues to political developments when he first arrived on the Moscow scene simply because he could not read between the lines of the Soviet press. He could only grasp the literal meaning of an editorial, but much later he was able to "feel" the interplay and crosscurrents of Communist Party politics and rivalries. Duranty conceded that it took him about five years before he could grope his way "through the fogs of lies and rumors, of my ignorance, and of the bewildering difference between Russian and non-Russian mentality in the first place and Bolshevik and non-Bolshevik mentality in the second place."

Reading between the lines is still the most valuable skill of a Moscow correspondent, acquired only after years of reading and understanding the lines themselves. Since the Communist

Party follows Lenin's dictum that it serves as organizer, agitator, and propagandist, the press reveals the Kremlin's concerns and what the leaders wish to communicate to the masses. An experienced correspondent who knows Soviet and Russian politics, history, economics, and culture can read *Pravda, Izvestia,* and the *Literary Gazette* to mine nuggets of gold.

Walter Duranty learned another lesson that could be included in a primer for Moscow correspondents. In December 1927, at the Fifteenth Congress of the Communist Party, Joseph Stalin dealt a final blow to Leon Trotsky's political ambitions by expelling him from the party and exiling him to Alma-Ata, a remote town in central Asia near the Chinese border. One morning a few weeks later, Duranty and Paul Sheffer, correspondent for the *Berliner Tageblatt,* were tipped that Trotsky, his wife, and two secretaries were to leave Moscow that afternoon. They drove to the Kazan Station to witness his departure. All the entrances to the station and the crowded platform where several thousand Russians had gathered were guarded by GPU security troops. After showing their press credentials, Duranty and Sheffer were admitted to the platform, where they found places on a flatcar directly facing the international sleeping car of the train, bound for Tashkent on the first leg of the journey. About ten minutes before departure time, the crowd stirred and a buzz of voices echoed through the cavernous station. Down the narrow passage between spectators standing on both sides of the platform moved a little procession headed by two uniformed guards, then a woman, three men with porters carrying baggage, followed by two additional guards. One of the men was short and erect and wore an Astrakhan hat pulled down over his ears, a thick muffler, and a heavy fur coat. As he strode along, the crowd murmured, *"Vot Trotsky!"* ("There's Trotsky!"). With head held high, glancing neither to the right nor to the left, he, with the woman and the three other nonuniformed members of the group, disappeared into the car.

Walter Duranty returned to his office and wrote a story reporting the departure, which was quickly passed by the censor. Two days later, Paul Sheffer, greatly excited, came to see Duranty. Sheffer had learned from an unimpeachable source that it was not Leon Trotsky they had seen at the station but someone impersonating him. The real Trotsky and his wife were taken from their home the following day and driven by car to Lubertsi, some twenty miles from Moscow, and there put on the Tashkent train. Later Duranty learned that an actor who had played Trotsky in a Russian Civil War film had played a similar but briefer role at the Kazan station. For Duranty, the lesson of the story was clear. When someone later asked how he handled news in Russia, he replied, "My first rule is to believe nothing that I hear, little of what I read, and not all of what I see."

This was a sound admonition to any reporter covering the Soviet scene, but in subsequent years Walter Duranty failed to follow his own advice.

4

Concealing Stalin's Famine

I had no intention of being an apologist for the Stalin administration; all that I was thinking of was that I had "doped out" the line that the administration must inevitably follow, and when it did follow that line I naturally felt that it was right.

Walter Duranty
The New York Times
1921–34

Against the background of desperation and enthusiasm and pitiless bigotry, against the life and death struggles amidst which we foreigners had our sheltered alien being, the breathless race of American newspapermen to file an emasculated, blue-penciled little dispatch ninety seconds before a rival was, in sober fact, grotesque.

Eugene Lyons
United Press
1928–34

In 1930, six American correspondents stationed in Moscow were trying with only moderate success to report on a country that covered one sixth of the earth and eleven time zones, with a population of 176 million comprising some 115 ethnic groups and a political system vastly different from any other in the world. They represented the two major wire services, the Associated Press and the United Press; *The New York Times;* the *Chicago Daily News;* and *The Christian Science Monitor.*

Although there were about the same number of correspondents in the capital as had arrived on the train from Riga in August 1921, in the course of the decade the institution of Moscow reportage had taken root. The Soviet government, accepting the presence of foreign journalists as a necessary evil, had established agencies and procedures for dealing with them. Under the aegis of the Press Department of the Commissariat of Foreign Affairs, a censorship system screened outgoing dispatches, eliminating "unfavorable" or "negative" reports. The secret police, under various acronyms over the decade—CHEKA, GPU, OGPU, NKVD—included surveillance of the correspondents as part of their regular responsibilities. Severity of censorship, however, varied during the decade according to the level of tension inside Soviet society. For example, during the bitter power struggle that ultimately resulted in Joseph Stalin's triumph and Leon Trotsky's exile, secrecy was so tight and censorship so rigorous that it was virtually impossible to report the conflict. But after total victory, when Stalin permitted his archrival and Mme. Trotsky to leave the country unscathed in 1929, GPU agents quietly urged several American correspondents to file the story, even to bypass censorship by phoning the news directly abroad. The reason for this departure from the rules was murky, but no correspondent was punished for this serious infraction.

By 1930, American newspapers and wire services had established a framework for operations in Moscow. Bureaus were opened and equipped; correspondents were provided with secretaries, translators, cars, and chauffeurs. Budgets were allocated to cover cable costs, salaries, office and apartment rental, travel, and other expenses. Newspapers touted the opening of a Moscow bureau as evidence of the broad coverage provided their readers.

Selection of correspondents, the key factor in the coverage, was, however, very much a haphazard procedure. The choice was often based on who was available for the assignment or located nearby, thus reducing the cost of travel. Special knowledge of Russia or ability to speak the language was not a factor. An exception was the *New York Herald Tribune*'s Joseph Barnes, an experienced reporter assigned to Moscow in the mid-1930s, who had studied Russian at Harvard. He may have been the first American newsman academically trained in the language before going to Moscow. The theory in the newsrooms was that a resourceful, aggressive professional with solid reporting experience abroad or at home could handle the assignment. Given the prevailing censorship and the limited access to any information that was not official, this approach probably made sense. The chosen few, however, did not stay long. Since Moscow was considered a hardship post, most of the correspondents served only two or three years, sometimes less, and were then reassigned. Except for Walter Duranty, they did not remain long enough to become experts, nor did they intend to become Soviet specialists. Moscow was simply another post, like Paris, Tokyo, or London.

Russia in the 1930s was a correspondent's nightmare—or a dream assignment, depending on the individual's frustration threshold. There was much to be reported, but much could not even be seen, and even if seen, would not pass through the heavy hand of the censor. Stalin announced completion of the first Five Year Plan one year ahead of schedule in 1932 but never revealed the staggering human and material costs. Factories were built, but there was no equipment to install; machinery was sent to unfinished plants to rust on railroad sidings; untrained peasants fresh from the countryside were ordered to produce tractors and trucks, to construct smelters and oil refineries. Those who remained on the land were forced to pool their plots into collective farms, producing only shortfalls in grain and meat. Housing for the workers was neglected, safety conditions in factories were ignored. People were overworked and underfed—all in the name of "fulfilling the plan." At the same time, Stalin imposed new "labor discipline" on Soviet citizens, making it virtually impossible to change jobs and inflicting heavy punishment for a single day's absence from work without sufficient reason. Despite the awesome costs, the accomplishments were impressive: Output of machinery quadrupled, oil production doubled, electric power output increased 250 percent. Two huge iron and steel centers were built, Magnitogorsk in the Urals and Kuznetsk in central Siberia, providing the Soviet Union with a base for a modern metallurgical industry. Joseph Stalin himself warned that time was short: "We are fifty or a hundred years behind the advanced countries. We must make good this distance in ten years. Either we do it, or we shall be crushed." The date was February 1931, ten years before Hitler unleashed his armies against Russia.

*   *   *

One of the biggest stories of the early 1930s was the famine—
the worst since 1920–21—that took an estimated five million
lives. Although bad weather and the Kremlin's policy of
forcing peasants to deliver grain to the state at low prices
contributed to the meager harvest, the overriding cause was
Stalin's determination to smash peasant resistance to collectivization of their land, and the exile of millions of the more
enterprising and productive peasants, the so-called *kulaks*, to
work camps and prisons far from home—the beginnings of
the Gulag Archipelago.

The government was determined to conceal the story,
fearing that if the famine became known abroad it would have
a devastating effect on Soviet prestige, particularly in the
world Communist movement. Furthermore, the news could
endanger fulfillment of the Five Year Plan in 1932. Since the
export of grain was Russia's principal source of hard currency,
foreign knowledge of the famine might force the government
to reduce exports, resulting in a cutback of imported machinery needed for the plan. Rumors of hunger in the Ukraine,
the North Caucasus, and Kazakhstan had reached Moscow via
returning travelers, diplomats, and Russians who had friends
and relatives in the afflicted regions. Several correspondents
were aware of the rumors, but since there was no mention of
famine in the newspapers, they knew that anything they wrote
would be killed by the censor.

Eugene Lyons of the United Press was among those who
had known about the famine for several months but as a wire
service reporter required to cover all breaking news and
respond to a stream of queries and requests from New York,
he could not risk leaving Moscow. Unique among the Americans, Lyons had worked for four years as an editor in the New
York office of TASS before being hired by UP for the Moscow
assignment. Karl Bickel, the agency's president, personally
recruited Lyons because he believed that sending a known
Soviet sympathizer might induce the Russians to treat the UP
more favorably than the Associated Press, providing it with
more interviews and greater access to government officials—a

naïve assumption, as events were later to prove. Passionately pro-Soviet although not a member of the U.S. Communist Party, Eugene Lyons, twenty-nine, arrived in the "land of our dreams" with his wife, Billy, and five-year-old daughter Eugenie in 1928. In a few years his enthusiasm waned, replaced by revulsion and bitter disillusionment with the brutalities of Stalin, the toll of human life and dignity exacted by collectivization, and the growing regimentation of Soviet society. By the beginning of 1933, Lyons had no qualms about reporting the famine, which he regarded as another of Stalin's crimes, if he could only confirm the news and slip the story past censorship.

In March 1933, Lyons' secretary, Natalya Petrovna Shirokikh, spotted a reference to food shortages in *Hammer* (*Molot*), a newspaper published in Rostov-on-Don. At last, thought Lyons, here was official confirmation in the press and a story that the censor could not kill. After filing a brief cable and well aware that the UP would not permit him to leave Moscow, he tipped off two colleagues whose newspapers encouraged them to travel: William R. Stoneman of the *Chicago Daily News* and Ralph W. Barnes of the *New York Herald Tribune*. The next day they went to the railroad station with Barnes' interpreter Oskar Emma, bought tickets, and departed for Rostov. For almost two weeks, the correspondents toured the area south of the city, talking to peasants about the grain shortage and local conditions. They watched as armed GPU security forces herded kulaks and their families onto freight cars taking them to distant exile. GPU agents finally arrested the newsmen and put them on a train for Moscow, but the Americans had their story.

Knowing that the censor would never pass their dispatches, Stoneman and Barnes sent them out of the country with two friendly German fur buyers returning to Berlin. The eyewitness accounts made the front page of the *News* and the *Herald Tribune,* but they so alarmed the Press Department that it immediately banned foreign correspondents from the famine areas. To add defiance to injury, Stoneman's story appeared under a Rostov dateline.

The phone call from the Press Department was not long in coming. Both Barnes and Stoneman were summoned to an audience with a furious press chief, Konstantin Oumansky, who charged them, as they were well aware, with violating censorship regulations. Stoneman, a tough, aggressive twenty-nine-year-old who had learned his craft covering crime and politics in Chicago, coolly replied, "If you want to criticize anybody, you can go right across the street to the GPU, to Lubyanka, and criticize the GPU, which is responsible for exiling the villagers and stealing grain from them."

Not many correspondents talked that way to Oumansky, but Stoneman, the son of a Congregational minister, was not timid in conversations with Soviet officials, especially the police. During an earlier visit of his to Stalingrad, the GPU phoned and ordered him to report to its headquarters. On arrival, he demanded an explanation from the officer on duty, who replied that he was not obliged to explain anything.

"Well," Stoneman shot back, "then I don't have to come to your goddamn office and tell you anything about myself."

Neither Ralph Barnes nor William Stoneman was punished for breaching regulations, although the violation caused great embarrassment for the Soviet government. In later years the pair most certainly would have been expelled, but such harsh action was rarely used until after World War II. Stoneman remained in Russia for two more years and then departed with his wife and daughter like an ordinary tourist.

The famine story, like the famine itself, was not dead. An enterprising reporter for Britain's *Manchester Guardian,* Gareth Jones, traveled to Moscow as a tourist in March 1933 and took a train to Kharkov, carrying a knapsack stuffed with canned food. Touring the region on foot, he was able to confirm what Barnes and Stoneman had reported. When Jones returned to England, his eyewitness reports in the *Guardian* created a furor. Moving quickly to head off any further reporting on the famine, the Press Department resorted to blackmail. An important international story was looming: The Soviets were preparing to put on trial six British engineers accused of sabotaging turbines and other machinery sold to the USSR by their own firm, Metro-Vickers. Konstantin Oumansky made it clear that unless the correspondents repudiated the Jones report, they would not receive press credentials to cover the trial. After discussing the matter, the newsmen agreed that "compelling professional necessity" required that they work out a deal with the Press Department. Whether they received approval from editors back home for this arrangement is unknown, but they invited Oumansky to meet in a hotel room to negotiate what was, in effect, the terms of surrender. The correspondents bargained over language and details, but agreement was reached on a formula that would repudiate Gareth Jones.

"We admitted enough to soothe our consciences," Lyons wrote later, "but in roundabout phrases that damned Jones a liar. The filthy business having been disposed of, someone ordered vodka and *zakuski* (canapés), Oumanski joined the celebration, and the party did not break up until the morning hours."

Until then, Walter Duranty had been downplaying the story and had even denied that there was a famine. In March 1932, when reports of hunger were already reaching Moscow, he advised the *Times* "to the best of my knowledge there is no famine anywhere although partial crop failures [had occurred in] some regions." In November he wrote that despite the fact that living standards of a "large number of peasants" had fallen, there was "neither famine nor hunger," and a week later he predicted "nor is there likely to be."

Obliged to respond to the Jones story on the famine, Duranty refuted it. Whether his report was a result of the agreement with Oumansky or of his own convictions cannot be determined, but without leaving Moscow, since travel to the Ukraine was banned, he wrote that Jones produced a "big scare" based on inadequate information. He asserted that "there is no actual starvation or deaths from starvation," but in the same paragraph he conceded, "there is widespread mortality from diseases due to malnutrition"—a semantic distinction that in plain English meant many people were dying. Even after the trial ended with the conviction of several of the engineers, Duranty continued to soft-pedal the famine. When his competitor Ralph Barnes returned to New York and wrote an uncensored story reporting that at least one million Russians had perished from hunger in 1932, Walter Duranty's response from Moscow in the *Times* three days later again showed his reluctance to report anything negative about the Soviets:

> The excellent harvest about to be gathered shows that any report of a famine in Russia is today an exaggeration or malignant propaganda. The food shortage which has affected almost the whole population last year and particularly in the grain-producing provinces—the Ukraine, North Caucasus, the lower Volga region—has, however, caused heavy loss of life.

For whatever reason, Walter Duranty was still playing with words, refusing to admit that there was scarcely a difference between a famine and heavy loss of life, especially for the victims.

In September, when it appeared that good weather and a successful spring planting ensured a plentiful harvest, the travel ban was lifted. Duranty was the first to leave Moscow, thanks to the Press Department, which gave him a two-week head start on the other correspondents. His first story set the tone for the rest of his dispatches, reporting that he had seen only well-fed peasants and plump babies; large stocks of vegetables, milk, and eggs in village markets; and "mile after mile of reaped grain in the fields."

When Walter Duranty returned to Moscow, however, he told a different story. At a dinner party attended by Eugene Lyons; his wife, Billy; and *New York Times* correspondent Anne O'Hare McCormick and her husband, Duranty described what he had actually seen in "brutally frank terms and they added up to a picture of ghastly horror." His estimate of the number of Russians who had died of hunger was "the most startling" Lyons had yet heard.

"But Walter," exclaimed Anne McCormick, "you don't mean that literally?"

"Hell, I don't," replied Duranty. "I'm being conservative."

The first comprehensive report on the famine, one that was dramatically dissimilar from Walter Duranty's, appeared in *The Christian Science Monitor* under the by-line of William Henry Chamberlin, the newspaper's correspondent in Russia since 1922. Published after he had left the Soviet Union in 1934 with no intention of ever returning, the articles described his extensive travels in the Ukraine and the North Caucasus with his Russian-speaking wife, Sonia. He saw barren fields, wasted and deserted villages, gaunt peasants, and whimpering babies. Everywhere he went, he heard the same account: Ten percent of the population had died from hunger and disease. This time there was no American Relief Administration to feed the starving. After the trip, Chamberlin returned to Moscow, packed his bags and notes, and left Russia to tell the story.

Like Eugene Lyons, William Henry Chamberlin had arrived in Moscow with strong pro-Soviet sympathies that quickly dissipated when they encountered the reality of Stalin's Russia. He spent much of his time traveling, a luxury that few of the other correspondents could afford, and gathering material for two books that have since become standard reference works: *The Russian Revolution* and *Russia's Iron Age*. When he returned to the United States he wrote a lengthy series on his experience, "a debt of honor to my readers for failing to report fully what happened in Russia after 1929 because of the censorship."

Walter Duranty's coverage of the famine was consistent with much of his reporting from the Soviet Union, slanting stories to fit his own vision of men and events. Unlike Eugene Lyons and William Henry Chamberlin, he arrived in Moscow with no basic sympathy for Socialism, and he was certainly not "redder than a rose," as George Seldes had described another correspondent. Chamberlin has suggested that Duranty sold out to the Russians in exchange for special treatment, presumably Katya and a private apartment, but he has presented no hard evidence. On the other hand, Malcolm Muggeridge, Moscow correspondent for the *Manchester Guardian* in 1933–34, probed for psychological reasons, convinced that Duranty's favorable coverage of the Soviet regime and his admiration for Stalin's brutal methods was "in some way getting back for being small . . . and not having the aristocratic lineage and classical education he claimed to have." William Stoneman saw Duranty differently: "He was amoral without any deep convictions about the rights and wrongs of communism."

Freudian analysis aside, Duranty's reporting created concern where it was most important: in the bosom of *The New York Times*. Managing editors, beginning with Carl Van Anda, who sent him to Moscow in 1921, and continuing with Frederick T. Birchall and Edwin L. James, who kept him there, were dissatisfied with his performance, especially when the newspaper, because of Duranty's dispatches, became known as the "Uptown *Daily Worker*." By August 1933, *Times* publisher Adolph S. Ochs was having second thoughts about his man in Moscow, concluding that although Duranty had been given "the widest latitude because of our confidence in his integrity and his alertness and ability to send authentic news, there have been indications for some time past that he is relaxing in his attitudes to his duties and not keeping us fully informed." Nonetheless, the *Times* retained him in the post, presumably because his retirement was imminent. Another reason may have been the Pulitzer Prize that Duranty won in May 1932 for his Moscow reporting that, according to the jury's citation, "show profundity and intimate comprehension of conditions in Russia and of the causes of those conditions. They are marked by scholarship, profundity, impartiality, sound judgment, and exceptional clarity and are excellent examples of the best type of foreign correspondence."

All the newsmen in Moscow wanted to interview Stalin. They wrote letters but received no answers; they phoned his secretariat but no one ever called back. They badgered the Press Department and were told that the request was being studied. Editors back home sent cables and urgent letters requesting the general secretary to receive their Moscow correspondents, citing "informed sources" in Riga and Warsaw who reported that Stalin had been assassinated, that Marshal Klimenti

Voroshilov, commissar for war, was conspiring against his master, and that Red Square was covered with corpses.

Like the others, Eugene Lyons had also written letters, the latest on November 22, 1930, requesting "only two minutes" of Stalin's time to confirm that he was still among the living. The next day Lyons' phone rang and a man speaking good English asked:

"Mr. Lyons? This is Comrade Stalin's office."

A skeptical Lyons replied, "You don't say! How interesting! Give him my kindest regards, and Mrs. Stalin, too."

The voice insisted, "But this *is* Comrade Stalin's secretary. Comrade Stalin has received your letter and wished me to tell you that he will be glad to talk to you in one hour—at five o'clock, that is—in his offices at the Central Committee of the party."

Lyons could scarcely believe his good fortune with what could be the scoop of a lifetime. No foreign correspondent had interviewed Stalin since 1927.

Central Committee headquarters still stands today where it stood in 1930, on Staraya Ploshchad (Old Square) near the Kremlin. Lyons was there at the appointed time with his friend Charles Malamuth, a professor of Slavic studies at the University of California, who agreed to serve as an interpreter should Lyons' Russian fail, an unnecessary precaution since Stalin provided his own translator.

Lyons was ushered into a waiting room unlike any Soviet office he had ever seen, "quiet, orderly, unhurried, and efficient, devoid of the trappings of power, curiously austere and self-assured, without elegance, gold braid, or shrieking symbols: power naked, clean, and serene in its strength." He then entered an inner office where Stalin, attired in his customary tunic unadorned with decorations, offered his hand and a smile, "remarkably unlike the scowling, self-important dictator of popular imagination." They sat down at one end of a long conference table, and instead of pulling out a pipe, Stalin surprised Lyons by offering him a cigarette and lighting one for himself.

For over an hour, Lyons asked Stalin a range of questions

covering relations between the United States and Russia, the progress of the Five Year Plan, and expectations of a world Communist revolution, but it was his first query that provoked a laugh:

"Comrade Stalin, may I quote you to the effect that you have not been assassinated?"

"Yes, you may," Stalin said with a smile, "except that I hate to take bread out of the mouths of the Riga correspondents."

After the political questions, Lyons asked Stalin about his family, and for the first time the Soviet leader revealed that he was married and had three children, one of them, Svetlana, still in school.

When the interview was over, Stalin asked whether he could read the cable, offering Lyons both an adjacent office and a Latin-script typewriter on which to work. Tea and sandwiches were served and Stalin occasionally stuck his head through the door to ask if anything was needed. When Lyons finished writing, the official interpreter read the story to Stalin and to Marshal Voroshilov, who had been present during the interview. They were both amused by references to Stalin's appearance and to his family. Other than a few nonpolitical changes suggested by Stalin, the story remained intact. Lyons, however, was taking no chances. He asked the Soviet leader to sign one copy to facilitate approval by the censor. Stalin picked up a pencil, scrawled across the top page, "More or less correct," and signed his name.

Eugene Lyons thanked Stalin and drove to the Foreign Affairs Commissariat to submit his cable to the censor, but everyone had left for the day. He then drove to Comrade Podolsky's apartment and handed him the dispatch. The Press Department official glanced at the signature, uttered the Russian equivalent of "I'll be damned," and collapsed in a chair. For once, a UP story was transmitted without changes.

Lyons' coup jolted the Moscow press corps, and congratulatory cables from the UP and its newspaper clients poured in. Envious colleagues phoned to find out how he had obtained the interview. Walter Duranty, however, was annoyed that *The New York Times* and he, the dean of correspondents who had been reporting from Moscow since 1921, had not been granted the interview. Duranty hounded the Press Department until he obtained an audience a few weeks after the UP newsman. Unlike Lyons or any other reporter, Duranty was favored with a second interview, in December 1933.

The choice of interviewer often depended on luck and timing. When it suited their purpose, Soviet officials chose any request for an interview, probably from the top of the pile. Lyons may just have been lucky, since there was no special reason for the UP to win the prize. If AP correspondent Stanley P. Richardson had sent Stalin a letter one hour after Lyons, he might have obtained the interview. Another lesson for reporters: The summons to the Central Committee came with one hour's notice, just enough time to change clothes, grab a notebook, and head across town. For Eugene Lyons, this only confirmed that, in a one-man news agency bureau, the correspondent must stay close to the office at all times.

In the lives of the American reporters, the most decisive factor was censorship. To get a story or a fact through the censor's net with minimal deletions was the daily challenge that correspondents dealt with in different ways.

When Linton Wells arrived in Moscow for INS in 1932, he told press chief Konstantin Oumansky that he would report nothing he believed to be untrue and would submit everything he wrote to censorship. However, if he knew that his facts were correct, no matter what the source, or if the information had already appeared in a Soviet publication and consequently was transmittable, then he would consider it "privileged and you cannot deny me the right to dispatch it. Whenever you do this, you ought to know that I shall feel justified in sending it out of the country by any means possible."

Oumansky replied, "I don't think we're going to get on well together."

"Well," countered the thirty-nine-year-old correspondent, "at least we know where we stand."

Another American who had few friends in the Press Department was Junius B. Wood, one of the finest reporters on the *Chicago Daily News* and a veteran war correspondent. A crusty, pipe-smoking graduate of the Chicago school, he enjoyed writing stories that he knew would offend the censors. When, for example, the Soviet government, seeking to halt the black market in rubles, announced that only foreign currencies would be accepted in certain restaurants and hotels, Wood wrote a cable that did not pass the censor. The lead:

THE SOVIET GOVERNMENT TODAY REPUDIATED ITS OWN CURRENCY.

Wood's successor, William Stoneman, never hesitated to evade censorship, usually sending out his dispatches with departing travelers, as evidenced by his reportage of the famine.

"If the story was important and interesting," he told me, "I would send it out and take the consequences. Or let my paper take the consequences. If anything happened to me as a result of a story I sent, it was a matter between the *Chicago Daily News* and the Soviet government."

The authorities seemed to take a relaxed view of censorship violations by Stoneman and Wells, who were probably not the only ones to flout the rules. Before Linton Wells left in 1934, the Press Department even gave him farewell dinner, complete with expressions of hope that he would soon return.

A basic policy established by the Press Department was that any published information, having passed the internal censorship, would be approved for transmittal by foreign correspondents. An enterprising reporter, however, would include additional data from other sources or his own observations to flesh out the story. For example, if he wrote a piece about Soviet agricultural "achievements" based on an article in *Pravda,* he might also include a quote from a diplomat or Russian who had just returned from the Ukraine casting doubt on those claims, leaving it to the censor to strike out the comments. Much of what a correspondent was actually permitted to transmit was what he and the censor agreed on. Bargaining took place face-to-face, a confrontation that was one of the crucial elements in reporting from Moscow. A correspondent without bargaining skills and tenacity soon found that his journalistic output declined in quality and quantity.

An example of this haggling occurred in 1933 when Stalin's forced collectivization policy ran into serious opposition in the Kuban region of the North Caucasus, a stronghold of independent-minded cossacks. Through one of his contacts, Eugene Lyons obtained copies of a local newspaper that bannered eight-column headlines announcing that the population of three entire villages had been packed into cattle cars by Red Army troops and shipped out to lumber camps. That meant everybody: men, women, children, the old, and the sick. The purpose of the mass deportation was to crush cossack opposition to collectivization.

Eugene Lyons wrote his story and took it to Konstantin Oumansky for approval, expecting that it would be passed without difficulty, since the information came from an official Soviet source. Although he was annoyed that Lyons had discovered such an "unfavorable" story, Oumansky could not forbid its transmittal. Groping for a way out, he asked:

"But Mr. Lyons, you say that forty thousand are involved in this mass deportation. Where did you get the figure?"

"That's simple. I looked up your latest official census. The population of three settlements as given there totals about forty thousand."

"All the same, I'm sorry, I can't let you use that figure. That was the population two or three years ago. How do you know what it is today?"

"All right—*you* tell me how many were deported! Surely someone in the government knows."

"No, your cable can't go unless you eliminate the figure. Just say that the inhabitants were exiled, without specifying the figure."

Lyons walked out of Oumansky's office, refusing to emasculate the story by filing it without the crucial numbers. A few days later he left Moscow for a vacation, transmitting the cable from the UP bureau in Berlin. The report created a worldwide sensation, with its specific details on the human cost of the collectivization drive. Konstantin Oumansky's reaction could only be surmised, but on his return, Eugene Lyons was not reprimanded for his failure to file through censorship.

The foreign correspondent was not the only victim of censorship. In an equally difficult and vulnerable position was the censor himself, since he was responsible for the political purity of the outgoing dispatches. One could easily imagine the scoldings they were subjected to by their superiors if by chance a story slipped through the net, or even a line or a paragraph that reflected unfavorably on the Soviet Union. Both censor and correspondent understood their symbiotic relationship, often collaborating to find acceptable language that would protect each partner to the transaction. In these cases, perhaps a more honest and accurate by-line would have been: Eugene Lyons and Konstantin Oumansky, United Press Staff Correspondents.

Unlike the agency correspondents who filed breaking news around the clock, the pace in Moscow for newspaper reporters or "specials" was leisurely in the 1920s. They filed one or two dispatches a day and then could relax. If a story broke late at night, despite the eight-hour time difference between New York and Moscow, the sixteen to twenty hours required for transmittal made it impossible to meet the deadline for the next day's paper. Since, under the circumstances, speed was not essential, the story was held over until the next day. Walter Duranty, for example, knew that a cable he delivered to the telegraph at 5:00 P.M. on Thursday would not reach the *Times* foreign desk before Friday between 5:00 A.M. and 9:00 A.M., much too late for the final edition's 3:00 A.M. deadline. Duranty's social life was enhanced by this schedule, permitting him to attend a party or enjoy a quiet dinner and file in the morning. By 1930, however, cable service had so vastly improved that he could file as late as 7:00 A.M. Moscow time

(11:00 P.M. in New York) and still get his story into the final edition of the *Times*.

What irked Duranty most, as it did the other correspondents, was the frequent late-night phone calls from the Press Department announcing that "an important communiqué"—no details—was available at the Foreign Affairs Commissariat and could be picked up immediately. This meant getting out of bed, driving across town, going through the Russian text with a translator, and writing a story, if warranted, at midnight or 1:00 A.M. for approval by the censor. Often the communiqués were only of marginal interest to American readers and not even transmitted: another wasted trip and sleepless night.

To ease the strain, Duranty hired Robin Kinkead, twenty-three, a year out of Stanford University, who showed up in Moscow a few days after Christmas in 1929 with little money, no job, and a great ambition to be a foreign correspondent. For an ungenerous fifteen dollars a week, Duranty, now forty-five, found himself an eager young assistant and legman who proved to be the best journalistic bargain in Moscow. Kinkead quickly learned his job, making it possible for Duranty to take longer vacations and go on lucrative lecture tours in the United States. But he also made mistakes.

In June 1931, two American pilots, Wiley Post and Harold Gatty, landed their monoplane *The Winnie Mae* in Moscow to refuel on a round-the-world flight. With Walter Duranty out of the country, Robin Kinkead was covering the arrival. Since the *Times* had obtained exclusive rights to Post and Gatty's personal story, Kinkead followed them around Moscow, nagging them for their report, but all he heard from them was "Get the hell out of here and don't bother us. We've got to rest!"

Instead of the personal signed story, Kinkead cabled a routine account of the landing. The next day he received a blistering wire from managing editor Frederick Birchall, demanding to know why. In desperation, Robin Kinkead asked Eugene Lyons for advice.

"Oh, for Chrissakes, someone should have told you. No

aviator writes his personal story. You write it! If they don't say anything, you make it up."

"But that's cheating," protested Kinkead.

"Well," replied the old wire service hand, "you can figure out what they *might* have said."

Robin Kinkead returned to the office, wrote a first-person account of the flight into Moscow, full of chitchat and colorful details, and dispatched it to New York. This time there was no angry cable from Birchall. The *Times* published the article about their heroic exploit, signed by Wiley Post and Harold Gatty—on the front page.

Life for the agency correspondents was very different from that of the "specials." Not only were they on duty twenty-four hours a day covering news in the Soviet Union, but they were also at the mercy of editors in New York who did not seem to realize that when it was 5:00 P.M. in Washington it was 1:00 A.M. in Moscow and urgent queries could not be answered at that time, if ever. Stanley Richardson of the Associated Press and his United Press competition, Eugene Lyons, left many Bolshoi Theater performances, dinner parties, and poker games in response to phone calls from the Press Department, which, as agency reporters, they could not ignore. If, on occasion, they were obliged to travel outside Moscow, they worked out a pool arrangement under which one reporter would cover the news for everyone else. In 1930, for example, the Press Department invited foreign correspondents to witness the opening of the Turksib railroad that connected the central Asia city of Tashkent to the Trans-siberian line, a mammoth engineering project. With Walter Duranty in the United States on one of his lecture tours, Robin Kinkead was again in charge of the *Times* bureau. Both the AP and UP correspondents decided to go on the trip, confiding their operations to the inexperienced cub reporter, a risky business for the agencies and for the newspaper. Fortunately, no big stories broke while everybody was out of town, in part because the news managers of the Press Department were also in Tashkent.

While correspondents agreed that travel, either arranged by the Press Department or privately, was the best way to find out what was going on in the country, only a few reporters like William Stoneman, Ralph Barnes, and William Henry Chamberlin could do so extensively. Stoneman and Barnes journeyed down the Volga to the Caspian Sea, to the Crimea, and to the Ukraine, almost anywhere they wanted except to Karelia and eastern Siberia, where the labor camps were located. Leaving Moscow was simple; since no permission from the Press Department was required, all one had to do was go to the railroad station and buy tickets. The wide latitude and freedom from deadline pressures that *The Christian Science Monitor* allowed Chamberlin provided him, of all the "specials," with greater freedom to travel. He found that the farther he traveled from Moscow, the more relaxed and communicative people became.

"The villages were never so cowed as the capital," he concluded. "There were fewer Communists, fewer police agents in and out of uniform, and the peasants, old and young, welcomed what was usually the unique occasion of meeting Americans."

Unlike the Russians around them, by 1930 the American correspondents were living well. Those who did not stay in hotels found comfortable apartments and acquired maids and cooks and chauffeurs. Walter Duranty left his storefront apartment for more spacious quarters on the sixth floor of a modern building; Katya and Michael moved with him. Joseph Barnes, who replaced Ralph Barnes (no relation) as correspondent for the *New York Herald Tribune* in the mid-1930s, rented a cozy log cabin, an *izba*, on the other side of the Moscow River. The house was later bought from its Russian owner by Edmund Stevens, who subsequently served as the wartime Moscow correspondent of *The Christian Science Monitor*. Stevens retained ownership of the *izba* for almost forty years, until it was demolished to make way for construction of an apartment building. Eugene Lyons, after living two years with Billy in a renovated stable that also served as the United Press bureau, moved into a mansion occupied by Dr. Armand Hammer, an American physician, entrepreneur, and acquaintance of Lenin; Hammer had obtained a concession from the government to manufacture pencils in the USSR. The new quarters, which were guarded by Dobermans, must have seemed like a palace, with a marble spiral staircase, rococo statuary, a vast kitchen, and a wood-paneled dining room that Lyons shared with his new landlord. Dr. Hammer's motives in opening his house to a correspondent were not entirely charitable, however. Since he was transferring ownership of his pencil enterprise to the Soviet government, he calculated that the Russians would be less likely to evict him with the UP correspondent on the premises. His assumption was correct, and Lyons and his family happily resided in the largest American home in Moscow for almost four years even after Hammer had departed.

Planning for the future, Eugene Lyons invested in an apartment in a cooperative building under construction financed by a group of Moscow literary figures. Since the writers desperately needed trucks to haul construction materials obtainable only with the hard currency, they offered Lyons an apartment if he would buy the vehicles. Lyons advanced the needed twenty-five hundred dollars and acquired what was to become the famous United Press apartment on Ulitsa Furmanova (Furmanov Street), which remained in the agency's possession for almost forty years, the only one owned by an American news-media organization in the Soviet Union. During that time it sheltered at least half a dozen UP correspondents, their wives, children, friends, girlfriends, cats and large numbers of mice. The celebrities who passed through its portals included Mrs. Eleanor Roosevelt, author Truman Capote, journalist John Gunther, U.S. Supreme Court Justice William O. Douglas, countless ambassadors, U.S. senators, members of the cast of a touring company of *Porgy and Bess,* and, of course, many Russians. What made the apartment even more valuable was that after Stalin's death in 1953, when almost all Western correspondents were obliged to live in ghettos for foreigners under twenty-four-hour surveillance by MVD or KGB guards who harassed Soviet citizens brave enough to enter the enclave, no security guards were posted outside the UP apartment. Russians could walk in and out unmolested, a prime source of information for the correspondents who lived and worked there.

Famine in the Ukraine and hunger in the North Caucasus did not affect the life-style of the correspondents. They were able to import supplies and, like other foreigners in Moscow, were permitted to buy food and liquor for dollars at special hard-currency stores operated by the Soviet government. As always the social scene was lively, with parties, dinners, and receptions offered by the diplomats, who invited the correspondents in the belief that they were the best-informed people in Moscow. Occasionally the correspondents would meet at the Hotel National for a friendly game of billiards. The big weekly event, however, was the dance at the Metropole, where Alexander Svartsman's band played traditional folk songs and popular Western tunes. Virtually the entire foreign colony turned out for the event, as well as a large contingent of Russian girls who were there for more than foxtrotting. Two popular dance partners for the correspondents were the Gillis girls, Faye and Beth, daughters of J. H. Gillis, an American mining engineer who had supervised construction of two electrolytic zinc plants in the Soviet Union. Faye Gillis, an expert pilot, was the first and probably the last American woman to fly Red Air Force planes. She later married INS correspondent Linton Wells. Walter Duranty also attended the dances, but because of his wooden leg, he did not get onto the floor frequently. According to Robin Kinkaid, he spent most of the evening engaged in his favorite pastime, "romancing some dame."

The correspondents were not always filing serious political and economic stories; they also wrote features that illuminated other aspects of Soviet life. In 1934, for example, there was much skepticism outside Russia about the cadaver in Lenin's tomb: Was it genuine, or just a stuffed dummy? To dispel such aspersions on the revolutionary leader and the Soviet Union's most revered relic, the Press Department invited the correspondents to Red Square for a personal inspection of the remains. On hand for the guided tour were the two scientists who had embalmed Lenin in 1924, Professors V. Vorobev and B. Sbarsky. As the fascinated correspondents watched inside the gloomy crypt, the Russians raised the glass case under which Lenin's body lay, the upper torso garbed in a khaki tunic with a single decoration over the heart, hands folded over heavy red embroidery that covered the lower half of the body. Then they briskly tweaked the ears and pinched the cheeks to demonstrate that the corpse was real, explaining how the organs had been removed after Lenin's death ten years earlier and replaced with chemicals. The Russians treated the corpse in a businesslike fashion, as if they were teaching an anatomy lesson to a class of medical students, displaying no awe toward the remains of the man who had led the Bolsheviks to power and was venerated by millions.

When the United States and the Soviet Union established diplomatic relations in November 1933, the American correspondents hoped that the Russians, seeking to improve their image in the stronghold of capitalism, would become more open and more forthcoming with interviews and special trips and might even ease censorship. Initially a new atmosphere of friendliness toward Americans did prevail, with a round of government receptions and interviews, including a meeting between the correspondents and President Mikhail Kalinin. In an unusual gesture, Stalin departed from the fiction that he was only a party official without government responsibilities and entertained U.S. Ambassador William C. Bullitt. Within a few months, however, it became clear that little would change. Bullitt, who had known Russia during the heady days of the Revolution, was depressed by the repressive atmosphere he saw around him. Furthermore, he believed that Foreign Affairs Commissar Maxim Litvinov, who had succeeded Georgi Chicherin and negotiated the recognition agreement in Washington, had deceived President Roosevelt with respect to the subversive activities of the Comintern in the United States, the settlement of Russia's prerevolutionary debts, and religious freedom for American nationals residing in the Soviet Union. The U.S. protest over the Moscow meeting of the Comintern in 1935 as a violation of the Roosevelt-Litvinov agreement was rejected by the Soviet government with the customary explanation that the organization, whose senior officials included many leading Russian Communists, was an independent body.

Contrary to expectations, the opening of a U.S. embassy in Moscow had only a modest impact on the American newsmen working there. They could now buy some American products previously not available in the hard-currency stores, such as pipe tobacco, and there were additional compatriots to invite to parties and dinners. Among the new arrivals were several choice social companions who were to play important roles in future Soviet-American relations: the brilliant, intellectual George F. Kennan and the shrewd and charming Charles E. (Chip) Bohlen. Only low-ranking officials then, both were destined to become ambassadors to the Soviet Union. Within a few years, however, the embassy became increasingly important for the correspondents as a place that could provide assistance when needed. The new ambassador, Joseph E. Davies, a political appointee who succeeded William Bullitt in November 1936, was particularly friendly toward American reporters and even interceded with Premier Vyacheslav Molotov on their behalf when they had problems. In 1934, however, the only indication that the Americans had arrived was the Stars and Stripes flapping from a balcony of the new embassy chancery on Mokhovaya Street, a modern building that faced vast Manege Square and the Kremlin.

During almost six years in Moscow, Eugene Lyons increasingly lost his enthusiasm for the Soviet regime as his dream collided with reality. He was transformed from a Communist sympathizer, first into a skeptical observer, then into a foe. Reflected in his stories, this change was beginning to be noticed both at the United Press and at the Foreign Affairs Commissariat. In the eyes of the Press Department, Lyons' report on the deportation of forty thousand peasants decisively pushed him over the line that separated "friendly" from "unfriendly" bourgeois correspondents. The dénouement came suddenly in November 1933 while Maxim Litvinov was headed for Washington to negotiate U.S. recognition of the Soviet Union, a particularly delicate and important mission. At that very moment, Russian and Japanese armed forces were involved in bloody fighting over violations of their common border in Manchuria, creating a potentially dangerous situation in the Far East. Although these incidents were common knowledge in Moscow among journalists and diplomats, there was no confirmation solid enough to file a story.

One evening, two Russian acquaintances whom Lyons suspected were GPU agents came to see him at his home, and after much drinking they revealed that Soviet forces had inflicted severe losses on the Japanese, including the sinking of naval vessels. Lyons considered the information worth a brief cable, taking the precaution, however, of describing it as an "unconfirmed report." Just as he finished writing his dispatch, the UP's London bureau phoned about another story, and before signing off, the editor at the other end asked the usual question: "Anything new in Moscow, Gene?"

Succumbing to temptation, Lyons read him the cable, uncleared by the censor, but as soon as he hung up, he knew he had made a dangerous blunder. Lyons immediately called London to kill the story, only to discover that the dispatch had already moved on all wires. Within hours it was on front pages around the world.

In unison, the Russians and the Japanese vehemently denied the story and denounced Eugene Lyons, but for different reasons. From Washington, Maxim Litvinov accused the Japanese of using Lyons to wreck negotiations with the United States, while Tokyo charged the Soviets were using Lyons to further negotiations. Webb Miller, UP bureau chief in London, phoned Lyons pleading with him to reveal his sources, but he refused, explaining as best he could that because the lines were tapped, disclosing the names would only subject his Russian contacts to reprisals. In retrospect, Lyons realized that he had indeed been manipulated, but if he had submitted the copy to the censor, he might have been spared. Since he was unwilling to name names, his credibility at the United Press was undermined and his value to the agency in Moscow was clearly at an end. Ed L. Keen, UP vice president for Europe, finally traveled to Moscow to inform Lyons that he was being recalled.

Eugene Lyons left Moscow in January 1934, but not before the Press Department honored him with a farewell lunch in an atmosphere of "polite, if strained cordiality." For the American reporter, it was a sad departure. Although he had come to detest the regime, he had also come to love and respect the Russian people. Now he was bidding *proshchai,* farewell, to them and to Moscow, "city of desperations and enthusiasm, beauty and squalor. The thought that I might never see it again was a vise, every turn of the train's wheels closing its arms more painfully on my heart."

During his six years in Moscow, Eugene Lyons must have filed from five thousand to six thousand cables and mail features covering an enormous variety of subjects, but whether they made any profound impression on the American public is doubtful. When he distilled the essence of his experience into a book, however, without the editorial assistance of Konstantin Oumansky, and infused it with a scathing appraisal of the Soviet regime, the result was explosive.

Assignment in Utopia, published in 1937, was the first major book by an American correspondent to tear aside the propaganda curtain that hid the harsh reality of the Stalinist regime: a bitter, angry work that could only have been written by a true believer whose vision of communism was destroyed by the Communists themselves. The evidence was eloquently—indeed, brilliantly—reported in its pages. Favorably reviewed by many critics, *Assignment in Utopia* was denounced by Soviet sympathizers and by American Communists, but Dorothy Thompson wrote in the *New York Herald Tribune:* "Of all the books on Russia written by Americans thus far, this seems to me the most important and the most moving."

Walter Duranty's departure from Moscow was far less dramatic than that of Lyons. In September 1931 Duranty had asked the *Times* to let him retire so he could work on his book and exploit the U.S. lecture circuit, where he was the most popular and best-paid authority on Russia. Apparently the newspaper was not ready to let him go even though covering Moscow was becoming too arduous for the forty-seven-year-old correspondent.

Before he finally relinquished his post in April 1934, Duranty sailed to New York on the *Berengaria* with Maxim Litvinov to cover U.S.-USSR recognition negotiations. The voyage with the commissar for foreign affairs must have been especially satisfying for Duranty since, without a doubt, his reporting from Moscow had helped create a climate in the United States that facilitated the establishment of ties between the two countries. On an earlier trip, he had been invited to lunch by Franklin D. Roosevelt, governor of New York and Democratic candidate for the presidency, who sought his views on Russia. Roosevelt had already made it clear that he would seek to establish diplomatic relations with the Soviet regime should he win the election. Duranty strongly believed that U.S. recognition of Russia was essential to counter the growing military strength of Nazi Germany and Fascist Italy. Indeed, despite his flaws as a reporter, during the years he covered Moscow, Walter Duranty informed the world that from the ashes of the tsar's empire a new power had risen that would have to be reckoned with and would henceforth play a paramount role in international affairs.

Walter Duranty's assignment in Russia was the longest of any correspondent in the history of the *Times* bureau, and although it created controversy inside and outside the newspaper, his own explanation for his fourteen-year stint is unassailable:

"Moscow is the most interesting place in the world and that as a newspaperman I would not change for any other assignment. It is interesting politically because there before your eyes is being created something wholly new in human history. Still greater in my opinion is what might be called the natural interest of Russia—its utter difference from anything one has known before and its Alice-in-Wonderland topsy-turvyness as compared with the Western World."

Most reporters who have covered Moscow since would probably share that assessment.

The controversy over Walter Duranty haunted him long after he left Moscow. Seen by many, including some of his fellow correspondents, as the preeminent expert on the Soviet Union, knowledgeable, balanced, and objective, he was viewed by others as an admirer of Stalin and an apologist for the Communist regime. Konstantin Oumansky, according to Malcolm Muggeridge, was always pointing to Duranty as an example for other journalists.

Even Joseph Stalin pronounced judgment on Walter Duranty during his last interview with him in 1933, a year of widespread famine, the exile of millions of peasants to Siberia and the Far North, forced collectivization, and enormous and widespread suffering. Few of these developments were reported by Duranty, or, if he did write about them, it was in a guise that justified the human costs, rationalized with his favorite expression, "You can't make an omelet without breaking eggs."

Stalin could not have been unaware of Duranty's professional performance when he told him:

"You have done a good job in your reporting of the USSR. Although you are not a Marxist, you tried to tell the truth about our country and to understand it and explain it to your readers. I might say that you bet on our horse to win when others thought it had no chance, and I am sure you have not lost by it."

After his retirement, Walter Duranty continued to work for the *Times* on a retainer with the understanding that he would serve in Moscow for several months a year. He did return to Russia on several occasions, but he spent most of his time in the United States on the lecture circuit promoting his best seller *I Write as I Please,* and writing other books. In 1940, he returned for the last time to the Soviet capital, where he seemed quite lost and out of touch. He even bet a fellow reporter a hundred dollars that the Nazi-Soviet Nonaggression Pact, signed in August 1939, would last because "Hitler and Stalin aren't that crazy." Walter Duranty finally settled down with a wealthy widow among the palm trees in Orlando, Florida, where he died on October 4, 1957, at age seventy-two.

*   *   *

Eugene Lyons left the United Press after he returned to New York and spent the rest of his working life as a prominent and articulate anti-Communist. He published eleven books; edited the *American Mercury*, a monthly magazine that opposed America's wartime alliance with Russia; and was a senior editor of *Reader's Digest* for many years. Lyons died in New York on January 7, 1985, at eighty-six, surviving all the Soviet bureaucrats who caused him so much grief. Konstantin Oumansky was killed in an airplane crash in 1945 en route to Mexico City, where he was the Soviet ambassador. The other censors disappeared during one of Stalin's many purges. But Dr. Armand Hammer, eighty-nine, Lyons' former Moscow landlord, in mid-1987 was still thriving as chairman of Occidental Petroleum Corporation and making lucrative deals with the Russians.

William Henry Chamberlin reported for the *Monitor* from Paris and Tokyo before retiring from journalism in 1940 to write books and lecture at various universities. He died in Switzerland in 1969 at seventy-two. William Stoneman abandoned journalism in 1945 to join the United Nations as the official spokesman for Trygve Lie, its first secretary-general. Stoneman died in 1987 at eighty-three in Saint Germain-en-Laye, a Paris suburb. Ralph Barnes, who went on to become a distinguished foreign correspondent for the *New York Herald Tribune*, was shot down covering a bombing raid over Yugoslavia in 1944.

By 1985, Robin Kinkead had long retired to Bolinas, California, a picturesque beach town north of San Francisco where he was writing his memoirs. Following his stint with Duranty and then heading the Reuters Moscow bureau, he decided to quit journalism and after six years in the U.S.S.R. returned to the United States in 1935. He undertook various writing assignments, including a WPA guide to California, a tour of duty with the Office of War Information, and a public relations post with Pan American World Airways. At eighty, he looked back at his years in Moscow without nostalgia.

"I'd had my fun as a glamorous and dashing correspondent—even with a trench coat for a while. . . . But as the years went by, I got more and more fed up and wasn't meeting any interesting women. Besides, I could see that I was in danger of becoming a drunk.

"I was fed up with being in Europe and away from my homeland—not a flag-waving thing. I just wanted to be on my own soil, with my own people."

5

Covering the Great Patriotic War

It's very dangerous at the front. Aren't you afraid?

There's only one thing I'm afraid of. That's going home without having finished my job.

> Margaret Bourke-White, *Life* photographer,
> to Deputy Commissar for Foreign Affairs
> Solomon A. Lozovsky

We do not recognize the institution of war correspondent.

> Nikolai Palgunov
> chief, Press Department
> Commissariat of Foreign Affairs

Henry Cassidy was sunning himself on the terrace of the Riviera Hotel in Sochi, a health resort at the foot of the towering Caucasus Mountains. A few yards away, the waves of the Black Sea sparkled as they surged over the breakwater onto the seaside promenade. For the thirty-year-old Associated Press correspondent, a quiet, peaceful, and well-merited vacation was about to begin. The date was Sunday, June 22, 1941.

As Cassidy strolled back to the hotel through the garden, he saw a crowd gathered in front of a loudspeaker. Foreign Affairs Commissar V. M. Molotov, in a flat, emotionless tone, was broadcasting a terrifying message to the Russian people:

"Today at 4:00 A.M., without any claims having been presented to the Soviet Union, German troops attacked our country, attacked our borders at many points, and from their airplanes bombed our cities. . . . This unheard-of attack upon our country is perfidy unparalleled in the history of civilized nations. . . . The Soviet government has ordered our troops to repulse the predatory assault and to drive the German troops from the territory of our country. . . .

"The government calls upon you, citizens of the Soviet Union, to rally still more closely around our glorious Bolshevik Party, around our Soviet government, around our great leader and comrade, Stalin. Ours is a righteous cause. The enemy shall be defeated, victory will be ours."

Cassidy was stunned. He had received a cryptic telegram from his assistant Robert Magidoff in Moscow that morning, SAMELOT SEICHAS (AIRPLANE IMMEDIATELY)! Now he knew what it meant. He had only one thought: to return to Moscow as quickly as possible. The long-expected war had begun, and the biggest story of his professional career had caught him stranded in a small town eight hundred miles from his typewriter. Nor did he know whether he would be able to return to his post, since all civilian aircraft were grounded; the only way to get to Moscow was to walk or take a train, if trains were still running.

In Moscow, at about 7:00 A.M. that same morning, the telephone rang in Henry Shapiro's bedroom. The United Press bureau manager, the only other full-time American correspondent in the Soviet Union, picked up the phone and heard the trembling voice of his friend Hermann Poerzgen of the *Frankfurter Zeitung* calling from the German Embassy.

"What we expected has happened. I am interned at the embassy and I want to say *Auf Wiedersehen* under better circumstances."

After weeks of rumors, German armies, preceded by waves of bombers and fighter planes, were rolling across the Soviet border. The entire world had heard the news, except the Russian people. For them, the war became official only when Molotov made his announcement eight hours later. Even though the minuscule foreign press corps had already learned about the invasion from the BBC and the German radio, no correspondent was permitted to file a line until Molotov had spoken.

The invasion came as a surprise to neither the reporters nor the foreign diplomats alert to the many signs that war was imminent. Three German Army groups comprising three million men, including two hundred thousand auxiliaries from allied nations, in 162 ground force divisions, and 3,550 tanks had been massed on Russia's western frontiers, ostensibly engaged in training maneuvers. Winston Churchill, thanks to his access to secret Wehrmacht communications, knew of the invasion plans and tried in vain to alert the Russians to the approaching attack. Commissar Molotov had rejected the warnings as "provocations" designed to undermine friendly relations between Nazi Germany and the Soviet Union. Joseph Stalin himself refused to see British Ambassador Sir Stafford Cripps, who bore further urgent messages from the British prime minister.

Additional ominous signs were visible in Moscow. The German envoy, Count Friedrich Werner von Schulenburg, and his staff sent their families and furniture home. Dulcie, wife of U.S. Ambassador Laurence A. Steinhardt, flew to Stockholm with only the clothes she was wearing, while her husband prepared a backup embassy installation thirty miles north of Moscow, complete with tents, canned food, and power generators. The ultimate tip-off was the departure of the two beloved boxers of the German first secretary, Gebhart von Walther, a confidant of German Foreign Minister Joachim von Ribbentrop, on what was to be the last flight to Berlin. When Henry Cassidy left Moscow for his Crimean vacation a few days before the attack, Dmitri Popescu, secretary of the Romanian legation, asked him with some surprise, "Are you really leaving now?"

Cassidy, however, turned what began as a journalistic disaster into a triumph. A resourceful reporter who began his career on the *Boston Traveler* after graduation from Harvard in 1931, he had worked for the AP in New York and covered the Spanish Civil War and the fighting in France, remaining in Paris until it was captured by the Wehrmacht in May 1940. Because he was a correspondent of a neutral country, the Germans gave Cassidy permission to travel on a troop train to Berlin, then fly to Moscow, the post to which he had been reassigned.

At the Sochi railroad station, Henry Cassidy flashed his credentials and talked his way aboard a Moscow-bound train packed with soldiers and recruits. For the next two days, his slow trip across the Ukraine and central Russia enabled him to witness the Russian people girding up for war. Having been in Spain and France as a front-line correspondent, he watched for the key elements in the Soviet response to the attack: transportation, civil defense, and army mobilization.

When he arrived in Moscow, Cassidy immediately filed a report that surprised the rest of the world: Everything was going smoothly, trains were running, blackout regulations were stringently observed, farms and factories were working, and mobilization of reservists seemed to be on schedule. Most important, he wrote, there was no panic. Passed by the censor, the story made front pages across the United States under this headline:

IVAN GOES CALMLY TO WAR

In the first week of the war, German spearheads advanced over a hundred miles on a two-thousand-mile front. The Luftwaffe destroyed twelve hundred Soviet aircraft, most of them on the ground, and took three hundred thousand prisoners, some three thousand tanks, and over two thousand pieces of artillery in the capture of Minsk, Byelorussia's capital. Henry Cassidy's dispatch was the first good news to come out of Moscow, but his freewheeling tour of the Russian hinterlands, uncontrolled by the Press Department, was the first of its kind—and the last.

Cassidy later learned that the conventional wisdom in the United States and England held that Russia, like Poland and France, would quickly collapse under the Nazi onslaught. His story convinced some skeptics that the Red Army would stand and fight. Even the Soviet ambassador to Washington, Konstantin Oumansky, former chief of the Press Department and nemesis of the Moscow correspondents, cited Cassidy's article as proof of his government's confidence that it could stop the Wehrmacht. Otherwise, he reasoned, the AP reporter would

not have been permitted to wander freely around the countryside.

Editors in the United States responded by dispatching their
best reporters to cover the new war. Within a few months,
American correspondents made their way to Moscow to join
Henry Cassidy and Henry Shapiro, traveling by various
routes, some via the Mideast and Teheran, others by the
perilous voyage from England through the submarine-
infested waters of the North Cape to Murmansk. Among the
first to arrive were A. T. Steele of the *Chicago Daily News,*
Cyrus L. Sulzberger of *The New York Times,* Wallace Carroll of
the United Press, and later, Eddy Gilmore of the Associated
Press and Larry Lesueur of CBS. In Russia they found that
the rules of the game were starkly different from what they
had known in covering the war in the West. The Soviet
government, acting in a traditional manner, promulgated a
severely restrictive coverage policy because of historical xenophobia, the need for wartime secrecy, and profound suspicion
of its new British ally. Joseph Stalin, who a month earlier had
replaced V. M. Molotov as chairman of the Council of People's
Commissars (premier), had not forgotten that His Majesty's
government was under the leadership of that ardent anti-
Bolshevik Winston Churchill, who in 1919 had urged President Wilson to destroy the young and fragile Soviet state. The
Russians still remembered that England had furnished arms
to generals fighting the Red Army and had occupied Murmansk and Archangel in 1918. More recently, they recalled
Neville Chamberlain's capitulation to Hitler at Munich. Stalin,
still doubting the British commitment to total destruction of
the Nazi regime, was concerned that England would prefer to
see Germany and the Soviet Union bleed each other white,
leaving the British Empire triumphant and intact. The Americans, not yet allies until Pearl Harbor, were tarred with the
same anti-Soviet brush.

Nevertheless, despite reservations and suspicions, the Soviets were obliged for political reasons to reach some accommo-
dation with the foreign correspondents. Stalin realized that if
he wanted critical supplies from the Allies—tanks, munitions,

gasoline, trucks, and food—he had to convince them that Russia had the will to fight and that the materiel would not fall into German hands. Only credible reporting from foreign correspondents to the outside world, mainly American and British, would achieve that goal. Like Lenin facing the harsh reality of the 1921 famine and the need to accept American correspondents with American food, Joseph Stalin also knew that in return for Allied aid, he was obliged to permit Allied reporters to cover the war.

To deal with the unprecedented situation, the Foreign Affairs Commissariat designed a system to provide the correspondents with the barest amount of information necessary to establish credibility and, at the same time, to ensure minimal exposure to battlefields and physical danger. As far as the Press Department and its chief, Nikolai Palgunov, were concerned, reporters could not have the freedom they had had during earlier fighting in France and later with Allied armies in the invasion of Europe and on the North African fronts. They would not be permitted to follow Red Army infantrymen and tanks through the snow and mud, to witness great battles, to fly missions with Soviet aircraft, or to visit munitions factories transported by train to safe havens behind the Ural Mountains. They would work under rigid control, subject to the usual strictures regarding access to Soviet officials, to information, travel, and an even harsher and more severe censorship. Just as Maxim Litvinov had viewed them in 1921, foreign correspondents in 1941 were still regarded as an evil, but a necessary one.

A week after the war began, the Press Department invited the correspondents to the former Greek legation building, where Solomon A. Lozovsky, a deputy commissar for foreign affairs, announced that the government had established a Soviet Information Bureau (Sovinformburo) to furnish them with news of the war. He himself would hold regular press conferences, something that had never been done before by a high Soviet official. Lozovsky, a bearded, witty old Bolshevik who spoke fluent English and French and had lived in Paris and Geneva, served as the Kremlin spokesman for the first six months of the war. As the Germans neared Moscow, he grew increasingly evasive and uninformative, and attendance at his briefings dwindled.

The principal source of information about the course of battle was a daily communiqué distributed—in Russian—at the Foreign Affairs Commissariat between 2:00 A.M. and 3:00 A.M. A steel-helmeted soldier delivered the copies to a Press Department secretary, who then handed each correspondent the text describing the military action on all fronts, often with deliberate imprecision. As soon as their interpreters had whispered the translation, the reporters began pounding out copy on typewriters kept permanently in the large, sparsely furnished room that served as the press center. When they had finished, two or three censors were waiting to review the dispatches, wield their black pencils, and stamp the seal of approval. Only then could the cables be sent to Central Telegraph for transmittal abroad.

Since competition among the news agencies was especially fierce, they used every possible means to speed transmission of the dispatches, including fleet-footed couriers. Henry Cassidy employed a fifteen-year-old girl with the unlikely name of Venera—Venus—who sprinted the entire distance from the Press Department to the telegraph, over a mile, clutching his copy. During one tense night, Harold King, Reuters bureau chief, and Henry Shapiro started pushing and shoving each other to get first to the only map of Russia in the room and pinpoint a location mentioned in the military communiqué. King, who towered over Shapiro, ended the fight by tearing the map off the wall, leaving the UP correspondent sputtering in anger and frustration.

In addition to the official communiqué, the other information source was *Red Star,* the official army newspaper, which had hundreds of its own correspondents at the front. The newspaper provided the American reporters with the only combat details and human-interest features they were able to transmit until they were finally permitted to tour the battle-fields themselves.

*   *   *

In the early weeks of the war, air raids on Moscow were frequent. As soon as the sirens began to scream, correspondents working in the Press Department, together with the censors, rushed downstairs to a comfortable underground shelter. They sat there for hours sometimes, awaiting the all-clear signal, their stories unwritten. Usually they slept, while Nikolai Palgunov passed the time quizzing his staff on literature with such questions as, "How many short stories did de Maupassant write?" "Who wrote *Gulliver's Travels*?" "What was the title of Jack London's story about a sea captain?" Outside the bombs were falling, anti-aircraft fire thundered, and searchlights probed the dark skies. The shared danger, however, did not make the censors any more amenable when it came to the copy. During the first six months, when the war news was so bleak, correspondents were permitted only to quote the communiqué; they were not allowed to evaluate the military actions it described. On some nights they could send only the text of the communiqué unaltered and were not even permitted to take the third or fourth sentence and make it the lead of the story. As the war progressed and the Red Army began to push back the Wehrmacht, censorship eased slightly, but it was always severe, and its harshness occasionally produced peculiar results. Because of the high cost of living at the Hotel National, Margaret Bourke-White, a *Life* photographer, frequently pressed her editors for additional funds. When her ruble account was running low, she once cabled New York:

MUST ASK FOR ANOTHER THOUSAND DOLLARS BECAUSE REGRET LIVING COSTS RISING ASTRONOMICALLY.

After the censor wielded his black pencil, the transmitted cable read:

MUST ASK FOR ANOTHER THOUSAND DOLLARS BECAUSE REGRET LIVING.

At 8:00 A.M. on September 15, 1941, a small group of reporters waited outside the Foreign Affairs Commissariat, chatting quietly. Within a few minutes, they got into five M1 sedans and drove off. Eleven American and British journalists were on their way for their first look at the Red Army in action. The long-sought tour of the battlefields was about to begin.

The correspondents were driven to Yelnya, or what remained of the town, about 150 miles southwest of Moscow, recaptured by the Red Army from the Germans a week earlier. Among them were Henry Cassidy; Wallace Carroll of the UP; C. L. Sulzberger of *The New York Times;* A. T. Steele of the *Chicago Daily News;* author Erskine Caldwell, reporting for *PM*, and his wife, Margaret Bourke-White, a challenge to German sharpshooters in a flaming red coat. They were accompanied by Press Department representatives, officer-guides, and armed chauffeurs who carried hand grenades in their tool kits.

During the three-day trip, the correspondents interviewed Major General Vasili Sokolovsky, chief of staff for the Western Front; Soviet fighter pilots who had just bombed the Smolensk airport held by the Wehrmacht; and three German crew members of a downed Junkers 88. In Vyazma, where they spent the first night, they were rudely awakened in the morning by German bombs that fell close to their hotel. No reporters were hurt, nor was the Press Department censor, Comrade Anurov, who was found in his bed unscathed but framed by a window sash that had fallen on him so precisely that he looked like a picture.

In Yelnya they saw a graveyard of shattered houses, ravaged streets torn by tank treads and pockmarked with water-filled bomb craters. Along the way they passed still-smoldering villages that had been burned to the ground, muddy fields slashed by antitank ditches, and communications trenches where the Germans had begun to dig in. The devastation was worse than anything Henry Cassidy had seen on the Western Front. One night, the reporters were taken to within seven hundred yards of the Germans' lines, where they caught a glimpse of Russia's new secret rocket weapon, the Katyusha. Everywhere they were feted with lavish dinners that included caviar, champagne, chocolate, and other delicacies, not the usual military fare. On their return to Moscow the correspondents were at long last able to file stories datelined: "With the Red Army."

All the correspondents were pleased with the trip to Yelnya, and so was the Press Department. It became the model for subsequent visits to the front. Structured like peacetime group tourism perfected by Intourist, the Soviet travel organization, the visits followed rigid itineraries managed by military guides accompanied by interpreters and Press Department censors. Interviews were allowed only with carefully selected officers and soldiers, often within artillery range of the enemy. But those reporters who could speak Russian, such as Henry Shapiro, Edmund Stevens of *The Christian Science Monitor,* and Alex Werth of the *Sunday Times* of London, were able to talk to anyone they could find. Even though the Soviets completely controlled their movements, reporters could still get a real sense of the sights and sounds of battle.

On October 15, 1941, as German armies closed in on Moscow, Joseph Stalin ordered a general evacuation of the city. Most of the children had already departed by train or truck, and many civilians had fled. Now members of the diplomatic corps, officials of the Foreign Affairs Commissariat, Bolshoi Theater artists, and foreign journalists were sent to Kuibyshev, a provincial town on the Volga some five hundred miles southeast of Moscow. All Russians who could work or fight were ordered to remain behind. Stalin himself remained in the Kremlin. At Spaso, the residence of Ambassador Steinhardt, thirty-two American diplomats and correspondents assembled for departure, not knowing whether they would ever return. A special train took them to their destination, where they were to spend the next seven months while the ferocious battle for Russia was fought on the Western Front.

In Kuibyshev, the correspondents lived in the shabby Grand Hotel, which had one bathroom on each floor and a restaurant that served beef stroganoff every day for dinner. As soon as the reporters arrived, the Moscow routine quickly resumed:

military communiqués were distributed, cables dispatched abroad, and Solomon Lozovsky held his press briefings. The Soviets tried to make the newcomers feel at home, presenting weekly performances by the Bolshoi Ballet. Moscow's Gastronom, the special food store for foreigners, opened a well-stocked branch, and even the commission store was moved from the capital's Stoleshnikov Street to a location across from the hotel so the diplomats and correspondents could shop for antiques. Kuibyshev, however, was not Moscow. To pass the time between communiqués, the reporters roamed through the city, drank cheap and plentiful vodka, and played endless games of poker.

Kuibyshev's tedium was alleviated in November by the arrival of a new contingent of correspondents from the West. Eddy Gilmore of the AP had shipped out from Scotland in October on the British freighter *Temple Arch* headed for Murmansk with supplies for the Red Army. With him on the perilous route were Walter Kerr of the *New York Herald Tribune;* Larry Lesueur of CBS; and Ralph Parker, a British journalist covering for both *The New York Times* and *The Times* of London. On board they stood watch with the crew, manning machine guns against submarines and dive bombers. Their vessel, loaded with two thousand tons of TNT, survived the voyage, but they saw several slow-moving freighters sunk by torpedoes. By the time the convoy approached Murmansk, German troops had occupied the city, forcing the ships to continue to Archangel, 350 miles farther southeast. Boarding a train headed for Moscow, the correspondents meandered around northern Russia for two weeks, trying to escape the Germans who were bombing the rail lines. Finally the correspondents debarked in Kuibyshev for a joyous meeting with their Moscow colleagues. At the hotel, Lesueur gazed at the beef stroganoff in awe, his first decent meal in over two months. Before he could taste it, a British correspondent sitting next to him snatched the plate and scolded the waiter, "How many times have I told you to heat the plates before you serve the food!" The chastised waiter returned it to the kitchen while Larry Lesueur fumed.

*   *   *

In mid-December, after the Red Army stopped the Wehr-macht tide before Moscow, thirteen correspondents were flown to the capital to visit the battlefield, then returned to Kuibyshev. For the next five months they were moved back and forth by the Press Department from the Grand Hotel to various fronts until the threat to Moscow had eased; and in May 1942, all the reporters returned to the Soviet capital. Except for Henry Cassidy, who had a small apartment in the Arbat district, the correspondents were lodged in an impro-vised wartime press center, the Metropole Hotel. Gloomy and cavernous, "Mother Metropole" was like a college fraternity house where the foreign journalists lived, worked, drank, caroused, played poker, and entertained a large contingent of Russian maidens. Through its corridors passed dozens of reporters for British, American, and French news agencies and publications during the four years of war. The Associated Press, the United Press, *Time*, CBS, *The New York Times*, the *New York Herald Tribune, Collier's*, and the *Chicago Daily News* had offices scattered through the hotel, which usually doubled as accommodations for the correspondents. Working together for most of the day, the reporters ate together in the Metro-pole dining room, where their ration tickets entitled them to fare superior to what was available to the Russians. At times even the Metropole faltered, and the evening meal consisted of thin soup, black bread, and vodka. The Soviets took seriously the slogan "Everything for the front."

In the midst of Allied conviviality was a small group of Japanese correspondents whose country was at war with the United States and Great Britain but not with the Soviet Union. This created protocol problems for the Russians, who sought to keep the American and British correspondents separate from the Japanese. In the Metropole, this was virtually impossible. After Pearl Harbor, for example, every time their armies scored a military success, the Japanese marched trium-phantly into the dining room, waving bottles of vodka and singing patriotic songs. The Allied reporters then rushed back to their offices and listened glumly to shortwave news broad-

casts to find out what disaster had befallen their forces in Asia
and the Pacific. Sensitive to the feelings of Russia's allies, the
Metropole management finally moved the Japanese into another dining room.

All the foreign correspondents regularly wrote to Premier
Stalin requesting an interview or soliciting his views on various
timely subjects, but never receiving a reply or even an acknowledgment. Late one Saturday night in October 1942, a Press
Department secretary phoned Henry Cassidy. Mr. Palgunov,
she said, wanted to see him immediately. "It is very important." Cassidy quickly hung up, dressed, and for the next
forty-five minutes stumbled through the blackout from his
house in the Arbat to the Commissariat. When he arrived, he
was immediately admitted to Nikolai Palgunov's inner sanc-
tum.

"The document that you are waiting for is here," announced
the press chief, handing him a sheet of paper. Across the
bottom, inscribed in violet ink, was an unmistakable signature:
"J. Stalin."

Henry Cassidy had received a reply to his latest letter to
Stalin, written only twenty-four hours earlier, with three
questions on the relations between the Soviet Union and the
other Allies, including one on the importance of a second
front in Europe. Stalin's reply was terse: 149 Russian words
that made headlines in the West. A second front, he wrote, is
"very important" in the current situation. Furthermore, Allied
aid to the Soviet Union "has so far been little effective"
compared to "the aid that the Soviet Union is giving the Allies
by drawing upon itself the main forces of the German Fascist
armies."

Typed on plain white paper without a heading, the letter
carried nothing to indicate its origins except for the bold
signature.

Cassidy was delighted. He had obtained what every Moscow
correspondent dreamed about: an exclusive statement by
Premier Stalin on an important subject. But fate and the time
difference between New York and Moscow were to play a

mean trick on him. Since it was too late to make the Sunday morning newspapers in the United States and no afternoon newspapers were published that day, he delayed cabling the story for twelve hours, then filed it at noon for the Monday morning papers. Afterward, in a gentlemanly gesture, he shared the story with his colleagues, including his competitor Henry Shapiro, rather than have them receive queries from their editors. The other correspondents quickly wrote their stories and sent them to the Central Telegraph.

What Cassidy did not know was that communications had been interrupted between Moscow and the West, and his cable was still sitting on a clerk's desk when the other dispatches were submitted. As soon as communications were restored, the last cable—on top of the pile—went out first, and the first was dispatched last—Henry Cassidy's. He was beaten on his own exclusive.

Since there was some doubt at the AP in New York that Stalin had actually addressed the letter to Henry Cassidy, he radioed a facsimile. At the telegraph, a clerk pointed out that the note was not signed by Stalin. The signature was imprinted with a rubber stamp, a detail that Cassidy cabled to New York. Apparently Stalin was informed about this discovery. When Cassidy received a second letter from him a month later with favorable comments on the American landings in North Africa, Stalin signed it with a dark blue crayon. The signature was unmistakably genuine. Both letters, now framed, are displayed on the living room wall of Henry Cassidy's New York City apartment.

When the first Stalin letter was published in *Pravda, Izvestia, Red Star,* and other Soviet newspapers, Henry Cassidy became an overnight Moscow celebrity, since it was addressed to him personally. In addition to congratulatory messages from his wife, Martha, who was living in London, and Kent Cooper, general manager of the AP, the more tangible reward for such instant fame was the four bottles of wine he was able to purchase in the store for foreigners, instead of the usual ration of one. More important, however, was the delivery of Cassidy's car from Kuibyshev within forty-eight hours after he had received the letter. He had been waiting for it almost a year.

A few days later, a recently arrived British correspondent stopped him in the corridor of the Metropole, asking:

"I say, old boy, when one corresponds with Stalin, how does one deliver the letter?"

Although the letters were a triumph for Henry Cassidy, they were a professional disaster for Henry Shapiro. Furious and frustrated, he complained bitterly to Nikolai Palgunov, although he knew that the press chief was powerless to help. Shapiro could do little more than send his own questions to the Kremlin and hope for a response. Although he was UP bureau manager and dean of the press corps, a Moscow correspondent since 1934, these were hardly reasons for Stalin to answer. Besides, when Shapiro asked writer Ilya Ehrenburg, who was highly regarded by the Soviet leader, to intercede on his behalf, the reply was blunt:

"With your name, you'll never get an answer."

Unlike most Moscow correspondents, Henry Shapiro, then thirty-six, came to journalism in a roundabout way. Born in Romania and raised in New York, he earned a Harvard law degree after graduation from New York's City College. On the advice of one of his professors, he departed for Moscow in 1933 to study Soviet law. While attending lectures at the Law Institute, he quickly learned Russian and soon began working part time as a translator for American and British reporters he had met in the small foreign colony. Ralph Barnes hired Shapiro as an assistant to read the newspapers and, eventually, to cover stories. In 1935, when Robin Kinkead returned to the United States, Shapiro inherited the Reuters job, moving over to the United Press in 1936. A year earlier he had married a twenty-year-old blue-eyed beauty, Ludmilla Nikitina, daughter of a professor of economic geography at Moscow University, a marriage that survived the vicissitudes of war, years of separation, and threats of arrest and exile.

A few days after Cassidy received his second letter, Nikolai Palgunov phoned Shapiro with some good news: His long-sought trip to the Stalingrad front, where a fierce and gigantic battle between the Red Army and the Wehrmacht was under way, had been approved. This was not group tourism; Henry Shapiro would tour the front alone—an exclusive that would compensate for Stalin's letters to Cassidy. Palgunov gave Shapiro short notice. Be at the Moscow airport the next day at 9:00 A.M., he said. Rising early that morning, the UP correspondent donned a U.S. Army uniform (like the other American correspondents, he was accredited to the Persian Gulf Command) and headed for his car. The old Chevy would not start in the below-zero weather. When the UP chauffeur arrived, he managed to get the car moving, but they reached Central Airport 30 minutes late, just in time to see a Soviet DC-3 take off. An angry Red Army colonel, the escort officer, told Shapiro that the plane could not be held up any longer. The other passenger, Major General Patrick Hurley, special envoy of President Roosevelt, was furious at being delayed by a mere correspondent. Hurley insisted that the plane leave without Shapiro, and it did.

Sick with disappointment, Shapiro once more turned to Nikolai Palgunov, who promised that a trip would be quickly arranged—by train. Within a week, accompanied by a staff colonel, Shapiro was heading southeast, toward Stalingrad. When he arrived at the front, he toured the combat zone for a week, interviewing generals and privates, visiting advance headquarters where he saw battlefield maps showing that Red Army troops had closed a trap around the Sixth Army of German General Friedrich Paulus, while troops of Field Marshal von Manstein were still trying to reach the Volga from the west. One of the Russians he interviewed was the chief political commissar on the Stalingrad front, an officer named Nikita S. Khrushchev.

What Shapiro saw at the Stalingrad front convinced him that he had witnessed the beginning of the end for Germany. On his return to Moscow, he wrote eight articles predicting that the Russians would crush the Germans and go on to win the war, a risky prognosis in November 1942. When he submitted the articles to Nikolai Palgunov for censorship, he expected they would be quickly approved. To his astonishment, the press chief vetoed the entire series because "they are too optimistic."

Shapiro protested to no avail, but he refused to accept Palgunov's decision as final and immediately sent a letter to Premier Stalin thanking him for the opportunity to go to the front. He also enclosed copies of his articles, mentioning that they were being reviewed by the Press Department and expressing hope there would be no difficulties because of his optimism about a Soviet victory.

About an hour later, Palgunov summoned Shapiro to his office.

"If you make a few changes," he announced, "I think I can let the articles go."

Shapiro chuckled to himself, made cosmetic alterations in several articles to pacify the censor, resubmitted them, and Nikolai Palgunov stamped them with the official seal. Everything passed except one single piece of information: the name of the commanding general of the Stalingrad front.

"You know we don't publish the names of our generals. We don't want the Germans to know who the commander is," Palgunov explained.

Shapiro handed Palgunov a leaflet dropped over the German lines by the millions urging General Paulus and his troops to surrender. It was signed General Konstantin K. Rokossovsky, commanding general, the Don front.

Nikolai Palgunov, the supreme bureaucrat, shrugged.

"I still cannot pass that. It has never been officially announced."

Without mentioning Rokossovsky, Henry Shapiro filed his story, the first eyewitness report on the Battle of Stalingrad, an exclusive of major importance that made the front page of *The New York Times* and other newspapers in the Allied countries. His colleagues at the Metropole were envious, but the United Press was delighted. So was General Hurley. A few months later, when Shapiro encountered him at the Teheran airport, Hurley told him that officials in the Pentagon refused to believe his own optimistic report on Stalingrad, but "your articles started coming in and confirmed everything I had said."

Although the Press Department easily controlled the correspondents, the reporters were not without weapons in their struggle for greater freedom to cover the war. They brought the bureaucrats to their knees in a confrontation over coverage of the first shuttle bombing flight of U.S. Air Force Flying Fortress B-17s in June 1944. The shuttle run was permitted by Stalin after repeated requests from President Roosevelt for the use of bases in the Ukraine to receive bombers from Italy and England that had dropped their loads on targets in Germany, Romania, and Hungary. The aircraft were to reload, refuel, and fly back, hitting more targets on the way. Appropriately dubbed "Operation Frantic," this was to be a showpiece of American-Soviet military cooperation and an important story for the American newsmen. They had already been alerted to the mission by General John R. Deane, chief U.S. military representative in Moscow, who was particularly eager to have the correspondents at the air base to cover the operation.

At 1:30 A.M. on June 1, the phone rang in Harrison E. Salisbury's quarters in the Metropole. The Press Department was calling to advise him to be at the airport at 6:00 A.M. for a flight to Poltava in the Ukraine to witness the landing of the first shuttle bombing mission. Salisbury, thirty-six, who had arrived in Moscow in December 1943 to relieve Shapiro temporarily for the UP, checked with William H. Lawrence of *The New York Times*, Richard E. Lauterbach of *Time*, and David Nichol of the *Chicago Daily News*, all living down the hall. He discovered that they had not been invited to make the trip. Only six of the forty Moscow correspondents were scheduled to go to Poltava, and of those, two were Americans: Harrison Salisbury and Eddy Gilmore. The Press Department had decided that the agencies could cover for the entire American press corps. At 6:00 A.M. every American correspondent in Moscow, including those barred from the trip, was at the airport demanding to go to Poltava. And not only the Americans, but also all the foreign correspondents, including Communist sympathizers, were there. For once there was a united front among the reporters. At an impromptu meeting, they immediately agreed that all would go or no one would go, and they stood firm. General Deane, who was working behind the scenes to increase the number, later called the joint action "the first labor strike in Soviet Russia."

After two hours of arguments, which included frequent phone consultations between Press Department officials at the airport and higher-ups at the Commissariat, the Russians yielded. They announced that everyone would be flown to Poltava.

The following day, at the air base, Russians and Americans witnessed a magnificent and inspiring sight: seventy-three silver-winged Fortresses flying in perfect formation through the overcast. They were precisely on schedule after a fifteen-hundred-mile flight from England, landing one at a time, bomb bays empty, on a steel-matted runway built in several weeks by hundreds of Russian women. This extraordinary feat, however, ended in catastrophe. A few nights later, German bombers destroyed fifty Fortresses on the ground, killing two Americans and more than thirty Russians. The only defense the Red Amy could muster against the Luftwaffe was a few anti-aircraft batteries, which failed to down a single plane. Although there were no recriminations on either side, it was a military disaster for the Americans and a political embarrassment for the Russians.

The Press Department dealt with the air raid in its usual fashion: It barred correspondents from filing the story. Not until the end of 1944, when William L. White, an editor of *Reader's Digest* and an eyewitness to the raid, published a condensed version of his book *Report on the Russians* in the magazine, did the incident become known to the American public.

Although U.S. newspapers did not report on the Poltava raid, they carried another story that almost cost the United Press its Moscow bureau. A Spanish diplomat walked into the UP's London office on a Sunday in February 1944 and announced that he had heard from a reliable source that during the Teheran Conference of November 1943, where the Big Three celebrated Winston Churchill's sixty-ninth birthday, Joseph Stalin had struck the bald pate of Marshal Semyon K. Timoshenko, one of the Red Army's top field commanders, with a bottle of champagne. The marshal allegedly had downed too much vodka and was making pronouncements unacceptable to Stalin in the presence of President Roosevelt and Prime Minister Churchill. Transmitted by London to New York and promptly put on the national wire by a junior editor without checking, the story was killed a few hours later, but not before it was broadcast on radio. Unfortunately for the UP, Marshal Timoshenko was not present at the Teheran Conference. The story was a fake or a plant. At his press conference the following day, President Roosevelt laughed it off as a fabrication. The United Press immediately issued a retraction.

In Moscow, Deputy Foreign Affairs Commissar Vladimir G. Dekanozov summoned Harrison Salisbury to his office and demanded an apology—promptly; otherwise the UP "would not have the possibility of having a correspondent in Moscow." The threat was clear: The UP bureau would be closed; Salisbury and Meyer Handler, the second correspondent, expelled; and Shapiro, on a lecture tour in the United States, would not be able to rejoin his wife and daughter.

Hugh Baillie, president of the news agency, cabled apologies to Premier Stalin and Foreign Affairs Commissar Molotov, but this did not satisfy the Soviets. They wanted a public apology distributed to the UP's client newspapers, which the Russians expected would be published on front pages in the United States. After negotiations between Salisbury and the Press Department, agreement was reached on a statement that was cabled to New York and moved on the national wire between 2:00 and 3:00 A.M. on Sunday, an hour when few editors were watching the teletype machines. As far as can be determined, no newspaper in the United States printed a word, but the Russians were satisfied. Nikolai Palgunov phoned Salisbury at the Metropole with the glad tidings, "Mr. Molotov considers the incident now closed."

Nevertheless, the Soviets conveyed an ominous message to all Western correspondents: They were hostages for any story about Russia dispatched from any other bureau of their newspaper or agency. If the story reflected unfavorably on the Soviet Union or its leaders, the correspondents in Moscow would pay a penalty, probably expulsion, a powerful weapon in the Press Department's formidable arsenal.

If a print correspondent encountered difficulties reporting from Moscow, a radio correspondent fared even worse, being totally dependent on erratic shortwave radio transmissions to New York. Larry Lesueur, for example, found broadcasting a cross between a nightmare and an amusement park fun house. Everything that could possibly go wrong went wrong. One of that small band of brilliant reporters hired by Edward R. Murrow at the beginning of the war, Lesueur was a New Yorker who started in journalism with the weekly *Scarsdale Sun,* eventually moving to the United Press, where he worked as an editor. In 1939 Lesueur departed for Europe to look for an overseas reporting job. Joining CBS in London, he covered the "Phony War" from the Maginot Line. When the Wehrmacht struck at France, he retreated with the British armies to the English Channel and was evacuated to England, where he spent the next year covering the Blitz with Murrow. When the German armies attacked Russia, Lesueur, thirty-two, was assigned to Moscow, the first CBS correspondent sent to that post.

After he arrived in the capital from Kuibyshev, Lesueur broadcast live from a Radio Moscow studio, which meant that he had to be received in New York at the precise moment CBS had a scheduled newscast. If he was a few seconds early or late, he missed his slot. Given the vast distances and the eight-hour time difference as well as the inaccuracy of Soviet timekeeping, he was rarely received in New York. Although he conscientiously broadcast twice daily, he usually got a message from editor Paul White advising that he had not been heard. Lesueur also cabled his reports, which were read by a newscaster in the studio, but they lacked the immediacy and the drama of a voicecast from Moscow, with the crackle of static and interference in the background.

As a last resort, Larry Lesueur wrote Premier Stalin requesting better facilities in order to reach the eighty million people who regularly listened to CBS, an exaggeration as he later admitted. Bad reception, he said, was depriving Americans of the news about the Red Army's heroic deeds and the sacrifices of the Russian people. A few days later, Lesueur was summoned to the Radio Committee and told that the Soviet government was taking steps to ensure that his broadcasts would be heard in the United States. The signal would be strong and clear. Lesueur returned to work, relieved. About a week later, he received a cable from White:

YOU ARE BEING HEARD IN SAN FRANCISCO BUT NOT NEW YORK. WHY?

Inquiring at Radio Moscow, Lesueur learned that his broadcasts were no longer transmitted to the United States via the Arctic, but by a circuitous route that included land lines to Sverdlovsk in the Urals, then shortwave to Vladivostok on the Pacific coast, and finally to Australia, where they were beamed to San Francisco. CBS asked him to obtain the frequencies the Russians were using so that its technicians could tune in more precisely. The Radio Committee refused to provide the information on the grounds that it was a military secret.

In June 1942, led by Henry Cassidy and Henry Shapiro, the American and British correspondents working in Moscow organized an Anglo-American Press Association to acquire some leverage with the Press Department. The Soviets had never allowed such an organization before, but since the members were now Allies, it was hoped that the group might be sanctioned. At an informal meeting, Shapiro was elected president and a British correspondent was elected secretary. Much to everyone's astonishment, Nikolai Palgunov announced that the Press Department had no objections but would require a formal constitution to be deposited with the authorities. Shapiro, a Harvard-trained lawyer, wrote a constitution acceptable to the Press Department, and the association became legal and operational.

The first official function of the new association was not unexpected. It gave a luncheon at the Hotel National, inviting all the Soviets that its members could not normally see: the editors of *Pravda* and *Izvestia;* writers Ilya Ehrenburg, Vera Inber, Alexander Fadayev, and Alexei Tolstoi; Alexander Shcherbakov, chief of the political section of the Red Army; the director of TASS; members of the Academy of Sciences; G. F. Alexandrov, chief of the Central Committee's propaganda department; and many others. Surprisingly, almost everybody showed up. The lunch may have been the high point of the association's existence, since the Press Department was unable or unwilling to deal with it. Occasionally Henry Shapiro would write to Nikolai Palgunov proposing a trip to the front, but these requests were ignored. The department rarely communicated with the association except when it wanted to reach the reporters and, rather than calling each of them individually, made a single call to the president, asking him to alert the others.

In mid-1944, the association became embroiled in a controversy over the impending publication of William L. White's book, written after a six-week trip to the Soviet Union with Eric Johnston, president of the U.S. Chamber of Commerce. Johnston had received red carpet treatment from the Russians, met with Stalin for discussion of postwar Soviet-American trade, and was provided with a private aircraft for an extensive tour of the Urals and Siberia. White's generally unfavorable picture of the Soviet Union was immediately attacked by a pro-Soviet organization in the United States, which demanded that American correspondents in Moscow denounce White's book as a disservice to the Allied cause. At a meeting of the association, a letter criticizing the book was circulated and, as far as can be determined, only two correspondents refused to sign it: Eddy Gilmore, who walked out of the meeting, and his rival, Henry Shapiro.

Pravda, of course, denounced the book as the "usual standard production of a Fascist kitchen, with all of its smells, calumny, unpardonable ignorance, and ill-conceived fury."

The association barely survived the end of the war. In May 1947, Mikhail Vasilenko, acting Press Department chief, summoned its president, Alexander Kendrick of the *Chicago Sun-Times*, and informed him that henceforth the organization must accept all foreign correspondents in Moscow, including representatives of Communist newspapers, an ultimatum he knew would be rejected. When the association refused, Vasilenko announced, "You are dissolved!" Since then, no attempt has been made to revive the organization.

A few months prior to its dissolution, the association appealed to the Soviets to once more suspend censorship, which had been permitted to lapse briefly after the war but then reinstated. Brooks Atkinson of *The New York Times* drafted the plea. Signed by all of the Western correspondents then in Moscow, including several pro-Soviet reporters, the letter was addressed to Foreign Minister Vyacheslav M. Molotov. By common agreement, no one filed a story on the appeal. Three weeks later, Yakov M. Lomakhin, the new head of the Press Department, summoned the association's president, Eric Darnton of Reuters, and its secretary, Farnsworth Fowle of CBS, to his office.

"In responding to your letter to Comrade Molotov," he announced, "I must inform you that your letter is without merit and cannot be taken into consideration."

The correspondents took the message back to the Metropole and informed their colleagues. Soon dispatches were going out to the rest of the world: The Soviet government had rejected a plea by Allied correspondents to ease censorship—not the last time that the request would be made, nor the last time the Soviets would say *"Nyet."*

British writer Phillip Knightley has called the Russian front "the most poorly reported part of the Second World War," with the Allied publics "receiving mostly a rehash of the Russian official communiqué." The major battles of Kursk, Moscow, and Sebastopol, the sieges of Stalingrad and Leningrad, he has charged, "never received proper attention." As a result, "the reader in the West remained largely ignorant of what was going on in the Soviet Union." Knightley accused the Western correspondents of being "unprepared" for the war "despite the fact that everyone knew that the two greatest powers of continental Europe were about to come to grips."

There is some truth to his charge: Only a handful of Western correspondents were in Moscow on the day the Germans attacked, but valid economic and news reasons justified the small number. Moscow had dried up as a news source over the previous five years, and foreign editors could not maintain a bureau that did not produce stories. The correspondents themselves could not be faulted. Even though they knew that war was imminent, they could neither cover an event that had not yet occurred nor, because of censorship, even speculate about it.

The system created by the Soviets to control news of the conflict, according to Knightley, was "so diabolical that to this day old war correspondents shudder when they recall it." Contrary to Knightley's contention, not one of the Americans who covered the war trembled with remembered indignation when they described their experiences to me. As long as the Red Army was retreating, recalled Henry Shapiro, the Soviets did not want any correspondents in the front lines. But when the Red Army started pushing back the Germans and winning battles, the Press Department arranged regular visits.

"The Americans didn't get what they expected—the ability to cover all aspects of the combat. But they didn't get that in Grenada, either," Shapiro pointed out.

Harrison Salisbury found the restrictions "tough and arbitrary" and missed the freedom of movement he had enjoyed elsewhere. "We were never able to go off on our own to where the guns were being fired in anger except by accident . . . but we were given extraordinary opportunities for seeing the Red Army. Like Oliver Twist, I wanted 'more'!"

Henry Cassidy strongly defended the Soviet policy. "We had as much opportunity to cover the war in Russia in '41, '42 and '43," he said, "as could have been humanly provided.

"We couldn't possibly go along with the troops. Most of the correspondents couldn't speak Russian. But the Press Department did provide very good conducted tours of the front. We went to a great many fronts: Moscow, Leningrad, Odessa, Kharkov, Kiev, Stalingrad. They were generous with trips that were really quite hard for them to organize. Security was always a problem. They didn't want anybody killed.

"Within the limitation they set on themselves, I think the coverage of the Russian front, given the size and the difficulties of getting around, was as good as could have been done."

At 2:41 A.M. on May 7, 1945, in a schoolhouse in Reims, Wehrmacht General Alfred Jodl signed a document of unconditional surrender in the presence of representatives of the Soviet High Command and of the Supreme Commander of the Allied Expeditionary Force. The war was over.

In Moscow, the government declared a holiday unprecedented in Soviet history. Nothing was organized, nothing planned: no parades, no speeches, no demonstrations. But hundreds of thousands of Muscovites poured into the streets to celebrate the end of a four-year nightmare to dance, sing, shout, embrace, and, when they could find the vodka, drink. Red Square was filled with soldiers and civilians thronging to the traditional meeting place to celebrate the great public occasion. On the balcony of the American embassy facing the Kremlin, George F. Kennan, the chargé d'affaires, waved at the cheering crowd below. He turned to Thomas P. Whitney, the twenty-eight-year-old economics attaché and soon to be AP correspondent, and asked him to run next door to the Hotel National to get a Soviet flag. When it was unfurled alongside the Stars and Stripes already hanging from the balcony, the crowd roared its appreciation. An American sergeant who stepped out of the embassy door at that moment was lofted into the air by cheering Russians and disappeared into the crowd. He returned to the embassy two days later, refusing to describe his experiences, but his grin showed that he had not suffered unduly.

On May 8, the Allies and the Germans signed another surrender document in a ceremony arranged by the Soviets in the ruins of Berlin. For the Russians, the war was now officially over. The American correspondents who had collectively reported the war from Moscow for four long and difficult years were not invited to attend. As Farnsworth Fowle put it with a trace of bitterness in his voice,

"We covered it from the Hotel Metropole."

6

The Cold War . . . Against the Correspondents

Every conceivable obstacle was put in the way of the foreign journalist who attempted to telegraph news. . . . The business of news gathering was under ban in the tsar's empire. The doors of the ministers of state were closed; no public official would give audience to a correspondent. Even subordinate employees did not dare to be seen in conversation with a member of the hated guild, and all telegrams were subject to a rigorous censorship.

> Melville E. Stone
> general manager, Associated Press
> (After visiting St. Petersburg, 1904)

There was an atmosphere of tension—it surrounded all of us, but you never let yourself dwell on that sort of thing. You just went ahead and did your job.

> Thomas P. Whitney
> AP correspondent, 1949–53

I had my own private hell when I would awaken at six o'clock on those dark Russian winter mornings and think about my problems.

> Eddy Gilmore
> AP correspondent, 1941–53

Walter Cronkite, the thirty-two-year-old United Press correspondent, stepped out on the street from the apartment building that housed the agency's office and promptly slipped on the ice-covered sidewalk. As he struggled to his feet, a man rushed up and asked if he needed help. Cronkite said with a smile, *"Nichevo! Spasibo!"* ("Everything's all right! Thanks!") When the Russian realized he was speaking to a foreigner, he quickly looked around to see if anyone else had witnessed the incident, then hurried away.

This brief conversation occurred in March 1948, a few months before Walter Cronkite and his wife, Betsy, were to

leave the Soviet Union. He wrote a story about the encounter
that I discovered when I rummaged through the UP files after
joining the bureau in December 1955. This was the lead:

> After almost two years in the Soviet Union, I had my first
> conversation today with a Russian "man in the street."

The story was killed by the censor.

Walter Cronkite did not mention the reasons for his limited
contacts with the "man in the street." He could not report that
the Soviet Union was engulfed by a wave of fear and terror
that menaced Russians and foreigners alike. The heroic
struggle of the people against the German invaders had been
swiftly followed by the Kremlin's war against the people,
waged by the secret police, a vast army of spies and informers,
utilizing a "judicial system" and the punitive network of
prisons and labor camps directed by the supreme leader,
Joseph Stalin.

Fanned by the growing hostility between the erstwhile Allies
over failure to agree on the fate of Germany and Eastern
Europe and exacerbated by mutual suspicion and outright
threats, a Cold War quickly emerged to dominate relations
between Russia and the West. Winston Churchill told the
world in March 1946 that an Iron Curtain had descended
across Eastern Europe, "from Stettin in the Baltic to Trieste
on the Adriatic," dividing the continent into a Communist bloc
and a democratic bloc. He called on the English-speaking
countries to form a political union and a military alliance to
defend themselves against the "growing challenge and peril to
civilization" from the Soviet Union. Stalin replied a week later,
charging that the speech was "a call to war against the USSR."
Within a year President Harry S Truman, at a joint session of
the U.S. Congress, proclaimed a policy that offered military
and economic support to any country, specifically Greece and
Turkey, resisting communism. The "Truman Doctrine" was a
direct challenge not only to Russia's growing domination of
Eastern Europe but also to the establishment of a Soviet naval
base on the Turkish Straits. In response, Stalin reversed the

demobilization of the Soviet Army and increased its strength from three million to more than five million troops by the early 1950s, half the wartime level. Furthermore, he accelerated efforts to break the American monopoly on nuclear weapons, and in September 1949 the Kremlin announced that it possessed the atomic bomb. Most important, to prepare for what may have appeared to him as imminent conflict with the United States, he ordered police chief Lavrenti V. Beria, head of the MGB, to cleanse the nation of real or imagined "enemies" in a reign of terror that matched the Great Purge of the 1930s.

For the next seven years, life in Russia was a nightmare for many of its citizens. Agents of the MGB were everywhere, watching and listening. Calls for "vigilance" against "enemies of the people" and "spies" screamed from the press, from the radio, and from posters. Tens of thousands of people were arrested on accusations by informers, beaten and tortured, forced to confess to nonexistent crimes, and sentenced to death or dispatched to prison camps in the Arctic or Siberia. Families and relatives learned long afterward about the fate of their kin. The "enemies" included writers, artists, actors, film directors, and intellectuals. Even such renowned composers as Sergei Prokofiev, Dmitri Shostakovich, and Aram Khatchaturian were sharply criticized for failing to adhere to the Communist Party's strictures on "Socialist Realism." In January 1949 the anti-Semitic policies of the Kremlin were publicly proclaimed when the Soviet press attacked a group of theater and literary critics as "homeless cosmopolitans." Most of them had Jewish names. The Yiddish Theater in Moscow was shut down, and its distinguished director, Solomon Mikhoels, died after he was "accidentally" run over by a truck in Kiev. Nikita Khrushchev, in his secret speech to the Twentieth Party Congress in February 1956, revealed that Mikhoels had been murdered.

During those seven years, the American correspondents worked under the most trying and frustrating conditions since foreign reporters were first admitted to Soviet Russia in 1921. In addition to having to contend with increasingly severe censorship and travel restrictions that limited them to Moscow and Leningrad, they also faced an open and official hostility toward Westerners that frightened off Russian contacts and friends and made it virtually impossible to establish personal relationships. In April 1947, Premier Stalin himself harshly criticized Western correspondents for portraying the Soviet Union "as a kind of a zoo" while censorship was suspended for a few weeks after the end of the war. He told former Minnesota Governor Harold Stassen that this angered the Russian people and "we had to resume censorship."

Stalin reminded Stassen of the Marshal Timoshenko incident, which he called a "rash and slanderous fabrication." He asked, "Are we expected to trust such correspondents?"

In June the screws turned tighter when a government decree forbade disclosure of "state secrets," covering a broad range of military and economic information. This included news of "negotiations and agreements with foreign countries, as well as any measures in the field of foreign policy and foreign trade not already disclosed in officially published documents." Although for many years foreign correspondents had worked under an unwritten Press Department rule permitting them to file anything that had already appeared in the Soviet press, they often tried to file "unofficial" material and negotiate it through censorship or even evade censorship. If they now sought to evade censorship or to file "unofficial" information, they faced up to twenty years' imprisonment in a labor camp. Both the source and the recipient of "state secrets" were imperiled by the decree. For example, if a correspondent met a Russian in a restaurant who "disclosed" his monthly salary, such economic information could not be used in a story without risk. Less than a year later, the government formally lowered an Iron Curtain between correspondents and Russians with a decree forbidding Soviet citizens from having any contact with foreigners, except through the Foreign Affairs and Foreign Trade ministries. A correspondent could no longer legally engage in conversation with a fellow passenger in the Moscow subway.

Innocent as it may have appeared, Walter Cronkite's pratfall story broke every rule in the book for correspondents. It conveyed information that had not been published in an official document—i.e., ice on the street; it was based on a conversation with a Soviet citizen not authorized by the Press Department. Above all, it implied that some Russians and some foreign correspondents were ignoring regulations, either deliberately or through ignorance.

A new system of censorship established in February 1946 moved responsibility from the Foreign Ministry's Press Department to the Main Administration for Literary Affairs (Glavlit), which came under the jurisdiction of the Central Committee of the Communist Party. Surveillance would be tighter, censorship harsher. Under this arrangement, dispatches were taken directly to a special office at the Central Telegraph, where a clerk seated at a counter window delivered it to unseen censors working behind a closed door. Correspondents were no longer permitted to see who was handling the copy, let alone argue or negotiate over a few phrases or a lead, as had been the custom for the previous twenty-five years. The process was carried out in total secrecy and anonymity.

Censorship was exercised only by *removal* of words, not by any additions, usually with a black pencil, a technique that provided ample opportunity to shape and distort the story. For example, if a correspondent wrote a cable that began:

PRAVDA ANNOUNCES SOVAUTO INDUSTRY EXCEEDED 1951 PLAN BY 16 PERCENT STOP ACTUAL FIGURES UNAVAILABLE BUT ANNUAL OUTPUT ESTIMATED AT 300,000 TRUCKS COMMA PASSENGER CARS LESSN ONE-TENTH US PRODUCTION STOP WAITING PERIOD FOR NEW CARS PROBABLY REDUCED FROM TEN YEARS TO NINE ENDIT

The cable that passed through the Glavlit meat grinder might have become:

PRAVDA ANNOUNCES SOVAUTO INDUSTRY EXCEEDED 1951 PLAN BY 16 PERCENT STOP WAITING PERIOD FOR NEW CARS REDUCED ENDIT

Even the truncated last sentence might not have passed, since it contained both favorable news (reduction in waiting time) and unfavorable news (there was a wait).

When the correspondent submitted copy, it bore his signature, press card number, and the words "My Corrections," to indicate that he agreed to any alterations made by the censor—in advance. Even so, the censor, after having slashed the copy, could then dispatch it overseas without the reporter knowing what had been removed despite the reporter's acknowledged right to review the cable prior to transmission, or even to withdraw it. Frequently the censor did not return the carbon copy in time for review or simply "forgot" to return it. By then the cable was on an editor's desk in New York or London.

In this unequal combat, the Soviet government held an array of weapons to cow the most intrepid reporters: fear, intimidation, and surveillance. Police agents in plainclothes trailed the newsmen, sometimes night and day. Phones were monitored; walls had ears. Individual travel was restricted to a radius of twenty-five miles around Moscow. Attacks in the press appeared almost daily, ranting against the American "spies" and "warmongers" dispatched by Wall Street to obtain intelligence information about the Soviet economy. The threat of arrest hung over every correspondent. Expulsion was another weapon—either directly by ordering a journalist to leave, or indirectly, by not granting a reentry visa when he left the country for vacation and was expecting to return. An all-embracing system was in place to achieve the Kremlin's goals: total control of information available to foreign correspondents, elimination of stories that could be considered unfavorable, and a reduction in the number of foreign reporters in the USSR, particularly from the United States.

At the end of the war, about a dozen American correspondents were working in Moscow, representing ten media organizations. Within three years, most of them were gone. Robert Magidoff of McGraw-Hill and NBC, who had been in Russia since 1935, was expelled in 1948, accused of spying by Cecelia Nelson, his American-born secretary, now a Soviet citizen. In

December 1946, when the Press Department banned all broadcasting from Moscow, CBS withdrew Richard C. Hottelet, who had arrived six months earlier. Joseph Newman of the *New York Herald Tribune* and Drew Middleton of *The New York Times* were denied reentry visas after they had gone abroad on vacation. *The Christian Science Monitor* closed its bureau and sent Edmund Stevens to Rome. By the beginning of 1949, the number of Americans reporting for the U.S. media had dwindled to four: Henry Shapiro, UP; Eddy Gilmore and Thomas Whitney, AP; and Harrison Salisbury, *The New York Times*. These men constituted the entire American press corps in Moscow from 1949 to 1953. Almost everything millions of readers in the United States and the rest of the world learned about the Soviet Union during those years came from them—and Glavlit.

During the Cold War period, the reporting barely reflected what was happening in the Soviet Union, although the correspondents were among the best in American journalism. While they were on the scene, however, their skills could be perceived only by what filtered through the censor. For example, when Golda Meir, the first Israeli envoy, arrived in Moscow in September 1948, she stayed at the Hotel Metropole where Joseph Newman was her next-door neighbor. She attended services at the synagogue and strolled the streets of the capital. Within a few days, as the news spread among Moscow's Jews, thousands lined up outside the hotel, hoping to see her and to obtain Israeli visas. Newman filed almost daily on this extraordinary phenomenon, but not a line passed Glavlit. Only when he left the country in June 1949 to marry Lucia Meza Barros, a Chilean diplomat he had met in Moscow, was he able to report the Meir story. Robert Magidoff wrote about the currency reform of December 1947, stressing that one of its effects would be to raise the standard of living of the Russian people. He added that the reform also resulted in a "substantial loss of savings" by requiring that "old" rubles be exchanged for new rubles at the rate of ten to one. When the cable came back from the censor, all references to the beneficial effects were retained; every reference to the negative impact was eliminated. Because he refused to transmit a skewed story, Magidoff withdrew the cable.

Drew Middleton still remembers the fate of an account he wrote after interviewing Marshal Georgi K. Zhukov in Odessa. Having met the *Times* correspondent earlier in Berlin, Russia's top soldier greeted him warmly, describing his new command as one of the most important in the Soviet Army, a statement that was far from true, since Stalin had exiled him from Moscow to this provincial post. When the long cable returned from the censor, it consisted of a single line:

MARSHAL ZHUKOV WAS IN ODESSA TODAY AND SPOKE TO CORRESPONDENTS.

Although the censors who actually handled correspondents' copy were anonymous, their boss was known. A minor official in the Press Department during the war, A. M. Omelchenko appeared at a Foreign Ministry reception on the anniversary of the Revolution in 1948. He was recognized immediately and besieged by correspondents who complained about how his minions were handling their copy. Omelchenko lectured them on the need to report the "truth," and if they did, they would have no difficulties. Thomas Whitney rejoined that Glavlit had killed a story that very day that he said was a "complete and accurate translation" of an article published in *Komsomolskaya Pravda*, with nothing added or subtracted.

"Do you wish to tell me that *Komsomolskaya Pravda* was printing untruths?" Whitney asked.

"Mr. Whitney," replied Omelchenko, "it's time you understood we have our own *considerations*."

The correspondents understood what Omelchenko meant: His neck was on the line for every single word that passed through Glavlit and was published under a Moscow dateline. They knew that people other than newspaper readers in the West were perusing the dispatches, among them Joseph Stalin himself, a notoriously impatient man. When there was even the slightest possibility that a story might seem unfavorable to the Soviet state or to the political health of Glavlit and/or A. M. Omelchenko, no chances were taken.

Glavlit used its powers both to create a favorable image of the Soviet Union and to penalize correspondents considered unfriendly. "They used the censorship to harass the correspondents, to punish them if they weren't behaving," recalled Joseph Newman, for whom the experience was "immensely frustrating.

"You'd write your story, then have it killed. Or they would hold it for hours. And if they wanted to be real nasty, they would hold the stuff overnight, or even for days."

Some American correspondents evaded censorship by sending story material through the diplomatic pouch. Since the practice was usually forbidden by the American embassy (it depended on the ambassador), they sometimes also used the services of other embassies. Drew Middleton sent "advisories" to Edwin L. (Jimmy) James, the managing editor of the *Times*, with background information on current developments. Harrison E. Salisbury did the same in 1949 when he succeeded Middleton, but his "advisories" were used by Soviet affairs specialist Harry Schwartz, hired by the *Times* to backstop its Moscow correspondent. Schwartz, a former Soviet affairs analyst for the wartime Office of Strategic Services who taught political science at Syracuse University, incorporated Salisbury's material in his analyses, which often were based on State Department information, academic sources, and his reading of the Soviet publications available in the United States. Eventually this arrangement created problems for the Moscow correspondent, whose censored reports seemed pro-Soviet to many *Times* readers. Salisbury urged his editors to precede his dispatches with a warning, "Passed by Soviet censorship," but they rejected the proposal.

"To this day," he told me, "I cannot understand why they wouldn't do it."

Occasionally a resourceful correspondent would trick the censor into passing forbidden stories. In April 1947, for example, Thomas Whitney noticed that Nikolai A. Voznesensky, the Soviet Union's top economic planner and a member of the Politburo, the ruling body of the Communist Party under Stalin, was absent from a meeting of the Komsomol, the party's youth organization. Voznesensky had been removed from his position as head of the State Planning Commission a month earlier, but there was no information about his fate. For Whitney, the tip-off was the attendance list at the Komsomol meeting published in *Pravda,* at which all the other Politburo members were present. Clearly, something ominous had happened to him. Since Glavlit would have killed any story suggesting that Voznesensky was in trouble, Whitney decided to send a "deadpan article" about the Komsomol meeting, describing the ovation for the Soviet leaders and including, as the newspaper did, their names in quotation marks. As he had hoped, the censor passed the story, but he was not confident that the editor on the New York desk would notice the omission of Nikolai Voznesensky's name. Whitney ordered the telegram transmitted three times and finally captured the attention not only of the foreign desk but also of someone who understood what he was really trying to convey. The AP carried the news of Voznesensky's ouster under a New York dateline: a scoop for the agency and for Thomas Whitney. Nine years later, Nikita Khrushchev revealed that Nikolai A. Voznesensky had been shot.

Playing games with Glavlit, however, was fraught with peril. As a result of the successful Voznesensky experience, Eddy Gilmore worked out an arrangement with New York to use the same trick for future purge stories. The foreign desk was instructed to watch for and study all transmitted lists carefully for omissions. Six months later, Gilmore cabled a story that listed the current members of the Politburo and had, by accident, left out the name of its only Jew, Lazar M. Kaganovich. In accordance with the prearranged plan, the AP put a story on the wires that Kaganovich had been purged, even making the front page of *The New York Times.* When it was confirmed that he was still a Politburo member in good standing, the AP was obliged to retract the story, and Gilmore was hard-pressed to explain the mistake. He squirmed out of it by blaming the Central Telegraph for an erroneous transmission.

Each correspondent dealt with the censorship in his own way. Edmund Stevens toed the line while he was in Moscow, but when *The Christian Science Monitor* reassigned him to Rome in 1949, he wrote "Russia Un-Censored," a series that won him a Pulitzer Prize. Eddy Gilmore filed colorful features about noncontroversial subjects such as racing at the Moscow Hippodrome and the hardy Russians who swam among the ice floes in the Moscow River. Drew Middleton used a technique honed to a fine art while reporting under wartime censorship in Europe: He tried—and occasionally succeeded—in getting sensitive facts through Glavlit by simply repeating them in the same dispatch. If one reference was eliminated, sometimes the second slipped through, conveyed in what he has described as "elliptical" language. The same technique was used by V. I. Lenin to evade tsarist censorship when he was writing articles for the Bolshevik newspaper *Pravda* published legally in St. Petersburg from 1912 to 1914.

For Walter Cronkite, however, working in Moscow was so frustrating and so unrewarding that he gave up after three months.

"I got defeated pretty early on," he confessed. "I went there with the thought that I hadn't read any stories about what the Russians are really like—it's time we find out. I'm going to be the guy who tells people, because the Russians are going to like my stories and I'm going to like the Russian people.

"But in a month or two, when I started to write that sort of thing, I realized they weren't going to let me tell these stories. . . . I said, 'to hell with them!' If they don't want me to write stories about the Soviet people, I won't write stories about the Soviet people!

"Really, at that point, I kind of turned off on the whole experience and sat on my rear end for the remaining year and a half. . . . I was a listening post for the UP. I wasn't a creative reporter. I was defeated, beaten by it."

Like many other reporters, Walter Cronkite quickly learned that goodwill and a desire to do an honest professional job could not dent the system. Moscow was his last foreign assignment for the UP before returning to the United States, where he joined CBS in 1950. Recruited by Edward R. Murrow, he went on to a brilliant career as a TV correspondent and anchorman. His departure from the agency may have been hastened by Leonard Lyons, a gossip columnist for the *New York Post*. Cronkite had told Lyons that before he left Moscow, a disapproving Soviet citizen had scrawled a huge dollar sign on the door of the UP office. Referring to the agency's merited reputation as a penny-pinching, shoestring operation, Cronkite added:

"If that Russian knew how the UP *really* operated, he would have painted a cents sign on the door."

When the item was published, it produced appreciative chuckles from Cronkite's colleagues but not from Earl J. Johnson, the editor and vice president of United Press.

In mid-March 1947, the Council of Foreign Ministers met in Moscow, bringing with it, according to Drew Middleton, "a breath of fresh air" for the resident correspondents. Almost a hundred reporters arrived from New York, Washington, Paris, and London to cover the meeting, one of the postwar series that sought Allied agreement on a common policy toward the defeated Third Reich. The bar of the Hotel Moskva, headquarters for delegates and journalists, which was well stocked with vodka, champagne, Scotch, and beautiful Russian women, was the scene of joyful reunions. Although the council meeting lasted six weeks, it was apparent from the start that there was no possibility of agreement between the Western nations, represented by U.S. Secretary of State George Marshall, Ernest Bevin of Great Britain, and Georges Bidault of France, and the Soviets, represented by Foreign Minister V. M. Molotov. The meeting soon dissolved into a dialogue of the deaf and mutual recrimination. It was clear to both sides that the Cold War would enter a more frigid stage.

If the meeting was a disaster for the diplomats, it was a blessing for the Moscow correspondents: The Soviet government suspended censorship for the duration. Although the Press Department did not actually announce it, all correspondents were quietly informed that they could phone stories directly to their home offices without going to the Central Telegraph, where Glavlit was located. Additional, but temporary, telephone booths were specially installed for the correspondents at the hotel.

The resident reporters took advantage of the new situation to transmit stories that Glavlit had previously killed or would not otherwise have passed. Drew Middleton, in particular, filed personal observations that were hardly likely to please the Press Department. In one dispatch he reported that the small plots tilled by individual peasants were more productive than the collective farms that were the pride and joy of Stalinist agriculture. He also wrote about grain that was rotting and/or sprouting in huge unprotected piles at railroad sidings because of a lack of both adequate storage facilities and transportation to ship it to the processing mills. The censors must have been furious with his report on the obsolete military equipment he had seen at Red Square parades. Two dated and poorly maintained Stalin T-54 tanks had broken down just at the entrance to the square, causing an embarrassing traffic jam within sight of Stalin and other Soviet leaders reviewing the parade from the top of Lenin's tomb.

Drew Middleton eventually paid the price for his temerity. When the ministers' meeting ended in April, he flew to Berlin on U.S. Ambassador Walter Bedell Smith's plane en route to a vacation in the United States. Before he left, the Press Department assured him that he would receive a reentry visa. When Middleton was ready to return in September, he applied for the visa, but it was never granted, much to the dismay of *The New York Times*.

Almost two years were to elapse before the newspaper regained its bureau, with Harrison E. Salisbury as correspondent under circumstances that raised some eyebrows in the newsroom. A tireless, resourceful journalist, the fastest rewrite man ever to head the cable (foreign) desk at the United Press, Salisbury had long sought to leave the agency and move to the most prestigious newspaper in the United States. However, in 1947–48 there were obstacles working against him. He was still recovering from nervous depression over the breakup of his marriage; the depression required treatment at New

York's Payne-Whitney Clinic. Furthermore, the newspaper simply wasn't hiring any new staff members.

Supported by several influential allies at the *Times*, Harrison Salisbury patiently lobbied for a job with managing editor Edwin L. James for many months. One day in 1948, James asked him if he would be interested in returning to Moscow, where he had briefly served with the UP during the war. The caveat was that Salisbury would first have to obtain a Soviet visa to get not just the assignment, but also a job with the *Times*. Although the newspaper had been trying to fill the post for almost two years, submitting visa applications for a number of staff reporters, no response or even acknowledgment had been received from the Russians. Nevertheless, Salisbury went to Washington, filled out a visa application, and, like the others, waited.

On December 24, 1948, Edwin L. James published an "Open Letter to Premier Stalin," requesting the Soviet government to permit the *Times* to send a correspondent to Moscow to help increase mutual understanding between the American and Russian people. Within a week, Harrison Salisbury received his visa. The question asked at the *Times* and elsewhere was why the Russians gave Salisbury the green light after turning down all the other candidates. Was it because his visa application was on top of the pile? And why would Salisbury, who wasn't even on the staff of the newspaper, be proposed by James? Had he turned to Salisbury as a "last chance," or were there other reasons? The answers to these questions are fuzzy indeed, but the fact is that only after he received the visa was Harrison Salisbury hired by the *Times* and appointed its Moscow correspondent. In effect he was selected for that important post not by the editors of one of the world's most influential newspapers but by the bureaucrats in the Press Department of the Foreign Affairs Ministry of the USSR.

By mid-1947, working conditions of the correspondents were "very much worse than they had ever been in Russia, by every comparison we were able to make," Reuters correspondent

David Brown wrote his managing editor in London. He considered it "barely worthwhile to maintain a bureau" since the cost of operations was not justified by the quality of the Moscow news report. Furthermore, the Ministry of Communications had just doubled the already exorbitant cable rates. Brown urged Reuters to consider closing the bureau in concert with AP and UP to dramatize and explain the intolerable conditions under which the correspondents worked. He conceded that the AP would be unlikely to go along, having "built up their Moscow coverage on a largely unwarranted prestige basis." Closure of the bureaus did not come to pass, but had all the agencies agreed, the move would have been unprecedented. Competition between the two American agencies, however, was too fierce to permit a retreat from Moscow.

Typical of the difficulties faced by the agencies was the experience of Don Dallas of Reuters, who filed twenty-nine separate cables in the first three weeks of March 1949. All were killed by Glavlit. A few months later, he asked to be relieved from his post because "present conditions are a tremendous strain on the nerves." Reuters granted his request and rescued him. His American agency colleagues were subject to the same pressures, but they were married to Russian women who could not obtain exit visas—and they were trapped. With the departure of Dallas, Reuters downgraded the bureau to a holding operation and entrusted the coverage to stringer Andrew J. Steiger, an American who was correspondent for the *Exchange Telegraph* of London and who had a Russian wife.

Access to information sources was never easy in the Soviet Union, but in the 1920s and 1930s correspondents could at least call on officials without much difficulty. Henry Shapiro once phoned State Prosecutor Andrei Y. Vyshinsky and arranged a meeting for two City College of New York professors who were visiting Moscow—on that same day. In the late 1930s, Robert Magidoff was asked by the *London News Chronicle* to find out whether Professor Otto Schmidt, the famed Arctic explorer rumored to have been executed, was still alive. Magidoff phoned Schmidt, who announced, "Well, I have not been shot," and was invited to his office to see that the explorer was still among the living.

After the war, however, requests for interviews with officials or visits to a factory or a school had to be made in writing through the Press Department, which generally ignored them. About twice a year, so-called press conferences were held at which an official distributed a mimeographed statement and then refused to answer questions on the subject. When a Soviet soccer team was scheduled to go to Sweden for an international match, the AP was forbidden to phone the Soviet Sports Committee for information on the team's departure date or for the names and biographical details of the players. Under a decree of January 1948, the news agency could direct such inquiries only to the Ministry of Foreign Affairs, whose interest in soccer was nil. If the correspondents could not secure information about a soccer game, the difficulty of obtaining data about annual steel production or the grain harvest can only be imagined. Added to the correspondents' problems was the ignorance and/or stupidity of editors in New York who requested stories that were either unfeasible or information that was clearly forbidden. Harrison Salisbury, while foreign editor of the UP in 1946, kept pressing Walter Cronkite to visit the famed monastery at Zagorsk—about 50 miles northeast of Moscow—to do a Christmas story. Under severe travel restrictions, as Salisbury should have known, Cronkite was unable to get there until Christmas of 1947. During the foreign ministers' conference, Hanson Baldwin, the *Times* military correspondent, sent Drew Middleton a cable from New York that must have provoked considerable suspicion in the MVD and the Press Department. He requested figures on Soviet Army strength in Germany, information that Middleton told me could have been furnished by the Pentagon or the U.S. Military Command headquarters in Heidelberg "down to the last platoon."

In the flood of Cold War editorials, attacks on the United States, claims of industrial achievements, and reports on the feats of heroic milkmaids and tractor drivers, the correspondents occasionally found a lighter side. In 1949, Kremlin propagandists launched a campaign to convince the Soviet people and the rest of the world of the superiority of Russian science and invention. As part of the effort to wipe out "kowtowing to the decadent West" and "eliminating the vestiges of capitalism in the consciousness of the people," the Soviet press published numerous articles claiming that Russians had been responsible for some of the major inventions and discoveries of the past hundred years, including radio, the airplane, synthetic rubber, the steam engine, the locomotive, the electric light bulb, penicillin, the harvester combine, and the discovery of the Antarctic continent.

This farfetched propaganda made good copy for the correspondents and provided some of the few amusing stories that emanated from Moscow during the Cold War years. In September 1952, just before the World Series, the magazine *Smena* announced that *beizbol* was not an American game after all but had been played in Russian villages for hundreds of years as *lapta*. The American version was a "beastly battle, a bloody fight with mayhem and murder" in which players are "slaves who are bought and sold like sheep. When they are worn out, and usually cripples as a result of injuries . . . they are thrown out on the street to die of starvation." Getting that story through Glavlit was easy, but the Russians did not know how foolish they looked in print.

Eddy Gilmore called it "Moscow Madness," an apt description of what happens to normal, conscientious reporters assigned to cover a police state. The physical environment of Moscow, a gray, grim city in prewar years but now even less attractive, cast a somber and depressing mood on its inhabitants. Many buildings were unoccupied. Unheated during the war, their floors and walls had been shattered by frozen pipes. The people who shuffled along Gorky Street were simply worn out, exhausted after four years of extraordinary sacrifice and belt-tightening. Shops were almost bare, and in the early postwar years, food was short in Moscow. At night, except for official vehicles, few cars moved on the dimly lit streets. Red stars glowing atop the Kremlin towers offered the only spots of color in the Soviet capital.

Under these conditions, together with the pressure and the frustrations of the job, the long hours, and the meager results, some of the reporters behaved less than admirably. Scenes at Central Telegraph occasionally looked like barroom brawls as agency correspondents punched and kicked each other to get to the single international telephone first. Sometimes the UP would tie up the line waiting for the censor to clear a story, while Eddy Gilmore cursed out Henry Shapiro, threatening him with bodily harm. On other occasions the situation was reversed and the AP, which usually had two correspondents to the UP's one, tied up the line. Each agency scored beats, transmitting a story a few minutes or a few seconds earlier to earn a congratulatory cable from New York, but the glory was fleeting, paid for with frayed nerves and sleepless nights.

Although "Moscow Madness" was a reality, the correspondents lived fairly comfortably at the Metropole or in their own apartments, attended dinners and parties in the small foreign colony, and went to the theater and concerts. Betsy and Walter Cronkite regularly entertained diplomats in their UP apartment, although after dinner they retired to a bedroom that was so cold that each had to sleep in half a fleece-lined leather flight suit they brought in from England. Eddy Gilmore and Thomas Whitney were able to rent *dachas*, small cottages, on the outskirts of Moscow, havens from the pressures and tensions of work. Harrison Salisbury shared the *dacha* with Whitney and his Russian wife, Julie, who planted the garden with roses, lilacs, dogwood, and raspberries. Whitney even mowed the lawn, much to the astonishment and amusement of Russian neighbors.

To ensure that correspondents would not be obliged to live like Russians, the Foreign Ministry accorded them the diplomatic rank of minister, a lofty status that provided certain privileges but none of the immunities enjoyed by real diplomats. They had the right to import a specific amount of tax-free food and liquor twice a year, including sugar, flour, butter, coffee, cheese, canned meats, condiments, even Soviet vodka—a welcome supplement to the sparse supplies available in Moscow. One of the most important items was toilet paper, which was rarely available in the stores and, even if available, was not of a quality to which the correspondents were accustomed. The challenge was to try to calculate in advance how much paper would be required to cover personal needs for a six-month period. The calculation became more complicated if the correspondent had a family, gave dinner parties and receptions, and received visitors at the office. Since there was also a weight limit on the semi-annual imports, he had to choose among paper, butter, and canned milk. On the other hand, a miscalculation could produce a shortfall with disastrous consequences. When Joseph Newman received permission to reopen the *Herald Tribune* bureau in 1947, he flew to Stockholm to buy clothes—and an ample supply of toilet paper.

Irrepressible Eddy Gilmore made a major contribution to the social life of the foreign colony by starting a jazz band—The Kremlin Krows—that became a fixture at diplomatic parties. Gilmore, who played drums, recruited the three other musicians from American embassy personnel. At one reception, a Soviet official frostily remarked that the painting on Gilmore's bass drum of the Kremlin towers and a flock of crows showed "disrespect" toward the Soviet Union and suggested that the band be renamed. The following day, Gilmore filed a story that could have made front pages in the United States:

THE KREMLIN KROWS—THE ONLY AMERICAN JAZZ BAND IN RUSSIA—WERE IN FULL FLIGHT TODAY TRYING TO GET AWAY FROM A PURGING PAINTBRUSH.

Glavlit pondered over the cable for twenty-four hours and finally sent it back to the chief Krow. The story now carried a lead that revealed the superb editing talent of the censors:

THE KREMLIN KROWS WERE IN FULL FLIGHT TODAY.

AP correspondent Gilmore killed the cable as rewritten by Glavlit and baptized the band The Purged Pigeons, a name requiring such lengthy explanations for those who hadn't known about the Krows that he tried again. This time the U.S. embassy painter carefully lettered on the bass drum: Joe Commode and his Four Flushers. When the rebaptized combo made its debut, the name produced chuckles from the Americans, but occasionally the wife of a foreign diplomat would address a request for a favorite dance number to the bandleader, Monsieur Commode.

Eddy Gilmore won a Pulitzer Prize for his reporting in 1947, provoking private cries of outrage from some of his colleagues. Walter Cronkite and Drew Middleton were furious that the award would be given to a correspondent whose dispatches were passed by the censor. The reaction was not personal, although Cronkite felt that Gilmore, likable, funny, and friendly as he was, had a little of the charlatan in him, but "to give a Pulitzer Prize for reporting that passes through censorship—any censor of any kind—that you don't even have a chance to correct—that's giving the prize to censorship. That's giving the Pulitzer to the idea of Soviet censorship. I found it terribly offensive."

Ludmilla Shapiro woke up in a cold sweat. Outside the United Press apartment, it was still dark, but she had heard a car pull up under the window. No knock on the door—this time. Julie Whitney, a talented musician, who had been looking forward to a career as a composer after a successful performance of her songs by orchestra leader Sergei Utyesov, was quickly expelled from the Composers Union and her songs banned from Moscow concert halls because they were "decadent" and "apolitical." Tamara Gilmore, mother of two young girls, was constantly pressured by the MVD to sign a statement renouncing her husband, which she refused to do.

The wives of American correspondents were treated as harshly as the hundreds of Russian women who had wed Allied military personnel, technicians, and diplomats during the war. Subject to a law passed in 1947 barring marriage between Soviet citizens and foreigners and applied retroactively, many women were forced to divorce their "capitalist" husbands who had returned home expecting that their wives would soon follow. The Soviet government refused them exit visas. Women were arrested and coerced into signing statements accusing their husbands of abandoning them. Those who refused were dispatched to labor camps for fifteen years.

Constant pressure on the correspondents' wives took its toll. Julie Whitney felt totally cut off from her own society, spending months at a time sitting at home reading, not even venturing to touch the piano. The only Russian she saw regularly was her ailing mother, who lived in Moscow. Tamara Gilmore was preoccupied with her children, but whenever she took them for a walk, a plainclothes escort would follow. Worried that her seven-year-old daughter Irisha might crack up under the strain, Ludmilla Shapiro sent her across town to live with her grandfather. She knew a family whose ten-year-old boy developed epilepsy after seeing his father taken away by police and did not want her daughter to risk the same fate. The Shapiros lived together as a family only on weekends, when the girl joined her parents in the UP apartment.

For Irisha Shapiro, the fear and pain were almost insupportable. Since she attended a Soviet school, her greatest concern was that she might be discovered to be an *Amerikanka*—an American. Some of her classmates, however, suspected that she was not only the daughter of a foreigner but also an American who was Jewish, a combination "tantamount to having leprosy." A girl once shouted at her, "You're an American kike—*zhid*" and stuck out her tongue. Irisha had never been so insulted. Trembling, she shouted back, "Kike yourself! My father is a Soviet diplomat!" Henry Shapiro, whose Russian was far from flawless, unlike other parents never attended any school functions.

Most terrifying for Tamara Gilmore and Ludmilla Shapiro was the possibility that their husbands would be expelled, that they would be arrested, and the government would take away their children and put them in orphan asylums or place them with Russian families—a frightening prospect for the fathers as well.

Appeals to the Soviet government to permit the Russian wives of Americans to leave the Soviet Union were to no avail. Mrs. Eleanor Roosevelt sent a personal plea to Stalin, as did former U.S. ambassador to Moscow Joseph E. Davies. When the issue was raised at the United Nations, the Soviets responded that if the women yearned to be with their husbands, why didn't the husbands remain with them in the Soviet Union? Underlying the Soviet policy was the conviction that, by marrying foreigners, the Russian women had sold their birthright and betrayed their country.

In January 1953, the predicament of the correspondents— and their wives—took a sharp turn for the worse. The Kremlin announced the arrest of a group of "saboteur-doctors" who had confessed to the murder of prominent Soviet leaders by misdiagnosing their ailments and prescribing lethal doses of medication. Six of the nine accused, all distinguished physicians, were Jewish and were said to be employed by an international Zionist espionage organization. *Pravda* attacked the state security agencies for failing to uncover the plot and called for elimination of "secret enemies of our people" who "with support of the imperialist world will continue to cause harm."

Suddenly the press was filled with appeals for "vigilance" and articles denouncing "Zionism—agent of United States and British imperialists." *Komsomolskaya Pravda* urged patriotic citizens to "expose unworthy persons. Do not be afraid to speak up!" A new kind of purge based on the latent anti-Semitism of the Russian people was being launched by Joseph Stalin, but nobody knew whom it was directed against. As the denunciations continued, the correspondents began to worry whether they were in line for "exposure," especially after *Pravda* announced the arrest of S. D. Gurevich, "an agent of a foreign intelligence service." A suave and affable man who had once lived in the United States and who spoke fluent English, Gurevich had worked for Western embassies and for several American correspondents.

With the link established, Stalin could put on a show trial, using hapless foreigners in the supporting cast to provide credibility to the proceedings. In the recent trial of Czech Communist leader Rudolf Slansky, the prosecution brought in an Israeli citizen to testify that Slansky worked with Israeli intelligence. Another precedent for a Moscow trial could be the recent arrest and conviction for espionage of the AP bureau chief in Prague, William Oatis.

Unprotected by diplomatic immunity and unwilling to leave Russia because of their wives, both Thomas Whitney and Henry Shapiro were prime candidates for a leading role in a Kremlin show trial. From the Soviet point of view, Whitney would make an ideal frame-up victim, having served with the Office of Strategic Services (OSS) during the war and the American embassy in Moscow before joining the AP in 1947. Henry Shapiro, dean of the press corps, a Moscow correspondent for almost twenty years whose wife came from a wealthy prerevolutionary family, was the only Jew among the American newsmen. The vulnerability of the American correspondents did not escape the attention of the U.S. embassy. Jacob Beam, the chargé d'affaires, summoned Shapiro to warn that he was in danger. You should leave the country, he urged, as quickly as possible. Henry Shapiro replied that he'd be happy to go, but only if his family departed with him, a most unlikely solution.

If the night is darkest just before dawn, then at 4:00 A.M. on March 4, the atmosphere in Moscow was opaque and grim indeed. A few weeks earlier, the Russians had severed diplomatic relations with Israel, a move clearly related to the "doctors' plot," although the ostensible reason was that someone had thrown a bomb at the Soviet legation in Tel Aviv. The Israelis, a convenient target, fit neatly in with the continuing anti-Zionist campaign waged by the Communist Party propaganda machine. Something was brewing, but nobody, certainly not the correspondents, knew what it was.

That night, Harrison Salisbury and Jean Nau of the French news service Agence France-Presse (AFP) were on duty at the

Central Telegraph waiting for *Izvestia*. By 6:00 A.M., copies of the newspaper still had not been delivered. Concerned about the delay, Salisbury phoned Thomas Whitney, "You'd better come down now. The papers are late. There's every indication that they have been held up for an important announcement." Salisbury also phoned Andrew Steiger of Reuters. Nau summoned Henry Shapiro. Within half an hour, five men representing the AP, UPI, Reuters, AFP, and the *Times*—the entire Western press corps except for Eddy Gilmore—were assembled in the small room. The atmosphere was tense. Whitney paced the floor. Shapiro puffed on a cigarette and whispered to Nau in Russian. Everyone thought the holdup was related to a dramatic development in the "doctors' plot," but they were wrong. The news that had delayed the newspapers was unrelated to the plot but to its instigator: Joseph Stalin had suffered a stroke and had lapsed into a coma.

Although the news was astonishing, an earthquake of a story and officially announced by TASS, the correspondents could not transmit a single sentence. Glavlit was holding up all cables until Radio Moscow announced the news on its 8:00 A.M. broadcast. Each man at the Central Telegraph knew what would happen: The radio monitor in London would pick up the TASS communiqué, translate it, and telex it to the news agencies, which would flash it around the world while their correspondents in Moscow—fuming and frustrated—were prevented from filing. As expected, a few minutes after the broadcast began, Glavlit released the cables approved for phoning to the West. Once again the system had triumphed, robbing the reporters of the biggest Moscow story in decades.

Joseph Stalin died the next day, but the news was not made public for twenty-four hours. When the American correspondents, camping at the Central Telegraph, received the announcement, they submitted their "flashes" to the Glavlit clerks and ordered telephone lines to London and Paris. Soon afterward, an official appeared and yanked the main cable out of the rear of the telephone switchboard.

"There will be no telephone calls abroad until further notice," he declared.

The Russian may not have known that Henry Shapiro had already managed to blurt out "Yes!" to a London editor who asked, "Is Stalin dead?"

The correspondents would not be permitted to file the story until someone higher up in the chain of command than Comrade Omelchenko gave permission. Again, Moscow Radio was the first to broadcast the news officially.

For the next three days, thousands of Russians, many sobbing, shuffled past Stalin's bier in the Hall of Columns, paying their last respects to the man who had guided their destiny for over twenty-five years. At 10:15 A.M. on March 9, Joseph Stalin's casket, draped in red with a plastic bubble over the head of the corpse, was borne from the Hall of Columns by senior party leaders including Georgi Malenkov, Lavrenti Beria, Nikita Khrushchev, and Vyacheslav Molotov, and placed on an artillery carriage. The funeral procession moved slowly across the broad expanse of Red Square to the squat marble Lenin mausoleum, on which the name of the new occupant was already carved. After brief eulogies, the pallbearers again shouldered the casket and carried it into the crypt. A few minutes later, the chimes of the great clock on the Spassky Gate struck noon while fighter planes streaked over the square, signaling the end of the funeral and the end of an era.

With the removal of Stalin's grip on Russia, life began to change, slowly yet inexorably. The new government, with Georgi Malenkov as premier and Nikita Khrushchev as the increasingly powerful party secretary, sent signals to the Soviet people and to the world that the country was beginning to take a different path. One of the first and most dramatic acts was *Pravda*'s announcement that the "doctors' plot" was a frame-up, the evidence forged, and the confessions obtained through "impermissible and illegal methods"—that is, by torture. The doctors had been released and were back at work. In another move, the government declared a broad amnesty for thousands of minor criminals and petty offenders, the first step in the dismantling of the Stalinist system of forced labor. The prices of bread, meat, sugar, vodka, and shoes were reduced. Popular grades of wheat flour were put on regular sale in Moscow stores for the first time in twenty years. More significant was the arrest in July of Lavrenti P. Beria, Stalin's police chief and the most feared man in the Soviet Union, charged with "criminal antiparty and state work." He was shot twenty-four hours after being tried and sentenced to death in December 1953.

The Kremlin's relations with the rest of the world were also changing. The USSR announced that it was abandoning all claims to Turkish territory. A clerk who had been confined to the British embassy grounds for several years to avoid arrest on trumped-up charges was permitted to return to England. Seven American civilians, freed from internment in North Korea thanks to the good offices of the Soviet government, passed through Moscow on their way home. A delegation of American editors visited Moscow, the first such group since 1947, and received red-carpet treatment from the Press Department. A veritable flood of news kept correspondents busy filing daily stories showing that the new government under Premier Malenkov was clearly breaking with the Stalinist past.

One day in mid-April, Henry Shapiro, Thomas Whitney, Andrew Steiger, and Eddy Gilmore were sitting in the office of the new U.S. ambassador, Charles E. Bohlen, who had served in Moscow as a young third secretary under William C. Bullitt, in 1934. Bohlen told them the good news: Secretary of State John Foster Dulles had authorized him to meet with Foreign Minister Molotov to request exit visas for their wives.

"Don't get your hopes up," he cautioned. "You know how touchy a subject this is . . . [but] the time is right."

Foreign Minister Molotov was noncommittal during the meeting, but instead of rejecting the request outright, as in the past, he replied, *Posmotrim.* ("We shall see.") Despite Bohlen's caveat, Molotov's remark offered a glimmer of hope. More important, the Soviet press had stopped attacking American correspondents as spies and warmongers, while Premier Malenkov was calling for improved relations with the West.

The new trend had surfaced earlier when Thomas Whitney gave a dinner party for the visiting American editors at the Aragvi restaurant, one of the best in Moscow. To his astonishment, Comrades Kartsev and Vavilov, a pair of senior Press Department officials he had invited pro forma, walked through the door of the private dining room—with Mme. Kartsev. The Russians exuded charm and amiability. Kartsev drew aside U.S. Chargé d'Affaires Jacob Beam and told him, "There have been many mistakes in the past. The important thing is that we must forget the past and start out anew."

Kartsev then raised his glass to toast the president of the United States, an act unseen in Moscow since the war. Some of the journalists at the dinner quickly swallowed their baked chicken and rushed to the Central Telegraph to file the story.

In early June, Ambassador Bohlen phoned Eddy Gilmore with glad tidings: "Well, boy, you're sprung. Tamara gets her visa." After years of fear and waiting, she was granted an exit visa for herself and the two girls. The wife of Robert Tucker, an embassy employee, received her visa next. Ten days later, Foreign Minister Molotov informed Bohlen that four more visas had been approved: All the wives and their children would be permitted to leave. Ludmilla and Irisha Shapiro were the last to go.

In 1963, at a Kremlin reception, Nikita Khrushchev was chatting with the wife of the Swedish ambassador, Mme. Rolf Suhlman, who was a descendant of Russian nobility. He told her that he was glad that she had married the diplomat "because it gives foreigners a good idea of what Russian women are like." Mme. Suhlman reminded him that for many years it was illegal for a Soviet citizen to marry a foreigner.

"Yes," said Khrushchev scornfully, "that was the barbarian—Stalin."

After a round of parties and farewells, the four correspondents and their families departed. Thomas Whitney was assigned briefly to the AP's London bureau and then to New York, where he worked as a foreign news analyst, focusing on Soviet affairs. In 1959 he left the agency, retiring to a small town in Connecticut. Julie resumed her musical career, re-cording several albums of Russian songs before dying of cancer in 1965 at age forty-six. Whitney, who had a superb command of Russian, spent five years translating Alexander Solzhenitsyn's epic work *Gulag Archipelago*, accepting no pay-ment for what he called a "duty of conscience." Eddy Gilmore was also assigned to the AP's London bureau; he succumbed to a heart attack in 1967. Andrew Steiger returned to Moscow as a stringer for various minor American and British publica-tions, barely making ends meet. He died in the late 1960s. Few of the American correspondents in Moscow even knew he was there. Of the four Americans who worked for U.S. news organizations, only Henry Shapiro became a "career" Moscow correspondent, returning in 1955 and, with time out for vacations, sabbaticals, fellowships, and lecture tours, headed the UP bureau there until 1973.

Harrison E. Salisbury remained in Moscow until September 1954, long after the others had departed. By then he was the most experienced and best-known American correspondent reporting from Russia. As the only correspondent represent-ing a daily newspaper, he traveled widely and wrote inces-santly, frequently making the front page with the big stories breaking after Stalin's death. After returning to New York, he wrote a series of articles under the title "Russia Re-Viewed" for the *Times* that won a Pulitzer Prize in 1955. That same year, he published his first book, *American in Russia*, and began to move up the newspaper's executive ladder to national editor and associate editor. Salisbury's career was not, how-ever, without controversy, especially when he obtained a visa for Hanoi during some of the most intensive fighting of the Vietnam War.

Long after his departure from Moscow, Harrison Salisbury remained committed to Soviet affairs, writing a number of books on the subject, including *900 Days*, a widely hailed account of Leningrad under German siege. He irked some of his former colleagues when he published a book in 1978 whose jacket cover announced that he spent "almost half his life in Russia." At age seventy, that would have meant he had lived in Moscow for at least thirty years, far more than the six years he spent as the *Times* correspondent and as an occasional visitor.

After almost half a century in journalism, Harrison Salisbury retired to a rambling Connecticut *dacha* at the end of a dirt road in a town called—Salisbury.

One nagging question about the Cold War period was whether Americans married to Russians soft-pedaled their reporting to avoid expulsion and threats to the safety of their families. The first to bring the predicament of the correspondents to public attention was Edmund Stevens, himself married to a Russian who, unlike the other wives, possessed an American passport and who could leave the Soviet Union at any time. In his Pulitzer Prize–winning series for the *Monitor* he pointed out that this situation gave Soviet authorities "a powerful lever" over the correspondents but stopped short of declaring that Eddy Gilmore, Thomas Whitney, and Henry Shapiro avoided filing stories that might be regarded as unfavorable by the Russians. Stevens failed to mention that, in any case, negative stories could not have gotten past the censor. Henry Shapiro has angrily rejected such allegations, stating the charges "are not only malicious, but ignorant.

"How could we have been influenced? Do you think that someone who was under that influence could report for forty years and send dispatches and articles which went to thousands of newspapers all over the world? Do you think anybody could get away with that? How long could he be influenced? How long would I have lasted? Who do you think my editors were? . . . Let one person show one line, one piece that I wrote, one paragraph that showed I wrote . . . !"

Whether the four Americans muted their reporting because of their families was of minor importance compared to the monstrous constraints imposed by the Soviet system and the censorship. Glavlit prevented not only the married men but also the unmarried man, Harrison Salisbury, from transmitting the full picture of life in the Soviet Union. Whatever filtered through the censorship was, by its very nature, only a small part of any story. On December 21, 1949, for example, all the correspondents reported Stalin's seventieth gala birthday festivities at the Bolshoi Theater amid tributes from the Soviet people. Could a reporter have included in the story that Stalin had sent millions of innocent people to labor camps, physically destroyed his old Bolshevik colleagues, and instigated a virulent anti-Semitic campaign against the Soviet Jewish intelligentsia? These details would have presented a well-rounded picture of his career, but no correspondent could have dispatched a syllable past Glavlit, nor would any have tried. If Americans did not get a complete and balanced report on the Soviet Union during the Cold War years, the correspondents were not at fault. They did their best; they were hard-working, diligent professionals, using wit and stamina to cope with an impossible situation. Curiously enough, the tension, the fear, and the pressure drove no one to drink or desperation and did not produce ulcers or nervous breakdowns. The feeling that enabled Thomas Whitney to retain his equilibrium was probably shared by his colleagues: the sense that he was "working on the most important news story in the world." In voicing this sentiment, he was no different from the Moscow correspondents who preceded and followed him. They all felt that, for better or for worse, they were recording history.

7

Khrushchev: Parting the Curtain—Partly

I never had the illusion that I was giving a balanced and comprehensive view of what was going on in a country where 90% of the area is out of bounds, you can't go places, can't talk to people, and can't ask questions. . . . My ambition was much lower . . . to give an accurate picture of what I had seen and heard.

> B. J. Cutler
> *New York Herald Tribune*
> 1956–58

Probably half the American correspondents in the last twenty-five years did not have enough training in [the] language, culture, and history of the Russian people. I am an example of it.

> John Chancellor
> NBC News
> 1961–62

Don't let the bastards grind you down. Stay healthy. Eat as well as you can.
> Robert Gibson
> *Business Week,* McGraw-Hill
> 1958–60
> (advice to a correspondent departing for Moscow)

One morning in mid-1954, Clifton E. Daniel, the newly assigned Moscow correspondent of *The New York Times,* sat at his desk at the newspaper's headquarters on Forty-third Street. Before him lay a blank yellow legal pad on which he itemized the stories he wanted to cover in the Soviet Union.

On the list was a visit to a collective farm, how the bureaucracy works or doesn't work, what people pay for food in the shops and markets, how workers and peasants live, how Russians amuse themselves, what they eat and drink, and reports on the myriad facets of life in post-Stalin Russia.

Daniel, forty-two, decided to report on the Soviet Union as if no one had ever been there before. Everything would be new to him, he reasoned, and therefore new to the readers of the *Times*.

Other correspondents had drawn up similar lists in the past, but few had been able to achieve their journalistic goals. They were caught and crushed not only by censorship but also by all the other barriers to reporting the reality of Soviet society. Nevertheless, history was on Clifton Daniel's side. With the death of Joseph Stalin and the gradual dismantling of the system's excesses, restrictions on correspondents became less onerous. Working conditions grew better, not the least improvement being the increase of international telephone lines at the Central Telegraph from one to four. Moreover, 1954 also marked the beginning of Nikita S. Khrushchev's ten years in the Kremlin, a decade when the Soviet Union began to play a highly visible role in international affairs, challenging the United States as the other superpower. At the same time, Russia's self-imposed isolation from the capitalist world was succeeded by an outreach policy that opened the country to Western influence. In the early part of the decade, for example, a series of agreements between the United States and the USSR on cultural and scientific exchanges, tourism, and air transport led to a dramatic increase in travel to the Soviet Union and the first trickle of Soviet visitors to the United States. Soviet achievements in space, the launching of *Sputnik I* and Yuri Gagarin, the first human to orbit the earth, provided reporters with front-page stories. As Kremlin diplomacy courted other countries, an unending and unprecedented stream of visitors flowed into Moscow: heads of state, Third World politicians, U.S. senators, peace delegations, clergymen, trade union leaders, newspaper editors, farming experts, athletes, and brain surgeons. An enterprising correspondent could often travel with these groups to parts of the country not normally accessible. Nikita Khrushchev, ebullient, garrulous, and peripatetic, made news whenever he traveled or opened his mouth.

If the Soviet Union was less threatening to personal safety

than during the Cold War years, it was also more of a professional challenge. Reporting opportunities suddenly exploded, covering a range of subjects undreamed of during the previous decade, requiring judgment and a sense of history that few correspondents possessed.

The Fourth of July 1955 was a cool, sunny day in Moscow. As in other U.S. embassies around the world, the American flag was flying high at Spaso House, the ambassador's residence. Several dozen diplomats, their wives, a handful of low-ranking Soviet officials, correspondents, and a few American tourists were gathered in the garden to mark Independence Day. As they sipped champagne and discussed politics, Avis Bohlen, a gracious and charming hostess, was moving among the guests, explaining the absence of her husband, who had been recalled to Washington for consultations on the forthcoming Geneva summit. Suddenly Russian voices were heard from the far end of the garden. Everyone turned and saw a remarkable sight: Led by Nikita Khrushchev himself, the senior members of the Communist Party Presidium shuffled up the driveway. Accompanying Khrushchev were Nikolai Bulganin, Vyacheslav Molotov, and Georgi Malenkov—the rulers of the Soviet Union.

To see so much power concentrated in such a small place was astonishing but not entirely unexpected. Since the death of Stalin, the Soviet leaders had begun to venture out of the Kremlin to attend national day receptions at various embassies, but this was the first time they had stepped inside Spaso. After the initial greetings from Chargé d'Affaires Newbold Walmsley and Mrs. Bohlen, the Russians were quickly surrounded by the American correspondents—Clifton Daniel of the *Times*, Charles (Chuck) Klensch of INS, Stanley Johnson of AP, Kenneth Brodney of UP—and two or three French and British correspondents, notebooks ready. Peppered with questions about the summit meeting, Khrushchev took it on himself to respond while the other Russians stood silently at his side. Quickly sketching the Kremlin's position with complete assurance, he made it clear that although Premier Bulganin would represent the Soviet Union at the meeting, he, Nikita Khrushchev, could expound that policy without consulting anyone else.

Mrs. Bohlen, annoyed that the party was turning into a press conference, asked Walmsley to terminate the interview. But he was just as interested as the reporters in hearing out Khrushchev.

"I'm very sorry, Avis," he replied firmly, "but I won't do it."

By the time Khrushchev finished speaking, the correspondents had their story. Clifton Daniel made the front page of the *Times* under a three-column head.

Nikita Khrushchev's frequent appearances at embassy and Kremlin receptions and on other public occasions was an unprecedented phenomenon in Soviet history. Compared to him, Lenin and Stalin were hermits, emerging only for important Communist Party and state occasions. At times Khrushchev attended two or three receptions a week, usually accessible to foreign correspondents, who immediately surged toward him to ask questions ranging from the future of Berlin to the impact of the weather on the grain harvest. The impromptu give-and-take between Khrushchev and the journalists came as close to a genuine press conference as had ever existed in the Soviet Union and produced far more news than those meetings arranged by the Press Department. The encounters also gave reporters unusual opportunities to observe the Soviet leaders closely, to watch them as they talked with the diplomats and with each other, to note their mannerisms and their dress, and eventually to see their wives, who also began to appear in public for the first time. At a French reception, for instance, I was not only able to determine that Khrushchev wore a shoe size smaller than my 6½D but also watched with admiration as he nibbled on a slice of *jambon* expertly balanced on his knife.

To deal with these new opportunities, the correspondents agreed on a system under which all information that came out of a reception was shared among them. The pooling took place at Central Telegraph when the correspondents met to file their stories. Agency reporters—AP, UP, AFP, and Reuters, all fluent in Russian—read from their notes. Other correspondents contributed to the general pool of information. Such an arrangement, in addition to being convenient for the reporters, also ensured an agreed text of what Nikita Khrushchev or Nikolai Bulganin had said, thus guaranteeing that everyone would file identical quotes. For those who knew no Russian, this system was their salvation. When the information-sharing was completed, each reporter was on his own. Agency reporters rushed to their cubicles to type their stories, ordered lines to London, Paris, or Frankfurt, and then prayed that the censor would pass their copy before the call came through.

For correspondents, the receptions, besides being sources of breaking stories, also provided opportunities to meet other members of the Soviet elite: actors, writers, scientists, musicians, ministry officials, and military leaders. In the course of one Kremlin reception I was able to chat with Galina Ulanova, the Bolshoi's prima ballerina, ask writer Ilya Ehrenburg about his forthcoming book, and complain to Press Department chief Leonid F. Ilyichev about the endless delay in getting responses from his staff.

One of the more memorable receptions took place at the Polish embassy in November 1956. NATO envoys led by U.S. Ambassador Charles E. Bohlen left the room after Khrushchev had attacked Britain, France, and Israel for the invasion of Egypt and hinting that God was on the side of Communists. Then he thundered a phrase that quickly entered the mythology of Soviet-American relations:

"We will bury you!"

As soon as the reception ended, the correspondents rushed to the Central Telegraph to report Khrushchev's dramatic pronouncement as a threat to the West and a warning that the Soviet Union would inevitably destroy the capitalist world. The interpretation of his remark was totally incorrect, but it carried weight because all the agencies and all the specials dispatched an agreed text. What Khrushchev actually meant was quite different, not implying any threat but citing a common Russian expression meaning, "We will survive you. We will be present at your funeral."

Ambassador Bohlen, whose Russian was vastly superior to that of the reporters, immediately recognized the phrase as a figure of speech "expressing confidence in prevailing over the long haul," as he later wrote. Presumably he advised Secretary of State John Foster Dulles that the USSR was not about to start a war with the United States. The erroneous dispatches, however, had already misled the American public.

At another reception, honoring cosmonaut Yuri Gagarin for his historic space orbit, Khrushchev exhibited the quick wit that fascinated the correspondents. I watched as Gagarin stood at rigid attention on the stage of the Kremlin's St. George's Hall, Khrushchev trying to pin a gold medal on his chest. Despite the Soviet leader's efforts, the pin could not penetrate the cloth. An embarrassed silence enveloped the white marble chamber as he continued to push. Soon a titter arose from the hundreds of guests, quickly turning to laughter. Gagarin began to smile and then to laugh as Khrushchev continued to press. Finally Khrushchev gave up, placed the medal in Gagarin's hand and turning to the audience with a grin, said:

"You see, comrades, how solid is our cloth. Even a pin cannot pass through."

Everyone in the audience knew that the problem was not the cloth but the shoddy workmanship of the pin. Khrushchev had managed to extricate himself from an embarrassing situation with grace and humor.

In July 1955, at Khrushchev's personal invitation, a delegation of American farm experts visited the Soviet Union to study agricultural practices. Accompanying the group was Irving R. Levine, an NBC radio and television correspondent based in New York. After arriving in Moscow, he persuaded the Press Department to accord him permanent accreditation with permission to open the first broadcast news bureau in the U.S.S.R. since 1947. For five months Levine was the only American network journalist reporting from Moscow. In December, CBS arrived on the scene in the person of Daniel Schorr, thirty-nine, a correspondent in the Washington bureau.

The Press Department was unprepared to deal with Levine. Since there were no transmission facilities at the Central Telegraph, where the censor was located, Levine was, like Larry Lesueur during the war, permitted to broadcast from the studios of Radio Moscow, surprisingly without censorship.

"I never had any problems, nor do I recall any restraints that I put on myself. I was just doing direct reporting on events," Levine recalled.

This happy state lasted until Schorr arrived; then Levine was ordered to broadcast from the Central Telegraph under the most primitive conditions. Worse, he was obliged to submit his copy to Glavlit before he could broadcast.

Schorr traveled to Moscow on a temporary assignment in 1955 to cover the trip of West German Chancellor Konrad Adenauer, the first German head of government to visit the Soviet Union since the end of World War II. Like Levine, Schorr was able to obtain permanent accreditation.

Daniel Schorr has not forgotten his initial broadcast from the Soviet Union. He sat in a glass-paneled booth at the Central Telegraph speaking into a microphone that stood on a wooden table. The echo produced by the bare glass almost drowned out his voice. He tried to muffle the sound by holding his fur-lined coat over his head and the microphone, but it was so dark inside he could not read the script that had been passed by Glavlit. Knowing that the censor was listening, he told the CBS technician at the receiving end of the broadcast:

"I hope everybody who is listening understands that what I am about to read is an approximation of what is in my script, but because of conditions, I cannot read my script, so any deviation from the original is not intended."

Daniel Schorr's appeal worked. The broadcast was transmitted as he ad-libbed it.

The arrival of the U.S. networks in Moscow marked the beginning of a new era in American reporting on the Soviet Union. In addition to radio broadcasts, film reports on Russia began appearing on American television, providing visual images of that hitherto mysterious land, its peoples, and its leaders. Correspondents using 16mm movie cameras shot everything they could aim at, even getting out-of-focus, underexposed film on the air, such was the hunger for footage. Moscow street scenes, the outdoor farmers' market, Sunday in Gorky Park, Soviet leaders at receptions, horse racing at the Hippodrome, and Red Square parades were all prime candidates for scarce time on the fifteen-minute evening news shows. Within a few years there would be "TV specials" and documentaries on such subjects as the artistic riches of the Kremlin, bear hunting in Siberia, championship chess matches, the Soviet woman, the Bolshoi Ballet School, and the Science City of Siberia, coordinated and narrated by a network correspondent using camera crews and technicians brought in from abroad.

Working the Moscow streets was fraught with difficulties for Irving Levine and Daniel Schorr. The Russians—still wary of Cold War spies—harassed the Americans as soon as they raised their cameras. Whether they were filming a taxi stand, a store window, people lined up in front of Lenin's tomb, or children ice-skating in a frozen courtyard, there were always outraged citizens who demanded that they turn away their cameras, or a militiaman asking for their identity cards. A scene would often be terminated by a large, hostile hand closing in on the camera lens. The other problem for the network reporters was how to send film out of the country. In principle, shipping undeveloped film was a violation of the censorship, but since the Press Department had no processing facilities, the correspondents had no choice but to break the rules. The only way to ship film was to entrust it to a departing traveler, a "pigeon," usually a tourist who would pocket the reel and carry it past customs inspectors. A network courier would meet the tourist at the airport in Paris or London and then rush the film to a continuing flight or to the laboratory for processing. Although the Press Department knew about the subterfuge, it chose not to interfere. Credit for initiating this system goes to Charles Klensch of INS, who arrived in Moscow in February 1955 and shot film for Telenews.

Some correspondents went to extremes to find a "pigeon." When Ambassador Charles Bohlen was leaving Moscow in

April 1957 en route to his new post in Manila, the State
Department sent a plane for him and his family. On the taxi
strip, in front of the entire diplomatic corps, senior officials of
the Foreign Ministry, the American colony, and the KGB,
Edmund Stevens, whose wife, Nina, was shooting for ABC,
walked up to Bohlen, shoved a reel of film at him, and asked
him to take it out. The ambassador froze at Stevens' audacity
but accepted the packet. At a U.S. embassy reception a few
years later, Stevens tried the same public approach with
columnist Walter Lippmann, who had just returned from the
Crimea after interviewing Nikita Khrushchev. The crusty old
man refused.

In May 1957, the Press Department phoned Daniel Schorr
regarding a CBS request to interview a senior Soviet leader on
Face the Nation. He was told that the senior official who had
agreed to the interview would not be Premier Bulganin, as he
had expected, but Nikita Khrushchev, apparently eager to
make his debut on American television. Delighted with the
news, Schorr immediately informed CBS in New York. After
lengthy and complicated negotiations over filming arrangements and translation procedures, agreement was reached.
CBS sent in three crews to shoot the interview. Just as the
program was ready to be filmed, everything came to a
screeching stop when Schorr submitted the three panelists'
names to the Press Department: Schorr; Stuart Novins, the
CBS moderator; and B. J. Cutler, the thirty-three-year-old
correspondent of the *New York Herald Tribune.* The Press
Department vetoed Cutler.

"We agreed to an interview with CBS," argued the Press
Department, "and not with any other correspondents."

"Yes," replied Schorr, "but this is the format of *Face the
Nation.* We always have a print reporter on the panel."

What Schorr could not tell the Russians was that there was
a sharp division within CBS over the propriety of exposing the
American public to Nikita Khrushchev. Some senior executives urged that CBS cancel the program because even in 1957
they questioned whether the Soviet Union and its leaders were

a legitimate news story. The Kremlin's brutality in crushing the Hungarian revolution a few months earlier had done little to enhance the Soviet image in the United States. Moreover, according to Schorr, CBS was still reeling from the confrontation between Senator Joseph McCarthy and Edward R. Murrow and charges that the network had harbored "Communist-leaning" reporters on its news staff. One result of this defensiveness was that CBS was unwilling to grant the Moscow bureau official status in order to avoid listing it in the company directory. Sensitivity over the Communist issue and possible charges that the network would serve as a channel for Kremlin propaganda made it essential to share the onus with a newspaper or magazine—whether the *Herald Tribune* or another publication was irrelevant. After consulting with Theodore Koop, head of the CBS Washington bureau who had already arrived in Moscow, Schorr told Press Department officials that if they refused to accept another correspondent, the interview would be canceled. In the meantime, he phoned CBS President Frank Stanton in New York to make certain that senior management supported his stand.

Knowing that the conversation was being monitored, Schorr asked Stanton to confirm that the company would not compromise on its position that there must be a non-CBS reporter on the program.

"Are you willing to scrap the whole thing if this condition is not met?"

"Yes," replied Stanton.

"Okay," said Schorr, "I think they will do it all the same, once they understand that it's not going to happen otherwise."

Within twenty-four hours, the Press Department yielded. *Face the Nation* was cleared for shooting.

The hour-long program was a remarkable coup for CBS, but it could just as well have gone to NBC. Since the Kremlin's aim was to present its views to the American public, either network would have served the purpose. CBS won the draw. Khrushchev must have been pleased with his performance, since the program was quickly reedited and presented on Soviet TV and in cinemas around the country. For the first

time, Soviet audiences saw their leader in action, defending
the Kremlin's intervention in Poland and Hungary, explaining
de-Stalinization policies, and calling for peace and friendship
with the United States.

In Moscow Daniel Schorr became an instant celebrity, but
Cutler, who had asked some skeptical questions about Khrushchev's claims that the Soviets were scaling back their armed
forces, was the villain of the piece. With his wife, Carol, he saw
the program in a Moscow movie theater. When the camera
turned on him, he heard a Russian behind him say with a
growl, "That's the spy." Cutler slumped down in his seat and
pulled his jacket collar over his face, hoping not to be
recognized.

The head-to-head rivalry between Daniel Schorr and Irving
Levine lasted the entire time they worked in Moscow. Schorr,
however, left in December 1957 for the CBS year-end news
roundup, knowing that the Russians would not give him a
reentry visa. Levine remained until 1959, when he was reassigned to NBC's Rome bureau. In the meantime, Schorr was
crisscrossing the United States on lucrative lecture tours,
regaling audiences with tales of life in Russia. Levine, however,
unknowingly had the last laugh. After his appearance in a
midwestern city, a woman rushed up to the stage, grabbed
Schorr's hand, and told him how much she enjoyed his
broadcasts from Moscow.

"I listened to you every day. Now I'm so delighted to meet
you in person—Mr. Levine."

Ambassador Charles Bohlen leaned back in his swivel chair
and puffed on a cigarette. All ten resident American correspondents were gathered in his office for the regular Friday
afternoon briefing. On the wall behind the ambassador's desk
hovered an expertly carved American eagle, wings outspread,
head cocked as if trying to overhear the chitchat among the
newsmen. (Four years later, U.S. Ambassador to the United
Nations Henry Cabot Lodge revealed that the wooden eagle
contained a listening device planted by the KGB!)

At 3:00 P.M., noting that everyone was present, Bohlen

extinguished his cigarette and posed the question that everyone in Moscow was asking:

"Well, gentlemen, what have you heard about the Party Congress?"

Scheduled to begin within a few weeks, on February 14, 1956, the Twentieth Congress of the Soviet Communist Party was expected to be a historic event. It was the first Congress since 1952, the first since Stalin's death, and nobody was certain what would emerge. The speculation was that Khrushchev would assume the mantle of the man who had dominated Soviet life and politics for almost thirty years.

The reporters had no information about the Congress. Equally important, they knew nothing about the arrangements the Press Department would make for coverage of the meeting: whether they would be admitted to the Kremlin, whether they would receive advance copies of the speeches, whether there would be additional international telephone lines at the Central Telegraph. Phone calls to the Press Department elicited the customary evasive response, "The necessary arrangements will be announced in due time." One week before the Congress was to begin, the Press Department informed the Western correspondents that they would not be admitted to the Kremlin, that the Sovinformburo would deliver texts of the speeches twice daily to the Central Telegraph, and that additional international phones would be operating temporarily.

For me, this was a big story. At age thirty-four, I had arrived in Moscow in mid-December 1955 with a Ph.D. in Russian history, six months in the Boston bureau of the United Press, and a year on the cable (foreign) desk in New York. With workable and soon-to-be fluent Russian, after seven years of academic and journalism training, I had finally achieved my goal: to cover the Soviet Union for a major American news organization.

On the morning of the fourteenth, the Central Telegraph was crowded with correspondents, translators, and bureau chauffeurs. Except for one man, the entire Western press corps was present, fifteen in all: John Retty and Sidney

Frank Bourgholtzer (NBC: 1961–63) aims his camera at a favorite and ubiquitous target: Nikita Khrushchev.
Courtesy Frank Bourgholtzer

Robert J. "Bud" Korengold (UPI: 1959–63; *Newsweek:* 1964–68) photographs Nikita Khrushchev on the way to vote in a Supreme Soviet election. Korengold is at right. Kenneth Bernstein, NBC correspondent, is filming the chairman. A few months later in October 1964, Khrushchev was deposed and succeeded by Leonid Brezhnev. *Courtesy Robert J. Korengold*

Robert C. Toth (*Los Angeles Times:* 1974–78) (right) with Jewish dissident Anatoly B. Scharansky. In 1978, Toth was arrested by the KGB and interrogated on his relationship with Scharansky, who was in turn arrested, tried and convicted of treason. Toth was permitted to leave Russia. Confined in a labor camp, Scharansky was freed in 1986 and now lives in Israel. *Courtesy Robert C. Toth*

Richard Nixon, after being de-feated for the governorship of California, started his political comeback with a trip to Moscow in 1965. Fred Coleman, AP, covers his tourist visit to the Kremlin. *Courtesy Fred Coleman*

Stuart Loory, CNN bureau chief, questioning Foreign Minister Andrei Gromyko during a 1983 press conference carried live from Moscow via satellite, a first for an American network. A "two-tour" correspondent, Loory had previously served with the New York *Herald Tribune* in 1962–64. *Courtesy CNN*

B. J. Cutler, New York *Herald Tribune* (right), and Richard O'Malley, AP bureau chief (second from right), at 1956 press conference examine radio equipment which Russians claimed United States dropped over Soviet territory to transmit intelligence information. A few weeks later, O'Malley was expelled for "currency speculation." *Courtesy B. J. Cutler*

The AP Moscow bureau poses for its portrait in 1963. Left to right: Preston Grover (bureau chief), Bill (translator), George Syvertsen (correspondent), Mila (translator), Tamara (translator), Nikolai (chauffeur), Reinhold G. Ensz (correspondent). Syvertsen was later assigned to Vietnam, where he disappeared covering a combat mission and is presumed dead. *Courtesy R. G. Ensz*

Serge Schmemann, *New York Times* (left), and Tony Barbieri, *Baltimore Sun*, enjoy caviar and vodka during their long trip on the Trans-Siberian Express in 1983. Schmemann, who speaks fluent Russian, spent almost seven years in Moscow, first for the AP, then for the *Times. Courtesy S. Schmemann*

The *Christian Science Monitor*'s Charlotte Saikowski, one of the few American women in the Moscow press corps during the early 1970s, poses for the traditional photo on Red Square. *Christian Science Monitor*

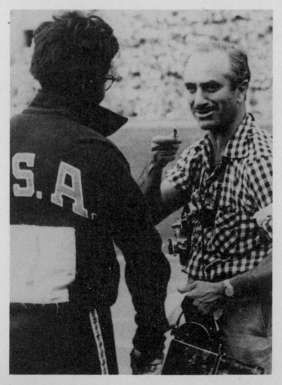

Whitman Bassow, UPI and later *Newsweek* bureau chief, covers first USA-USSR track meet in 1957. Track star Wilma Rudolph (left) sparked relay team that beat Russian women. *Courtesy Whitman Bassow*

Henry Shapiro, UPI's Moscow correspondent for almost forty years, interviews General Secretary Leonid Brezhnev in his Kremlin office in 1973. A Harvard-trained lawyer, Shapiro went to Moscow in 1933 to study Soviet law, stayed on to work as a correspondent briefly for the British news agency Reuters and then UPI. *Courtesy Henry Shapiro*

Larry Lesueur (right), the first CBS correspondent to broadcast from Russia, chatting with Eddy Gilmore, AP, and an unidentified U.S. Navy attaché at a military airfield near Moscow in 1942. Although the Russians gave Lesueur permission to broadcast, they refused to reveal the precise radio frequencies used by their transmitters to carry Lesueur's reports because they were "military secrets." *Courtesy Larry Lesueur*

From left: Whitman Bassow, UPI, Charles Klensch, INS, and Irving Levine, NBC, film new Soviet cyclotron in 1956. This was the first time Western correspondents had been permitted to visit Russia's big atom-research center at Dubna. *Courtesy Charles Klensch*

Daniel Schorr, CBS, taping on Red Square in 1956. Schorr scored a journalistic coup when he arranged a panel interview with Nikita Khrushchev on *Face the Nation*, the first time the Soviet leader presented his views directly to an American television audience. *Courtesy Daniel Schorr*

Bessie Beatty, *San Francisco Bulletin*, listens to V. I. Lenin on Red Square in 1922. Beatty covered the Bolshevik coup in Petrograd in November 1917, along with John Reed and Louise Bryant. *Slavonic Division, New York Public Library*

Covering a USA-USSR basketball game in 1957: (from left) Howard Sochurek, *Life*, Roy Essoyan, AP, and Harold Milks, AP bureau chief. Relaxation of tensions between America and Russia after Stalin's death led to an unprecedented increase in athletic competitions between the two countries in track, basketball, rowing, tennis, and hockey, with the brunt of the coverage falling on the agency reporters. *Courtesy Howard Sochurek*

Foreign correspondents in Kharkov en route to Dniepropetrovsk to attend inauguration of the huge new hydroelectric power station. Among them: Robin Kinkead, assistant to Walter Duranty, the *New York Times* correspondent (extreme left with .pipe); *Fortune* magazine photographer Margaret Bourke-White (in railroad-car entrance); author Louis Fischer; Anna Louise Strong, formerly of International News Service (center in light coat); at her left, William Henry Chamberlin, *Christian Science Monitor;* and his wife, Sonia. At her left in trench coat and fedora is Eugene Lyons, UP, and behind him is William Stoneman, *Chicago Daily News.* Trip was arranged by Press Department of the Foreign Affairs Commissariat. *James Abbe, courtesy Robin Kinkead*

In 1921, the *Chicago Tribune*'s Floyd Gibbons, a flamboyant, resourceful reporter, bluffed the Russians into granting him the first visa issued to an American since the Bolshevik revolution. Gibbons had threatened to fly to Moscow and land in Red Square if necessary in order to cover the famine that was devastating the country. With massive American food shipments and medical aid readied for delivery, the Russians could ill-afford to carry out a threat to shoot down the plane. Gibbons got his visa and scored a world beat on the story. *Courtesy Chicago Tribune*

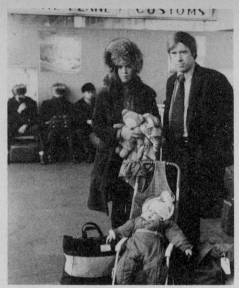 

Top left: AP correspondent George Krimsky, his wife, Paula, and daughter, Alissa, departing from Moscow's Sheremetyevo airport in 1977. Speaking fluent Russian, Krimsky was the agency's point man in covering dissidents. Expelled by the Soviets, he was accused of being an intelligence agent. KGB plainclothesmen in the background shield their faces. *Courtesy Associated Press*

Top right: Henry Cassidy, AP bureau chief, was vacationing at the Black Sea resort of Sochi on June 22, 1941, the day Hitler's armies invaded Russia. A report on his train trip to Moscow—IVAN GOES CALMLY TO WAR—was the first good news to reach the West after the Germans had knifed through Red Army defenses. *Courtesy Associated Press*

AP bureau chief Eddy Gilmore, his Russian wife, Tamara, and their two children finally leave Russia after being virtual hostages of the Stalin regime for almost eight years. Denied permission to depart with her husband at the end of World War II, Tamara received her exit visa after the death of Stalin in 1953. The wives of other American correspondents also left at that time. *Courtesy Associated Press*

Life photographer Margaret Bourke-White had the good fortune to be in Russia in June 1941 when the German invasion began. Her camera recorded some of the best photos of the early days of the war, including a memorable portrait of Stalin. She is photographing the first German aircraft downed by the Russians near Moscow. *Time Inc.*

Edmund Stevens, at various times correspondent for the *Christian Science Monitor, Look, Time,* and *Newsday,* by 1987 had spent almost five decades in Russia, far longer than any other American reporter in history. Speaking fluent Russian, he had wide contacts among intellectuals, artists, writers, and musicians. Stevens is shown here en route to Kharkov in 1943 to cover the trial of German POWs. Left to right: Soviet writers Alexei Tolstoi, Konstantin Simonov, and French correspondent Jean Champenois, Stevens, and UP's Mike Handler. *Courtesy Edmund Stevens*

Walter Duranty, correspondent of *The New York Times* from 1921 to 1934, was the most influential foreign correspondent of his era. A controversial reporter often accused of pro-Stalinist views, he nevertheless won a Pulitzer Prize for his dispatches and charted the transformation of Russia from a peasant country to a world power. In 1924, Duranty's foot was amputated following a train accident in France, but he returned to Moscow to continue his assignment. *The New York Times*

John Reed, Harvard '10, revolutionary romantic from Portland, Oregon, wrote the classic report on the Bolshevik Revolution, *Ten Days That Shook the World*. The book was published in 1919. A year later, Reed died of typhus in Moscow five days before his thirtieth birthday and was buried at the foot of the Kremlin wall. *International Publishers*

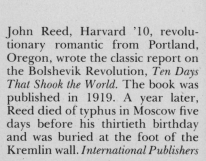

Drinking partners: Sam Jaffe, ABC, and Nikita Khrushchev exchange toasts. The network's correspondent in Moscow from 1961 to 1965, Jaffe's boasting about numerous contacts in the KGB led to rumors that he was a Soviet agent. Unable to obtain further employment with a major news organization, Jaffe sought to clear his name. In 1984, a federal judge announced there were no grounds to question Jaffe's patriotism. A year later, Jaffe died of lung cancer. *Courtesy Jeune Jaffe*

John Chancellor, NBC correspondent from 1960 to 1961, has admitted that he was inadequately prepared for the Moscow assignment. He quickly established himself as one of the more thoughtful and perceptive American correspondents, but after only thirteen months in Moscow, NBC reassigned him to New York to host the *Today* show. *Courtesy John Chancellor*

Robert Cullen, *Newsweek* bureau chief from 1982 to 1985, interviews an allegedly 109-year-old man in Kirgizia. Like many other American correspondents, Cullen was subjected to the KGB's "dirty tricks." *Courtesy Robert Cullen*

Eugene Lyons, United Press correspondent from 1928 to 1934, shed his pro-Soviet sympathies when he saw the realities of life in Russia. His angry, eloquent *Assignment in Utopia* was the first major American book depicting the repression and brutality of the Stalin regime. (This photo was taken when Lyons was in his mid-fifties.) *Courtesy Armand Grunberg*

Marvin Kalb, CBS correspondent from 1959 to 1963, was one of the rare network reporters with Russian-language training acquired at Harvard. After serving as the network's chief diplomatic correspondent in Washington for many years, he joined NBC, making occasional trips to Moscow. Here Kalb is doing a "stand-upper" for NBC on Red Square. *Courtesy Marvin Kalb*

Nicholas Daniloff, correspondent for *U.S. News & World Report,* was arrested in 1986 by the KGB and accused of spying for the CIA. His release in exchange for a Soviet U.N. employee caught buying classified documents in New York paved the way for the Reykjavik summit between General Secretary Gorbachev and President Reagan. *Courtesy U.S. News & World Report*

UPI correspondent Aline Mosby was drugged by KGB agents in 1961 during lunch at a Moscow restaurant. Western reporters agreed to kill the story at the urging of UPI bureau manager Henry Shapiro, who feared that she might be expelled or the bureau closed if the news was transmitted. *Courtesy Aline Mosby*

George Seldes of the *Chicago Tribune* was among the first American correspondents permitted to enter Soviet Russia in 1921. Two years later he was expelled for evading censorship. He is shown here as a war correspondent at the battle of Château-Thierry, France. *UPI/Bettmann Newsphotos*

Wieland of Reuters; Alex Shiray and Jean Nau of AFP; Richard K. O'Malley, Stanley Johnson, and Roy Essoyan of the Associated Press; Howard Norton of the *Baltimore Sun;* Jack Raymond and Welles Hangen of *The New York Times;* and B. J. Cutler, Daniel Schorr, Irving Levine, Charles Klensch, and Whitman Bassow. We chatted quietly while sipping coffee brought in thermos jugs by our wives. I sat alone in the UP booth at the old black Royal typewriter that had served many predecessors. Henry Shapiro was the only correspondent missing.

The morning dragged on as we waited for the text of Khrushchev's opening speech. At about eleven o'clock, the special UP phone rang. Shapiro was on the line.

"I got the Khrushchev speech," he said in a low voice. "Here's the lead."

Shapiro dictated several paragraphs.

"I'll phone later with more," he murmured, then hung up.

I typed the story and handed it to the woman behind the counter, trying not to attract the attention of the other reporters. The copy was quickly returned without any black pencil lines. Lyena, the blue-eyed clerk, looked at me as if to say, "Where did you get this from?" I ordered a line to London and was soon dictating to a deskman. Within minutes, the story was flashed to New York for transmission to thousands of newspapers and radio stations in the United States and around the world. Shapiro phoned every half hour to add to the story, while I repeated my calls to London. Three hours after the UP filed its first report, the Sovinformburo delivered copies of the Khrushchev speech—in Russian—to the impatient reporters. Within minutes, leads were written, phones ordered, and the wire service correspondents were dictating to Paris, Frankfurt, and London the speech that the UP had moved almost four hours earlier. By then, Richard O'Malley was getting "rockets" from the AP in New York, urgent cables demanding that he match the UP story. He strode up to my booth, shouting, "What the hell are you guys doing? Where did you get the speech? And where the hell is Henry?"

"It's none of your business where we got the speech," I replied, "and Henry—he's covering another story."

"Another story!" exploded O'Malley. "What other goddamn story is there in Moscow?"

The disaster for the AP continued for the next two weeks. Every day, Shapiro phoned me from somewhere in Moscow with the text of speeches by the top Soviet leaders—Foreign Minister Molotov, Premier Bulganin, Deputy Premier Georgi M. Malenkov, First Deputy Premier Anastas I. Mikoyan, and others. And each time, the UP scooped the AP by several hours. Not once did Shapiro appear at the Central Telegraph. Soon O'Malley was telling everyone who would listen that the UP bureau manager had been admitted to the Kremlin in exchange for certain unspecified services to the Soviets. Shapiro, however, was not inside the Kremlin but in the office of the Sovinformburo with its director, Valentin V. Mikhailov. His handling of the Congress story was an example of the astute way in which Shapiro operated, his knowledge of the workings of the system, and how he could manipulate it to the advantage of the United Press.

Shapiro had known Mikhailov during the war but lost contact with him during the Cold War days. After Stalin's death the acquaintance was resumed over occasional dinners and lunches. About a month before the Congress, Shapiro called on Mikhailov to discuss coverage. Knowing that the Sovinformburo always received texts of important statements for distribution to selected audiences, he asked if he could see the Congress texts in advance to avoid making mistakes in interpretation.

"If I have the text at least an hour or two earlier, then I can look through it and I can decide what's important. And I can do a much more accurate job."

A reasonable request, Mikhailov thought, and agreed to let Shapiro see the speeches. Every day of the Congress, Shapiro was at the Sovinformburo, reading the Russian texts, marking up the lead, and phoning the story to me at the Central Telegraph.

Henry Shapiro kept the secret within the UP, although he

did tell Daniel Schorr that "anyone could do it if they only thought of it." There was, however, no one else in Moscow who could have thought of it, much less accomplished what Shapiro had done.

The most significant story to come out of the Congress was not distributed by the Sovinformburo: Nikita Khrushchev's secret speech denouncing Stalin and accusing him of a long list of crimes, misdeeds, errors, and establishing a "cult of personality" to elevate himself "above the party and above the nation." Correspondents in Moscow were unaware that a special Congress session was convened on the night of February 24–25 to hear Khrushchev's historic exposé. Word of the speech began to leak almost immediately, however, after summaries were read at thousands of closed party and Komsomol meetings all over the Soviet Union. East European ambassadors, who received private briefings, cabled reports back to their capitals, revealing further details. The first concrete information disclosed to Western correspondents came from Ralph Parker, the British journalist who had briefly covered Moscow for *The New York Times* during the war. Subsequently he married the daughter of a Soviet general, and his growing sympathy for the Soviets led him to cut his ties with the West and remain in Moscow, where he wrote for the British Communist newspaper, *The Worker*. Parker, often serving the Kremlin as a conveyor of information, first spread the news of Khrushchev's speech at a French Embassy reception for former President Vincent Auriol on March 10. With only sketchy information and no official confirmation, none of the reporters could expect to pass a line through Glavlit. John Retty, the Reuters correspondent with close contacts in East European embassies, obtained a summary of the speech and left immediately for Helsinki to file the story, which was transmitted under a Bonn dateline. Retty was later forced to leave the Soviet Union. Harrison Salisbury in New York obtained a text that appeared in the *Times* on March 16, but it was the U.S. State Department that published a definitive version in June 1956. While the official Congress proceedings stated that a "closed session" took place on February 24–25, no details were provided on what occurred. The secret speech has never been published in the Soviet Union.

During the months following the Congress, correspondents filed dozens of stories reporting the dismantling of the Stalin myth as his statues and portraits began to disappear from public places in the capital, from subway stations, offices, theater lobbies, and stores—without any official explanation. During a visit to the Tretyakov Gallery with an American church delegation, I saw empty spaces on the walls from which paintings had been removed. As I rounded a corner, I saw two workmen carrying a huge portrait of Stalin. In response to my question, one explained that it was being "temporarily" put into storage. Two years later, when I returned to the gallery, the portrait was still in storage.

It was not, however, until November 1961 that the most visible symbol of the Stalin era—his embalmed corpse—was removed from the tomb on Red Square and interred at the foot of the Kremlin wall. Thereafter, correspondents were filing stories almost daily on the renaming of towns and cities, streets, mountains, canals, and lakes that had borne Stalin's name. Stalingrad—symbol of Russia's tenacity, heroism, and sacrifice—disappeared from the map and reappeared as Volgograd. Stanley Johnson of the AP added a personal footnote to the de-Stalinization campaign, reporting that the dictator had been painted out of a large canvas that hung in the lobby of the Metropole. According to Johnson, the painting had originally shown Lenin sitting in a chair reading *Pravda* to Stalin, but an artist had deftly removed Stalin and the picture now showed Lenin reading to himself. The story was distributed by the AP worldwide. Unfortunately for the news agency, Johnson's vision was faulty. When other reporters got callbacks from their editors to match the story, they rushed to the Metropole to view the painting. Sure enough, there was Lenin reading *Pravda,* and sure enough there was an empty armchair next to him, but clearly that seat had never been occupied by Stalin or anyone else. The painting was a copy of the original that hung in the Tretyakov Gallery. One reporter bought a postcard reproduction in the Metropole gift shop and sent it to his editor.

*   *   *

The changed character of the stories that developed during the last five years of the 1950s illustrated the complexities, frustration, and the sheer fun of reporting from Moscow. They ranged from the launching of *Sputnik I* and the beginning of the Space Age to the "kitchen debate" between Vice President Nixon and Khrushchev; from the performance of *Porgy and Bess* by an American opera company to a triumphant tour by violinist Isaac Stern; from an unprecedented visit of U.S. Air Force generals to the equally unprecedented visit of film producer Mike Todd and his wife, Elizabeth Taylor; and from the publication abroad of Boris Pasternak's *Doctor Zhivago* to his rejection of the Nobel Prize in 1958. What had not changed, however, was the old nemesis, Glavlit, lurking behind the green-curtained door in the Central Telegraph.

As the number of American correspondents increased, as the story opportunities multiplied, as the tide of tourists and official visitors rose (some ten thousand Americans visited the Soviet Union in 1956), even Glavlit could not control the outward flow of news as rigorously as it had in 1953. Moreover, many correspondents found ways to bypass censorship, risking at the least a scolding by the Press Department, an attack in *Pravda,* or, at worst, expulsion. Because of the nature of the medium, the network correspondents were most easily able to evade censorship. That they could ship undeveloped film by whatever means was in itself an erosion of Glavlit's control. Although their footage was usually shot in public view and under KGB surveillance, the "flimsy," the accompanying text shipped with the film, was not reviewed by the censor.

Still photographers faced the same challenge as the network correspondents in getting film out of the country. Howard Sochurek, thirty-four, a brilliant World War II combat photographer now working for *Life,* after a lengthy bureaucratic delay was permitted to shoot four days in the life of a Soviet schoolboy. His report would run side-by-side with a story of a high-school student from Evanston, Illinois. After shooting forty rolls of color film, Sochurek desperately sought someone to smuggle them out of the country: Deadline in New York was seventy-two hours away. Tracking down the only American tourist leaving Moscow that day in January 1958, he found his "pigeon" in the men's room at Vnukovo Airport. An awkward conversation and explanation took place, but eventually the American, who lived in Baltimore, agreed to carry out the film on one condition:

"I'll take the film if you guarantee that when I get to Paris— I'll get laid."

Taken aback by the unusual demand, Sochurek promised his best effort to comply. The American boarded the aircraft, coat pockets stuffed with film, passing through customs without difficulty. Sochurek phoned Paris to ask Loomis Dean, a fellow photographer in the *Life* bureau, to meet a friend at the airport. Dean being out of the office, the message was taken by Frank White, the bureau chief. With the KGB listening, there could be no description of the quid pro quo demanded by the "pigeon."

Dean was at the Paris airport to receive the forty rolls and to ship them on a New York flight departing ninety minutes later, but the American refused to hand over the film unless he was guaranteed a woman. No sex, no film.

The *Life* photographer finally got the film but only after agreeing to take the courier to a bar near the Champs-Élysées and introduce him to some of the ladies who frequented the establishment. "After that," said Loomis Dean, "you're on your own."

For *Life,* at least, the story had a happy ending. The film arrived in New York on time, and the magazine's editors were pleased with the exclusive, as was the Press Department. Howard Sochurek, who had only a temporary visa, received accreditation as permanent *Life* correspondent in Moscow, the first since the end of World War II.

As a network correspondent, Daniel Schorr frequently faced a dilemma. His radio circuit for New York was scheduled for a specific hour, and occasionally his script had not been cleared by the censor in time. When the circuit came up, he would have to choose between reading unapproved copy or losing the circuit. If he read uncleared copy, he might have gotten his story through, but he risked being cut off in midsentence. He never knew in advance what would happen. Schorr's competitor, Irving Levine, took the same risks. He once interviewed Senator Hubert Humphrey live at the Central Telegraph without submitting any copy to Glavlit, probably an unprecedented feat. When Van Cliburn won first prize in the Tchaikovsky international piano competition in 1958, Paul Niven of CBS drove him to the Central Telegraph and arranged for the twenty-four-year-old Texan to tell his mother the good news—on a CBS radio broadcast. Glavlit had no advance text but permitted Niven to complete the interview.

Evading censorship was not uncommon in the United Press bureau when I was working there. While almost all copy was filed through Glavlit, Shapiro and I often phoned stories from the office directly to London, Frankfurt, or Paris if we felt it was worth the risk. These stories were usually relatively "safe" official statements or declarations that had come off the TASS teletype located next to the phone. Since I could read Russian, it was a simple matter to dictate a lead directly from the official communiqué. I took the chance, not because I had a story that would not pass censorship but because I knew it *would* pass and the UP could beat the Associated Press. Some of the other correspondents, including AP reporters, knew that we were phoning stories from our office. Daniel Schorr was convinced that Henry Shapiro had some kind of arrangement with the Press Department that permitted him to bypass Glavlit. There was no such arrangement. We broke the rules because we thought we could get away with it—and we did. I was never scolded by the Press Department for bypassing Glavlit.

One of the rare times I deliberately risked expulsion by phoning a controversial story occurred in March 1958, when the United Press learned that Khrushchev would oust Premier Nikolai Bulganin and succeed him as head of the Soviet government. I phoned London and talked with William Sexton, bureau news editor, who was off-duty, enjoying himself at a cocktail party. Above the din of the conversation, clinking glasses, and music, and using the most elliptical language, knowing that Glavlit was listening, I conveyed to him the idea that major changes would take place at the highest levels; then the line was cut. The UP, on the basis of the phone call, put a story on the wires flatly stating that Khrushchev would oust Bulganin and take the premier's post for himself. The following day, at a meeting of the Supreme Soviet, Bulganin was demoted to head the State Bank, while Khrushchev was unanimously elected chairman of the Council of Ministers. The Press Department never raised a fuss about the evasion of censorship by the United Press.

B. J. Cutler was a skillful writer who had covered New York local news for the *Herald Tribune* before the Moscow assignment. A master at slipping sensitive copy past Glavlit, he used a technique that he revealed only after he left Moscow. His normal procedure was to phone dispatches to the *Tribune's* office in Paris, where they were taped and monitored by a secretary. Unlike the other correspondents, who tried to insert an uncensored phrase or a sentence, he deleted a word or a phrase, thereby changing the thrust of a story. He correctly calculated that the censor's English was not good enough nor timing quick enough to cut the phone connection at the appropriate moment.

As an example, explained Cutler, he would write that he did not believe the Soviet government was not telling the truth when it announced a reduction in its military budget. If he dropped the second "not" the story was entirely different.

"People used to read my copy in the European edition of the *Herald Tribune* and say, 'How the hell did you get that through the censor?' I'd say, 'I don't know.' But now I can tell."

Press Department officials never caught up with Cutler but would occasionally call him in and complain about what appeared in the European edition. His reply:

"Look, you people have censorship in this country. It's your problem to enforce it. If your censor doesn't do his job, why are you complaining to me?"

"They always thought that this was a reasonable argument."

Other correspondents also found ways to evade censorship. Jack Raymond, thirty-eight, who in January 1956 succeeded ailing Clifton Daniel for nine months, phoned his stories to Prague while traveling in the Soviet provinces. A Press Wireless office established in the Czech capital after World War II was still operating and transmitted Raymond's copy to the *Times* office in London. Glavlit never saw his stories. Reprimanded on his return to Moscow by press chief Leonid F. Ilyichev, he promised to abide by the rules, but he continued to break them on subsequent trips.

"I did it only because I was rambunctious and didn't want the nuisance of going through Glavlit and having the stories held up," Raymond told me.

Correspondents perfected other ways to outwit Glavlit, mainly by using language or references that the censor did not understand. When Marshal Konstantin K. Rokossovsky, the Soviet World War II hero who had been appointed Polish defense minister by the Kremlin to ensure Warsaw's loyalty to the Communist bloc, was decorated by the Polish government in the early 1960s, Tom Lambert of the *Herald Tribune* wrote a short dispatch that put the news in perspective. Aware of Polish antipathy for the Russians, he wrote that Rokossovsky "was held in the same esteem in Poland as General Sherman in Atlanta."

"I liked that story," Lambert confided. "It zoomed right past the censor."

Cutler wrote a feature on an exhibition by Sergei Gerasimov, whose chief claim to fame was his ability to paint flattering portraits of Stalin in heroic poses. Cutler praised Gerasimov's art, adding that a room filled with his paintings had the same effect on a viewer as Nembutal. The censor, unaware that this was far from complimentary, passed the copy. A few days later, Cutler's KGB acquaintance, who understood the irony, phoned to let him know that the phrase had not passed unnoticed.

"Nembutal," he sniffed, "very funny!"

A reporter who trifled with Glavlit always risked the supreme penalty: expulsion from the USSR, usually for "violating the rules regulating the conduct of foreign correspondents." But what were these rules? When I arrived in

Moscow in December 1955, a U.S. embassy official gave me a mimeographed translation of a one-page document distributed by the Soviet Foreign Affairs Ministry. It listed a number of restrictions that applied to diplomats as well as to journalists. These included prohibitions on taking photographs of military installations, bridges, railroad terminals, bodies of water, ships, and members of the armed forces; it specified that no foreigner could travel forty kilometers (twenty-five miles) outside of Moscow without permission of the Foreign Ministry, and procedures for communicating with government agencies. It failed, however, to specify how a correspondent carried out his or her duties, including the most important requirement that all dispatches had to be filed through the Central Telegraph, and the censorship. Instructions to file in this manner were transmitted verbally, not by the Press Department but by the other correspondents. The regulations were sufficiently vague to enable the Press Department to accuse a correspondent of "violating the rules" without the need to be specific. Many correspondents have stood on the carpet in a Press Department office listening to such accusations, and when requesting specifics were told, "You know what we're talking about." Most of the time the correspondents did not know.

Roy Essoyan of the Associated Press knew why he was expelled. In the summer of 1958, rumors were circulating in Moscow about a serious rift between the Soviet Union and China, on ideological and military grounds, even though both sides sought to maintain a surface unity. Although these rumors were reported from outside the USSR, no correspondent had been able to write about them under a Moscow dateline. Glavlit's severity was absolute. Essoyan was able to transmit a few sentences during a phone call to the London bureau before being cut off. The AP moved the story on the wires. While the news was not earthshaking, Joseph Alsop, a political columnist for the *New York Herald Tribune* who had visited Moscow earlier that year and knew how the system worked, wrote that since Essoyan's story had passed censorship, then not only was it true, but also the Russians wanted the entire world to know about it.

The Soviets reacted quickly. When Harold K. Milks, the AP bureau chief, who had been out of the country on vacation, stepped off the plane at Vnukovo Airport, a Press Department official was waiting to escort him to the Foreign Ministry. On arrival, he was told that Roy Essoyan would be expelled from the USSR "for violating the rules regulating the activities of foreign correspondents." The AP correspondent and his family left Moscow in a few days.

In 1956, Milks' predecessor Richard O'Malley was expelled after less than six months in the assignment. He was accused of "currency violations" by the Press Department. Since most correspondents were buying rubles on the black market unhindered by the authorities, none of the other reporters took the official explanation seriously. O'Malley's transgressions were more serious from the Soviet point of view. A belligerent man who disliked his assignment, he did not conceal his animosity toward the regime. Shortly after O'Malley left Moscow, a KGB agent disclosed to another American correspondent the real reason for his expulsion: The Russians regarded him as unstable, behaving in an irrational manner, and capable of transmitting a false story that could have "started a war between our two countries."

"So we just couldn't have a man like that working for the AP, the most important American news agency."

This was not the only time the Russians exhibited such sensitivity. A few years later, the Press Department quietly informed the U.S. embassy that *Newsweek* would be well advised to recall its correspondent because his carousing with women, drinking, and unseemly behavior would inevitably result in expulsion, an act the Soviet government sought to avoid. Within a few weeks, *Newsweek* ordered the correspondent to return to New York and fired him, not only because of his behavior, but also because he was not covering his beat and was failing to file stories. When his successor arrived in Moscow and began to drive *Newsweek*'s red Mercedes around town, he was frequently accosted by blowsy women who rushed into the street expecting to find the former correspondent behind the wheel.

Charles Klensch, the thirty-three-year-old INS correspondent, begged to be expelled. After three years in Moscow he decided he had had enough. In February 1957, he cabled his editor reminding him that his tour of duty was over and requesting a new assignment. One week later, he was summoned to the Press Department and ordered to leave the country. The reasons were vague, but press chief L. F. Ilyichev accused him of passing "anti-Soviet" publications to a student. What probably annoyed the Russians even more was a home-made Christmas card that Klensch and his wife, Copper, had sent to their friends and also to Nikita Khrushchev and Nikolai Bulganin. It depicted the INS reporter in a Russian costume, holding a vodka bottle in one hand and mistletoe in the other, dancing on Red Square, while Copper walked behind him barefoot and carrying a Christmas tree over her shoulder. That, too, was "anti-Soviet."

Like Glavlit, the KGB was omnipresent and omnipotent, intervening in and seeking to control the professional and personal lives of the correspondents. In addition to tapping phones; using listening devices in the walls and fixtures of apartments, offices, and hotel rooms; and physical surveillance by plainclothesmen, KGB operatives sometimes sought to ensnare the correspondents. When a new reporter arrived in Moscow, he often received a phone call from a Soviet journalist inviting him to lunch. The Russian would appear at the restaurant with another man, clearly working for the KGB. During the vodka-laden meal, the agent would offer to make things "easier" for the newcomer—access to officials, exclusive stories, female company—in exchange for some friendly collaboration. When the advances were rejected, the KGB usually left the correspondent alone. For many Americans, however, it was a scary and unnerving introduction to the realities of reporting in the Soviet Union.

Typical was the experience of Robert Gibson, then thirty, who arrived in Moscow in 1958 to negotiate the reopening of the McGraw-Hill bureau, shut down with the expulsion of Robert Magidoff in 1948. A graduate of the United Press who had covered the Korean War, Gibson joined McGraw-Hill in

1953, serving in New York and London prior to the Moscow assignment. For some reason he received VIP treatment and was lodged in the Sovietskaya Hotel, a facility normally reserved for senior foreign officials and guests of the government. Immediately after arriving, Gibson was invited to lunch at the Praga Restaurant by a Russian named Georgi, who said he worked for the Sovinformburo. At the appointed time, Georgi appeared in one of the Praga's private dining rooms with Filip Krasnov, who was presented but not introduced to Gibson. Barely had they been seated when they both accused Robert Gibson of being a spy, "like your predecessor."

"It's ridiculous," replied Gibson. "I'm not a spy. I'm a journalist. I'm here to do one thing—to arrange my accreditation as a correspondent. I'm insulted that you would even consider me to be a spy. And I don't want you to say that to me again."

About a week later, the three met once more for lunch. This time Georgi, who spoke fluent English, pushed a piece of paper at Gibson and instructed him to write down the names of diplomats at the U.S. embassy.

"Now," he ordered, "tell us what they do."

Gibson scribbled their official titles, which the Russians knew, and pushed the paper back across the table. Georgi insisted, "Tell us what they really do. And we also want to know what the ambassador talks about at his Friday briefings."

Robert Gibson refused, but the Russians did not give up. Over several weeks these luncheons continued and finally ended in a climactic argument when Gibson reminded them that at first he was accused of being a spy for the United States and now they were asking him to spy for the Soviet Union.

"I sure as hell don't intend to do that!"

Krasnov threw his napkin on the table and stormed out. The two men finished lunch in silence.

"It was the strangest meal I ever had," Gibson recalled.

Irving R. Levine's baptism of fire also occurred at the Praga, the KGB's favorite restaurant for entertaining foreign correspondents. After losing broadcast privileges for several days for evading censorship, he was invited to dinner by a KGB agent he had met at the Stanislavsky Theater. The Gibson scenario was repeated: The KGB man arrived with another Russian who spoke fluent English. After a few polite exchanges, they came to the point: Would Levine meet with them periodically and tell them what other reporters and U.S. diplomats were saying and thinking? Levine refused.

They showed him a copy of a letter he had sent to a friend in New York containing a joke about Khrushchev. It's against the law to ridicule our leaders, they warned. They also showed him the cover of *The New York Times Magazine* with photos of Khrushchev, which they said had been found in the wastebasket of his hotel room. Each photo was embellished with moustache and spectacles, "a criminal offense in the Soviet Union."

"You ought to think about our suggestion. We can make life easier for you."

Levine left the table and returned to the hotel. He made a quick trip to New York to consult with William McAndrew, president of NBC News, and Robert Kintner, president of NBC. The KGB attempt to coerce him was "unnerving," he told them, but he insisted "that it would in no way" affect his reporting. Levine returned to Moscow and resumed broadcasting. Although the KGB agents phoned several times offering to make "life easier" for him, they did not invite the NBC reporter to the Praga again. After a while, the phone calls stopped. The KGB had given up on Irving Levine.

Then there was the sex gambit, with which the KGB seemed to have had little success, but not for lack of trying. As in earlier years, there was always a number of American correspondents in Moscow, married and unmarried, who were vulnerable to the charms of ballerinas, girls who wanted to improve their English, visitors from Leningrad or Kiev spending a few days in Moscow, jazz fans who wanted to talk about Stan Kenton, students who wanted to talk about Picasso, and occasionally ladies of the night. On their travels, correspondents would invariably meet a woman on a train or in a hotel dining room who was attractive, spoke English, and was available for conversation and companionship. They were the successors to the *"mozhna* (may I?) girls" who during wartime were on the phone to the newly arrived correspondent within minutes after he checked into the Metropole, asking, *"Mozhna* come to your room?" Most American correspondents were well aware of the dangers involved in affairs with Russian women and resisted temptation, but others said, "What the hell! I'm covering a story in which women play an important role. What better way to find out what they think and feel and know than by sleeping with one?"

One of my unforgettable encounters with a femme fatale occurred on the *Red Arrow,* the overnight train I took to Leningrad in February 1958 to write a story on the Hermitage Museum. Since the Soviet railway administration ignored the sex of passengers in assigning reservations, I was not surprised to find that I was sharing a sleeping compartment with an attractive, well-endowed blonde whose name I still remember because it was so un-Russian: Karolina. We shared a bottle of champagne, which she had providentially packed for the trip, while my contribution to the evening consisted of two Cadbury chocolate bars, reminiscences of World War II as a U.S. Air Corps radio mechanic in North Africa, and responses to her questions about life in the United States. Karolina said she worked for an unidentified government agency and had been in Moscow briefly on business. At about 11 P.M. I said good night, climbed into my upper berth, turned off the overhead light, and wriggled out of my clothes into a pair of pajamas, concerned that I might embarrass Karolina if I were to expose a bare ankle. But she was far less inhibited. Standing in the center of the compartment, she shed her clothes and wrapped herself in a diaphanous robe of obvious foreign origin. I could not take my eyes off her.

"Do you like me—a little bit?" she asked, turning slowly to reveal all her charms in the dim light.

I did not reply.

"I like you. You are an intelligent, handsome man. I have always wanted to make love to an American. I hope you will not deny me the opportunity."

"I have a wife and a child. I do not do such things."

"You will not regret it. Don't you want to know what a Russian woman is like?"

"I already know what they're like. I've read *Anna Karenina* and *War and Peace. Spokoini nochi.* Good night."

I turned to the wall. Karolina must have shrugged her slender shoulders, then slipped into her berth. Within a few minutes I could hear her breathing regularly. She had fallen asleep.

The next morning I wriggled back into my clothes and left the compartment while Karolina was still asleep or pretended to be. We did not speak to each other when the train arrived in Leningrad station. When she stepped out of the train, two beefy men greeted her, eager to hear her report.

Had I succumbed to Karolina's charms, I'm certain that the next step would have been a visit from the KGB and a request for information under the threat of blackmail. I doubt whether I would have had the temerity to do what a married journalist of another era had done when KGB photographers caught him in bed with a Russian woman. He coolly asked for a dozen enlargements.

In addition to the burden of dealing with the KGB and Glavlit, correspondents also had to worry about editors back home who knew little or nothing about working conditions in Moscow. Like many of their predecessors, these editors thought covering Russia was just like reporting from Paris, London, or Kansas City. They made unreasonable, often idiotic, requests for stories, reactions, and comments, ignoring a basic fact of geography: at 4:00 P.M. in New York and Washington, the big Kremlin clock struck midnight.

When Clifton Daniel, after months of waiting, finally was permitted to visit a collective farm, he wrote a long feature article for the *Times Magazine.* Sunday editor Lester Markel cabled back suggesting that Daniel should visit two or three more farms for comparison rather than base his story on a single farm, "so we can get a broader view." Replied Daniel:

THIS IS THE FIRST TIME IN TWENTY YEARS THAT A CORRESPONDENT OF NEW YORK TIMES OR ANY OTHER WESTERN NEWSPAPER HAS BEEN TO A COLLECTIVE FARM. IT'S LIKELY TO BE ANOTHER TWENTY BEFORE WE SEE ANOTHER ONE. IF YOU WANT TO WAIT THAT LONG—PLEASE DO. OTHERWISE PRINT ARTICLE AS SENT.

Lester Markel printed it—as sent.

Editors in the United States presumably understood Soviet sensitivity about queries related to military affairs, yet correspondents were always getting requests for defense establishment stories. The experienced Moscow correspondent usually responded to such queries with a cryptic negative cable, without an explanation. In the United Press bureau, the succinct response that always worked was perfected by Henry Shapiro:

YOUR [CABLE NUMBER] UNFEASIBLE SHAPIRO

During the peak of one of the recurring crises over Berlin, in 1959, McGraw-Hill correspondent Ernest Conine received a list of detailed questions from New York on Soviet civil defense preparations. Knowing that even the most discreet inquiries would get him into trouble, he cabled his editors that the information was secret. Apparently they were unaware that a decade earlier, a similar query to his predecessor Robert Magidoff led to a charge of espionage, expulsion, and the closing of the McGraw-Hill bureau.

Most "unfeasible" queries requested information that was either difficult to obtain in time to meet a deadline or simply not available to reporters. My favorite query came from a UP photo editor in 1957, when Khrushchev fired Bulganin and took the post of chairman of the Council of Ministers:

NEED SOONEST PIX BULGANIN HANDING KHRUSHCHEV KEYS OF OFFICE

This cable was phoned to me by a clerk at the Central Telegraph at 3:00 A.M. I wasn't sure whether the reference was to real or figurative keys, but my reply would have been the same in either case:

YOUR [CABLE NUMBER] UNFEASIBLE BASSOW

A favorite—and legitimate—query requested an official Soviet reaction or man-in-the-street comment on an event that occurred outside Russia—for example, to a statement by President Eisenhower. U.S. editors failed to understand that a correspondent could not obtain an immediate reaction from the Press Department and that it might be days before *Pravda* would comment, if at all. Nor would Moscow's man-in-the-street react to a statement or event that had not appeared in the Soviet press. American editors assumed that what appeared on agency wires in the United States was common knowledge. That may have been true elsewhere, but not in the Soviet Union. Not for years, when foreign editors back home had acquired a great deal more experience working with their Moscow correspondents, did the idiot queries begin to decline.

As Soviet society began to open up after Stalin's death, the work load for the correspondents became heavier. Pressure from editors, competition for stories, and dealing with the censor and the Soviet authorities meant working seven days a week, often ten to twelve hours a day. Agency staffs were small. The AP and the UP struggled along with two and then three correspondents. Doubling the staff would have barely been adequate to cover the explosion of news. International sports events, for example, rare under Stalin, proliferated as American and Soviet athletes competed in track, tennis, basketball, rowing, and hockey. They all had to be covered. As second man in the UP bureau, I was the one who shivered in twenty-five-below-zero weather reporting the world hockey championships at Lenin Stadium, where it was so cold that my ballpoint pen froze. Pencils from Armand Hammer's former factory worked perfectly.

The first visit of an American vice president to the Soviet

Union dramatized further the changed nature of Moscow news coverage. Richard M. Nixon arrived in Moscow in July 1959 to open a United States exhibition that was to leave a mark on his political career. In the famous "kitchen debate," he confronted an angry Nikita Khrushchev, and by all accounts defended the American Way of Life as if he were running for president. The debate took place in front of a "typical" U.S. kitchen, complete with refrigerator, stove, toaster, and other electrical appliances. As the two men argued, they leaned on a railing that separated the public from the exhibition area, surrounded by Soviet and American officials, KGB and Secret Service agents, and a swarm of White House correspondents flown in for the trip. The challenge to the reporters was to get close enough to hear what was being said.

Robert J. (Bud) Korengold, then a twenty-eight-year-old reporter for UPI (with the acquisition of Hearst's International News Service in 1958, the United Press became United Press International), solved the problem by sneaking behind the display area into the kitchen and sitting at Richard Nixon's feet.

"I had a ringside position for the whole operation," he recalled. "At one point I got so involved in trying to take it down that when Nixon interrupted something that Khrushchev was saying in the heat of the argument, I involuntarily looked up and shouted, 'Let him finish!' "

Howard Sochurek shot his finest photographs for *Life* by squirming under the barrier and lying full length on the floor under the noses of Nixon and Khrushchev, who were oblivious to his cameras.

What was so astonishing was that correspondents were able to move freely in and around obstacles and barriers to approach the two men without interference from the KGB or the Secret Service. When I arrived in Moscow four years earlier, it would have been impossible to bypass the control lines, and if one had dared to do so, a severe reprimand—or worse—would have come immediately from the Press Department.

*   *   *

Angelo Natale, AP correspondent in 1958 and 1959, once remarked, "You don't make friends in Moscow, you make family," but it was a family that experienced frustration, anger, and resentment largely provoked by and yet mirroring the pressure-cooker life in a Communist society.

"We were forced into situations where because we were all frustrated in dealing with the Soviets, we took it out in the way we dealt with each other. . . . We became as suspicious, as loyal and as disloyal, as helpful, as disruptive as the Soviets were toward us," Daniel Schorr has observed.

As an example, since all the correspondents worked at the Central Telegraph, they often left carbon copies of their dispatches lying around in their booths. Some reporters had no scruples about stealing the carbons and using them to write their own stories. Suspecting two of their colleagues, Schorr and Max Frankel of the *Times*, in the fall of 1957, concocted an elaborate scheme to punish the rascals. They arrived at the Telegraph one evening looking sufficiently secretive to arouse the curiosity of the other correspondents. With a Yugoslav delegation in Moscow, they had fabricated a story about the Soviets making outrageous demands on Marshal Tito and planted carbon copies to bait the trap. Within a few minutes they saw the INS correspondent and another American reporter surreptitiously retrieve the carbons, type their cables, and hand them to the Glavlit clerk. Since they were fake, the censor did not return them immediately. Undeterred, the INS man bypassed Glavlit by phoning his story to London from the Hotel National suite of his boss, William Randolph Hearst, Jr., then visiting Moscow. It is not known whether the story was actually moved on the INS wires in the United States, but a few days later, the correspondent accused Schorr of being "irresponsible" and violating journalistic ethics in perpetrating the deception. The stealing of carbons, however, stopped.

"Where else," asked Daniel Schorr, "would you distrust people enough to test them with a hoax? And where else would that hoax work?"

*   *   *

One of the most sensational stories of the first post-Stalin decade exploded on May 1, 1960, when an American U-2 reconnaissance aircraft was downed over Sverdlovsk, deep in the Soviet heartland. The dramatic announcement was made by Nikita Khrushchev at the opening session of the Supreme Soviet, the USSR's nominal parliament. The U.S. State Department, after having first claimed that the plane was on an unarmed weather observation flight, conceded that it was actually engaged in photo reconnaissance of Soviet territory after Khrushchev triumphantly told the same audience a few days later that pilot Francis Gary Powers had been captured. In August Powers was tried in the white-columned chamber of the House of Trade Unions, site of the purge trials of the 1930s. Like the earlier defendants sitting in that dock, Powers confessed to the crime, and he was sentenced to ten years' imprisonment.

For the foreign correspondents at the scene, the trial was theater on a grand scale, worthy of a Bolshoi production. The Hall of Columns was packed with members of the diplomatic corps, Soviet marshals and generals, representatives of the "toiling masses," uniformed security guards, and the international press, listening intently to the testimony. The U-2 pilot sat immobile on the stage, while his wife, Barbara, and his parents watched from a special section reserved for VIPs.

One of the most intriguing aspects of the trial was the role of Sam Jaffe, a thirty-year-old CBS reporter, sent to Moscow to back up resident correspondent Marvin Kalb, who had arrived three months earlier. Jaffe had been covering the United Nations for CBS, a secondary assignment but one that provided him with the opportunity to meet Soviet diplomats, many of whom worked for the KGB; these contacts were to prove helpful in his future career. A few days before the trial began, he was on a plane headed for Moscow sitting alongside Mrs. Powers, an attractive brunette. When I interviewed him two weeks before his death of lung cancer in January 1986, Jaffe claimed that he had no idea how or why this happened. As he walked down the ramp at Vnukovo Airport with Mrs. Powers at his side, there were surprised looks on the faces of the Americans who knew him. Even more curious was the coincidence that Jaffe and Barbara Powers were both lodged at the Sovietskaya Hotel. That night she asked him to drive with her to downtown Moscow to view Lubyanka, KGB headquarters, where she believed her husband was imprisoned. At 4:00 A.M. Jaffe phoned Kalb at the Metropole to tell him that they had talked to sentinels outside the building. Kalb warned him that investigative reporting was acceptable in Washington but not in Moscow.

Sam Jaffe was the only correspondent who had unrestricted access to Mrs. Powers and the rest of the family during the trial. At the Hall of Columns he was favored with a seat just a few rows from where Powers sat in the prisoner's box, while the rest of the press was farther back. By providing information that no other reporter could obtain, Jaffe helped CBS clobber the opposition. "He was fearless and fantastic," recalled Kalb.

When the trial ended, Jaffe returned to New York, where a few months later, James Hagerty, former press chief for President Eisenhower and then the new head of ABC News, asked him to go to Moscow to open a bureau. Jaffe eagerly accepted and was soon headed for Russia, but his peculiarly privileged position during the Powers trial had laid the foundation for the controversy that was to haunt his subsequent career: Was he or was he not working for the KGB, the CIA, or both?

By the mid-1960s, the number of American correspondents in Russia had risen to sixteen, with an equal number of Soviet reporters in the United States. The American public was obtaining news about Russia from two agencies, two networks, and seven newspapers and magazines, the most diverse range of sources since 1921. The AP and UPI each had three correspondents who filed staggering amounts of copy, reporting everything from ballet, art, steel production, dogs in space, fashion, chess, and politics to, above all, the highly visible and audible Nikita Khrushchev, who still appeared frequently at embassy receptions. Long days and sleepless nights took their toll on the reporters. Both Clifton Daniel and B. J. Cutler developed bleeding ulcers. Robert Gibson lost forty pounds. Other correspondents began to drink heavily. A number of marriages disintegrated as wives found it difficult to cope with life in a Communist society and the absence of husbands. The same hardships strengthened other marriages as the challenge of daily living brought couples closer together.

Seven years after Stalin's death, Nikita Khrushchev appeared to be in total control of the Communist Party and the government, but unknown to Kremlin-watchers and to correspondents, opposition to the flamboyant first secretary and his policies would soon coalesce inside the top leadership of the Communist Party. Catalyzed by the Cuban missile crisis in October 1962, other members of the ruling elite would force him from power within two years. Before he would disappear from the scene, however, Khrushchev would make a decision that forever changed the nature of reporting from Russia. He terminated censorship—the bane of the Moscow correspondents for over four decades.

8

The End of Censorship

I think I had extremely good relations with the Russians because I never got too close and never got too far away.

Seymour Topping
The New York Times
1960–63

I am proud I never made a major mistake embarrassing to my country or to myself in my journalistic career.

Sam Jaffe
ABC News
1961–65

Working in Moscow was one of the most important, exciting, and interesting experiences in my life. . . . It was such an incredible experience that if I die tomorrow, I can say that after having worked in Moscow, Peking, and Paris, I have no complaints.

Aline Mosby
UPI
1959–61

Edmund Stevens sat in his wood-paneled *Time* office, studied the blank sheet of paper in the typewriter, and began what might have been considered a presumptuous letter to Nikita S. Khrushchev, first secretary of the Communist Party and chairman of the Council of Ministers of the USSR. It proposed nothing less than the dismantling of the ponderous and stultifying system of censorship that had dismayed and frustrated all foreign correspondents reporting from the Soviet Union since the Bolshevik Revolution in 1917.

Stevens, the magazine's bureau chief since 1959, argued that censorship was ineffective, "a formality alien to the spirit of the times and not capable of improving relations between the USSR and other countries." Furthermore, he pointed out that the system had huge gaps, since correspondents could send out stories with any of the thousands of tourists who crossed the borders every week and so "bypass" Glavlit.

"Knowing your uncompromising attitude toward all kinds of bureaucratic routine and your desire to improve international relations in which the press plays a considerable role, I request your consideration of such frankness. I hope you will not take offense at my words or misinterpret them." The letter was dated February 12, 1961.

Edmund Stevens was not the first American journalist to make such an appeal to an all-powerful Russian leader. In January 1904, Melville Stone, general manager of the Associated Press, during a visit to St. Petersburg had presented a petition to Nicholas II requesting the abolition of censorship on outgoing dispatches. His arguments were remarkably similar to those of Stevens, pointing out that correspondents could evade censorship by sending their dispatches with couriers across the imperial borders. In addition, censorship undermined the credibility of the House of Romanov. Despite the opposition of his ministers, the tsar agreed, and for several months foreign correspondents could freely transmit their stories. But with the outbreak of the Russo-Japanese War in March, censorship was reinstated and remained in force in one form or another until the collapse of the Romanov regime, through the March Revolution in 1917, the Bolshevik coup in November, the Stalin years, World War II, and the post-Stalin era. Glavlit seemed a permanent fixture on the Russian political landscape.

Nikita Khrushchev, however, decided that the time for change had come. In March 1961, correspondents were summoned to the Foreign Ministry where Mikhail A. Kharlamov, head of the Press Department, announced the termination of censorship even though its existence had been officially denied for over forty years. Kharlamov deftly evaded the issue by cheerily informing the more than one hundred reporters present that "measures are being taken to facilitate communications between correspondents and editors at home.

"From this day forward, correspondents will be able to use facilities both at the Central Telegraph in Moscow and in their offices, homes, and hotel rooms to phone directly."

Kharlamov added that the ministry was studying how the new regulations would be applied to photos and TV films.

Lest reporters permit themselves to be carried away by their newfound freedom, Kharlamov warned that they would be held responsible for any "incorrect rumors" they transmitted. He also urged them to keep copies of their dispatches "in case any misunderstanding of your reports may arise."

"It reminded me of *Alice in Wonderland,*" thought UPI's Aline Mosby as she rushed back to the office to file the story—her first uncensored dispatch.

Edmund Stevens has refused to claim credit for Khrushchev's decision, convinced that abolition of censorship was inevitable and that his letter only accelerated the move. At U.S. Ambassador Llewellyn E. Thompson's July Fourth reception a few months later, a good-humored Nikita Khrushchev, who had been nursing a Scotch highball for almost an hour, approached Stevens and thanked him for the letter.

"I agreed with you and so ended censorship."

Behind the decision were other factors that Khrushchev must have considered. The Soviet Union, the most powerful country in Eastern Europe, was the only one that still resorted to prepublication censorship, whereas lesser powers such as Poland, Czechoslovakia, and Hungary did not. Such a distinction was probably deemed inappropriate for the leader of the Communist world. Perhaps the Kremlin—after forty-four years of Soviet rule—felt confident enough to permit correspondents to file without restraints, relying instead on its control of access to information to manage the news. Besides, the Press Department had other means of shaping the information flow: warnings to correspondents who crossed the unmarked line delineating fact from "rumor," withdrawing privileges, delaying interviews, denying permission to travel, and the ultimate punishments: expulsion and the closing down of a bureau.

For Robert Korengold, who reported under censorship and afterward, Glavlit's disappearance meant an enormous change in working conditions and life-style. The endless and wasted hours spent at the Central Telegraph waiting for copy to clear could be devoted to reporting. He no longer had to deal with the "enormously frustrating, wearing, mentally debilitating experience" of submitting his stories to the anonymous cable slashers behind the green-curtained door.

"You turned and you twisted stories and sometimes you got them through in such a fashion that the editors on the other side couldn't even understand the real import. It affected the way you went at stories and it affected the way you wrote them, knowing you had to pass through the eye of a needle," he said.

Seymour Topping, *The New York Times* correspondent from 1960 to 1963, found that he could at last sit down and write "in the same way that you would be writing a story if you were in Paris or London. Meeting deadlines was also easier. Under censorship, there was always a possibility that the story would not emerge from behind the green curtain for a considerable time and with cuts that required rewriting and sending it back again."

All correspondents appreciated the convenience of being able to phone from the office or their apartments, especially on freezing winter nights when London or New York would call for a follow-up to a broadcast on Radio Moscow. This used to mean getting out of bed, trying to get a cold car engine started, and driving to the Central Telegraph to file, something Walter Duranty bitterly complained about in the 1930s.

The full impact of censorship's demise took several years to penetrate the journalistic mind-set. At first, correspondents were wary, uncertain about how freely they could report since no one trusted the Soviets, knowing that surveillance continued, phones were tapped, and that they would be held accountable for whatever appeared in print or was seen or heard on the air. With the passage of time and with the appearance on the scene of a new generation of Americans who had never worked under Glavlit, reporting gradually became far looser and uninhibited. Correspondents could now begin to cover the entire spectrum of Soviet life accessible to them, including the seamier side: alcoholism, corruption, shoddy housing, the continued acute shortage of apartments, and the black market in scarce consumer goods. One area still forbidden was speculation about changes among top party and government leaders and gossip about their personal lives. A correspondent could report on what Khrushchev said at a diplomatic reception but could not report that he had drunk too much or that Muscovites were circulating disparaging jokes about him. Seymour Topping's dictum was not to report anything that was "not truly pertinent or important to understanding the Soviet Union." Gossip or snide remarks about the leaders, he believed, would only endanger his position. Most American correspondents adhered to the same operating principles.

With the end of censorship came the demise of the Central Telegraph as the Western correspondents' "club." Reporters no longer congregated in the plain, bare offices inside Entrance 12, where for almost fifteen years they had written their dispatches. From here the big stories had been transmitted to the outside world: the death of Joseph Stalin, the execution of police chief Lavrenti Beria, Nikita Khrushchev's appointment as all-powerful first secretary, Soviet possession of the atom bomb, de-Stalinization, the Kremlin's intervention in Hungary and Poland, the launching of *Sputnik I*, and the historic orbit of Yuri Gagarin. The Central Telegraph was where the correspondents had spent up to twenty to thirty hours a week in enforced camaraderie while writing stories or waiting for them to clear Glavlit. Vero Roberti of the Italian daily *Corriere de la Sera* has estimated that he spent no fewer than forty-five hundred hours there during the four years he served in Moscow.

More than a marketplace for the exchange of ideas, tips, philosophy, and gossip, the Central Telegraph sometimes generated news. One night in March 1958, we were gathered there following a reshuffle of the Council of Ministers of the USSR. Howard Norton of the *Baltimore Sun* wrote a risky and farfetched story predicting that Nikolai Bulganin, who had been succeeded by Nikita Khrushchev as chairman of the Council of Ministers, would be named to head the State Bank. The following morning, Bulganin was appointed to the bank post. Norton's feat astonished the other correspondents since he had no Soviet contacts, could speak no Russian, and his reporting was far from distinguished. The *Sun* reporter refused to divulge his source, but I knew the information came from a fifty-kopeck coin. Undecided as to what he should predict, Norton tossed the coin: heads for the chairman of the State Bank, tails for minister of defense—posts that Bulganin had held previously. Heads came up. Bulganin was transformed from premier to banker. And Norton had called it. He was a hero in Baltimore, but his envious colleagues at the Central Telegraph had another name for him.

Occasionally a reporter would be carried away by the heady competitive atmosphere generated at the Central Telegraph. In May 1960, the Soviets orbited two dogs, Byelka and Stryelka, inside a single capsule. The dogs were presented at a news conference at the Academy of Science, where their barking occasionally interrupted the scientists who explained the experiments that were performed in space. The long-range goal, of course, was to orbit a human being. When the correspondents returned to the telegraph to file the story, the *Daily Express* reporter jumped the gun—by a year. Instead of transmitting his dog story to London, he phoned something quite different:

I DRANK CHAMPAGNE WITH SIX SOVIET COSMONAUTS ABOUT TO GO UP IN SPACE.

That total fabrication was overheard by all the other reporters, who shook their heads in disbelief. Realizing he had been scooped by his rival, the *Daily Mail* correspondent wrote a story that was passed by the censor and shouted over the phone to his London editor:

PLANS TO SEND SIX COSMONAUTS INTO SPACE MYSTE-RIOUSLY SCRUBBED TONIGHT.

Also pure fiction! But some of the American correspondents received callbacks from editors who reasoned that where there's smoke, there's fire.

The Central Telegraph was also the scene of minicomedy. When the shah of Iran and the beautiful Empress Soraya paid an official visit to the Soviet Union in the mid-1950s, the prospect of their arrival created consternation in the ranks of Soviet officialdom. Protocol called for host country representatives to receive a reigning sovereign in morning coats, garments usually worn by actors representing wicked capitalists on the Moscow stage. Khrushchev, Bulganin, and other senior officials solved the problem by wearing dark suits at the airport, while foreign diplomats took their formal wear out of mothballs. Protocol also posed a sartorial challenge to the four agency pool correspondents selected to cover the state dinner offered by the shah in honor of the Soviet government. In order to be admitted to the dinner the newsmen were obliged to wear white tie and tails. Each reporter found a different solution. Stanley Johnson of the AP had his suit flown in from London by Moss Brothers, the royal outfitters. Alex Shiray of Agence France-Presse borrowed his costume from a French diplomat. Henry Shapiro proudly announced that his formal wear was hanging in the closet. Sidney Wieland of Reuters borrowed mine. His wife used safety pins to shorten the cuffs and sleeves.

While the pool reporters were at the dinner, the rest of us waited for them at the Central Telegraph. A few minutes past midnight, they walked in clad in the degenerate West's most elitist garb and clutching notebooks. We stared at them in awe and disbelief, and so did the Glavlit clerks behind the counter. Seeing them under the portraits of Lenin and Marx was so incongruous that everyone began to laugh. The biggest guffaw came later, when Sidney Wieland announced that Empress Soraya had kept Khrushchev, Bulganin, Molotov, and the entire ruling Communist Party Presidium waiting for over an hour while her personal hairdresser was fussing with her coiffure.

When Glavlit departed from the scene, technology arrived. In March 1962, the Soviet government leased a duplex teleprinter line to Reuters, the first foreign news agency ever to receive such a direct connection with its home office. The line permitted Reuters to transmit dispatches to London and to receive its own news service reports. The AP, UPI, and AFP obtained their hookups in May, thus terminating thirty years of reliance on foreign radio broadcasts for news of the outside world. Moscow was no longer an isolated outpost on the fringe of Europe but part of the international news network. Only Henry Shapiro among the American correspondents could remember that ten years earlier the four agencies had battled at the Central Telegraph for the single international phone.

Some American wire service reporters were far from delighted with the new arrangement, which bound them more closely to the home office. They were now at the beck and call not only of the foreign desk in New York but also of bureau editors in London, Paris, Rome, Tokyo, and Bonn, each ordering stories of interest to their local clients.

"The first thing New York asked us to do was send a daily weather report," grumbled one agency correspondent, "something we never had to do before."

No signs of the past now remain on Ogarov Street. With the number 12 long since removed from above the entrance, a massive gray padlock and a heavy link chain seal the doors against curious passersby and nostalgic correspondents.

The end of censorship coincided with developments in the Soviet Union that kept the Moscow dateline on page one and on the nightly newscasts. Beginning with Yuri Gagarin's earth-girdling voyage on April 12, 1961, and terminating with the ouster of Nikita Khrushchev on October 14, 1964, the correspondents covered on-again, off-again negotiations between the United States and the USSR on a nuclear test-ban treaty, the bitter ideological and political conflict between China and Russia and the futile efforts at reconciliation, and Khrushchev's further consolidation of power with the expulsion of his opponents from the Communist Party. Equally important, the correspondents chronicled the ferment in Soviet art, cinema, and literature, out of which came the most significant novel published since the Bolshevik Revolution,

Alexander Solzhenitsyn's *One Day in the Life of Ivan Denisovich*. The stark account of life in a forced-labor camp created a sensation in the Soviet Union and abroad, earning its author a Nobel Prize and expulsion from his homeland. Without a doubt, however, the Cuban missile crisis in October 1962, which could have led to a military confrontation between the United States and the Soviet Union, was for some correspondents the most important and most frightening story of the period.

"Those were the most exciting times in decades in the Soviet Union," recalled Robert Korengold wistfully, "and I lived through it."

Even without Glavlit, Moscow was still "the camp of the enemy," as Tom Lambert of the *Herald Tribune* put it, a post where tension and pressure rarely eased for the correspondents. The KGB was lurking in the background, while the Press Department continued to summon reporters for periodic scoldings. Soviet newspapers, especially *Pravda, Literary Gazette,* and the official newspaper of the Union of Soviet Journalists, *Zhurnalist,* frequently attacked American reporters for transmitting "lies and slanders" about the Soviet people. After a while one shrugged off the barbs, but the notoriety acquired by such publicity made it difficult to obtain interviews and to establish contacts with Russians.

Two months after the abolition of censorship, the Press Department sent a clear signal to the correspondents. Heinz Weber, a respected West German journalist who had been reporting from Moscow since 1959, was expelled for "illegally collecting data about the political and economic life of our country." In September, Botho Kirsch, correspondent for the *Frankfurter Rundschau,* suffered the same fate for "systematic disparagement of the policy of the Soviet Union and its leadership." No Americans were banished but the Press Department made it clear that it was prepared to use the harshest measures against correspondents who took advantage of their new freedom. At the end of 1961, the Press Department, in a goodwill gesture, invited a small group of correspondents, including Americans, to join an elk hunt in the forests of the Moscow region. The journalists came back with no elk but with an amusing and offbeat story.

In November 1961, Sam Jaffe returned to Moscow to open a bureau for ABC News. All three American networks were now operating in the Soviet capital, an array of talent and resources that would presumably provide increased radio and TV coverage for the American public. This was not quite what happened, however. Although the prohibition on shipping undeveloped film had been removed, Soviet suspicion of cameras was so ingrained that carrying one on the street continued to attract attention and hostility. When a reporter interviewed a Russian official using a pen to take notes, there was no problem. But if he walked in with a camera crew, everybody froze. This suspicion and distrust also applied to Soviet TV reporters. A revealing cartoon published in the satirical magazine *Krokodil* showed a collective farm director being interviewed by Russian television. A camera pointed at him and the scene behind: a dilapidated barn; a few scrawny chickens, a broken-down, rusty tractor; and a cow with visible ribs. The director pleaded, "Please, comrade, can this interview be conducted on radio?"

Requests to do "hard" or tough stories were almost invariably rejected by the Press Department, stories that dealt with real issues such as the life of an ordinary worker or a farmer; the impact of de-Stalinization; the controversies that were boiling up among the writers; and the fate of the Volga Germans, an ethnic group that had been forcibly removed from their traditional villages in southwestern Russia and shipped by Joseph Stalin to central Asia at the beginning of World War II. Even seemingly less sensitive stories encountered a "*nyet*" from the Press Department. When Marvin Kalb, twenty-nine, newly arrived in Moscow, told press chief Mikhail Kharlamov that one human interest story he was planning would be about the capital's efficient snow-removal system, the official demurred because it would show women sweeping the sidewalks with twig brooms.

"Why take pictures of the women?" Kharlamov asked.

"Because they're there."

"When we have communism, they won't be there."

"When you have communism, I'll come and cover snow removal then," snapped Kalb.

The plight of the network correspondents was alleviated somewhat with the establishment in January 1961 of a second Soviet news service, called APN or Novosti, described by TASS as "an independent information service providing news to Soviet public organizations with mass membership." While APN's main purpose was to provide feature articles to the Soviet media, Western reporters were advised that it was also available to produce articles; help arrange interviews with Soviet officials, especially outside Moscow, and provide TV crews for resident journalists—for a fee. Although the correspondents regarded the agency as an arm of the KGB, within a few years it became an important resource, expanding much-needed access to the Soviet establishment. On a daily basis, however, the TV correspondents, more dependent on the Press Department than were the print journalists, were often fed innocuous stories that they would have ignored in any other country. Typical was a one-day trip to Smolensk to cover the deactivation of a Soviet Army unit announced with great fanfare by Nikita Khrushchev a few weeks earlier. A dozen American correspondents made the trip to see the spectacle. On a military drill ground, they watched about a thousand men parade past a reviewing stand, halt, and salute as regimental flags were lowered. Rifles were stacked in neat piles, and at a command the troops were dismissed. Then everybody marched off with a precision worthy of the Bolshoi ballet. The video was good but the correspondents were barred from asking questions and were immediately put on the train for Moscow. For all anybody knew, the regiment could have marched back after the reporters left, picked up the rifles, and returned to the barracks.

Aware of television's impact on American public opinion, the Russians constantly sought to plant stories that would put the Soviet Union in a favorable light. In one instance, Sam Jaffe was tipped that Moscow's Orthodox Jews were again

being permitted to bake their own Passover matzoh. With a
Novosti crew, he was taken to a ramshackle house on the
outskirts of Moscow by a representative of the Central Synagogue to film five or six Jews baking matzoh. In an unusual
move, the Press Department gave him explicit permission to
ship the film to New York, to which Jaffe added several
packages of matzoh as evidence. The report was obviously
intended to persuade American viewers that Soviet Jews were
free to pursue their religious beliefs. Another example: Frank
Bourgholtzer, who succeeded John Chancellor as NBC correspondent, received a phone call in March 1965 from Novosti
with an unexpected offer, an interview with Aleksei Leonov,
the first man to walk in space. Accepting with alacrity,
Bourgholtzer asked New York to send in a crew and a
producer. Looking for a way to make the interview more
lively, Bourgholtzer suggested that the cosmonaut, who was
reputed to be an artist, draw some pictures to illustrate what
he was talking about. This was agreed, but a few days before
the interview, Leonov requested NBC to supply him with one
or two Magic Markers, nonexistent items in the Soviet Union.
When the NBC crew arrived, they brought in six dozen.

"Leonov was the happiest guy in Moscow when we gave
them to him," recalled Bourgholtzer.

During the interview, the Russian drew sketches of the
spacecraft, showing how he emerged from the porthole and
walked in space. He also drew sketches of his apartment house
in Moscow. The one-hour program, an NBC special, was seen
by millions of Americans and presented the undoubted
achievements of Soviet science and technology in a favorable
light, precisely what the Kremlin wanted.

"To this day," Bourgholtzer said, "I don't know why they
chose me."

A few years earlier, NBC had scored another remarkable
coup with a one-hour special on the Kremlin, the first time any
TV network had been able to film inside the historic site.
Permission was granted by Khrushchev himself after he was
accosted at a Turkish embassy reception by NBC producer
Lucy Jarvis, who had been getting the run-around from the

Press Department. George Vicas, head of NBC's European production unit, was brought in from Paris for the project, which ultimately required eight weeks of shooting in and around the Kremlin. Fluent in Russian, Vicas cajoled, threatened, and charmed the Soviets into giving him almost everything he wanted, including a scene showing the Kremlin walls surrounded by flames, a replay of the conflagration that destroyed a large part of the city in 1812. Dozens of Moscow fire engines sped to Red Square to put out the "fire" even though the authorities had been forewarned. The Soviets, however, rejected Vicas' request for a chorus to sing "Eternal Memory," a traditional melody performed at funerals of the tsars, claiming that they had not preserved that kind of music. When Vicas announced that he would be obliged to use the chorus of the Russian Orthodox Cathedral in Paris, the score was found within twenty-four hours, and the all-male choir of Soviet Radio and Television, the finest in the country, was made available to perform. The documentary, which showed the ancient churches with their icon-covered interiors and the treasures of the Kremlin museum against a background of Russian history, was a critical success for NBC and a political success for the Soviets.

Despite the easing of some restrictions, television correspondents faced the old problem of shipping film. The authorities were still less concerned about words than about pictures. For example, when Frank Bourgholtzer tried to send film of Moscow police roughing up unruly Arab students demonstrating in front of the American embassy, the Press Department advised him not even to try. Disregarding the warning, he packed the footage with film of a championship figure-skating match for which permission to ship had been granted, but the film never got to New York. A few days later, press chief Leonid Zamyatin summoned the NBC correspondent to the Press Department for a scolding and cautioned him not to do it again. Like his competitor, Marvin Kalb was also a victim of a disappearing shipment. He had shot some remarkable footage of the funeral of Boris Pasternak, the great poet and the author of *Dr. Zhivago,* catching the somber mood, the

weeping friends and admirers, the procession winding across
a snow-covered field to the open grave near three birch trees,
and the KGB agents busily photographing everyone present.
Kalb rushed to the airport and found a "pigeon" to take out
the film: an American woman headed for London. He
watched the plane take off, delighted with his coup. When a
CBS courier met her at the airport, she denied that she had
ever received the film. Something had happened on the plane
to make her change her mind.

Kalb was crushed when his editors told him the bad news.

"It was one of the greatest frustrations I have ever had as a
TV reporter," he told me.

Within a few years, the introduction of videotape and
lightweight videotape cameras would make it possible for the
three American networks to move their Moscow operations
into the high-tech age. They would be permitted to bring in
cameramen, soundmen, and other technicians to establish
ministudios that could produce complete and technically
perfect TV reports ready to be shipped to New York and go
on the air. When satellite transmission was introduced in the
mid-1970s, reports could be sent directly to the United States
and broadcast immediately. Correspondents could even arrange live feeds of public events, such as a Supreme Soviet
session, an interview with a track star, or a stand-up report on
a Kremlin arms control proposal. This would be very different
from the 1960s, when NBC's John Chancellor, assisted by his
wife, Barbara, set up a sound camera and lights in his office
and spoke his piece.

One morning in mid-August 1962, Alexei Y. Popov, deputy
chief of the Press Department, sat behind his desk in the
Foreign Ministry and peered at me through his metal-rimmed
glasses. He was blond, balding, and spoke in his most cold and
official manner.

"Mr. Bassow," he said, "I have asked you to come here in
order to read you an official statement of the Soviet government."

The statement was brief. I was accused of "violating the

standards of behavior of foreign correspondents in the USSR" and writing "crudely slanderous dispatches about the Soviet Union, which have evoked the righteous indignation of Soviet public opinion." Consequently, I was ordered to leave the Soviet Union within seven days.

I was stunned. I knew I had been skating on thin ice since censorship was terminated, filing stories that had displeased the Press Department, but they were honest, factual, and as balanced as I could make them considering the constraints imposed by the Soviet regime.

"What dispatches are you referring to? What behavior standards did I violate? Please give me some examples."

"You know what I'm talking about. I don't have to be specific."

"My conscience is clear. I have been an objective observer of your country and have written the truth as I saw it. If this displeases you, so be it."

I stood up and walked out. There was no protocol handshake.

My two-year stint as *Newsweek* bureau chief had come to an abrupt end. In August 1960 I had returned to Moscow to open the magazine's bureau after an interlude in New York as the Carnegie Press Fellow at the Council on Foreign Relations and a year with CBS News. Working for a weekly, after three years with UPI Moscow, gave me the time to do the longer, more reflective reports on a wider range of subjects than was possible with the agency. And there were many fast-moving developments in those two turbulent years, beginning with the trial of U-2 pilot Francis Gary Powers, a series of remarkable Soviet space exploits, the renewal of the de-Stalinization campaign, and the Vienna meeting of President John F. Kennedy and Nikita Khrushchev that sparked a series of East-West confrontations over Berlin. During that time I also wrote extensively about art, music, ballet, and film—Soviet cultural life virtually unreported by the other correspondents and of which I was particularly proud.

Now my career as a Moscow correspondent was finished, and as I drove back to my apartment in *Newsweek*'s red

Mercedes I kept thinking: "What did I do? What brought this on?" Was it the story I had filed from Tashkent during Benny Goodman's tour about an air raid drill and blackout that I had witnessed and that no other American correspondent had reported? Was it because I had tried to interview a black American teenager from Newark whose father had sent her alone to the Soviet Union for the education he claimed she could not receive in the United States? I had attempted to see the director of the school she would be attending without going through the Press Department, a technical violation of the rules but hardly a cause for expulsion. Was it the story on alcoholism that had been sensationalized by a *Newsweek* editor in New York without my knowledge or approval? But surely the Press Department knew precisely what I had written. Was it because my contacts and friends, acquired after working in Moscow for over five years, had provided me with direct access to members of the Central Committee? Or was it that I spoke fluent Russian and did not require the services of a KGB interpreter? Or perhaps I had just been in Moscow too long to suit the authorities. By August 1962 I had served longer in Moscow than any other American correspondent except Henry Shapiro and Edmund Stevens. Now I would have the additional distinction of being the first American expelled since the termination of censorship.

More likely what precipitated my expulsion was a mail feature on Soviet humor I had written three weeks earlier, titled, "What Makes Ivan Laugh." Since the story was held over for lack of space and rescheduled for a subsequent issue, an editor cabled a routine request to "freshen" the story. By coincidence, I ran into Feliks Soloviev, my KGB baby-sitter, at the Hotel National cafe, and he reminded me of a joke that had kept Muscovites chuckling after Khrushchev ordered Stalin's remains transferred from the tomb on Red Square to the foot of the Kremlin wall.

A little boy asks his grandmother about Lenin.

"Ah, he was a great and good man."

"What kind of man was Stalin?"

"Sometimes he was good and sometimes he was very bad."

"And Grandma, what kind of man is Khrushchev?"

"When he dies, we'll find out."

Delighted with the "freshener," I delivered it to the Central Telegraph for transmittal to New York. It was never sent. Someone in the Kremlin, probably Khrushchev himself, did not find it amusing.

On the TV news that evening, an announcer told the Russian people that *Newsweek* correspondent Whitman Bassow had been deprived of accreditation and expelled from the USSR for violating "standards of behavior" of foreign journalists working in the Soviet Union. The news was carried by Radio Moscow and published in *Pravda* and *Izvestia* the following day. Within hours, the phone began to ring. Russian friends were calling to extend their regrets and asking when they could come to say good-bye. I was astonished that they would risk bidding farewell to a man who was being expelled by their government for conduct regarded as anti-Soviet. For me, this was dramatic evidence of how much things had changed since the death of Stalin. I could easily imagine what would have happened to Russian friends of Robert Magidoff had they dared bid him farewell when he was expelled in 1948. And they came. First Volodya, a jovial photographer who worked for *Soviet Sports;* his wife, Olga; and five-year-old daughter Lyuba, who often played with my four-year-old Fern. Elizabeth also arrived with her daughter, Irina. Elizabeth's father, a senior Soviet diplomat when Maxim Litvinov was Foreign Affairs commissar, had been eased out of his post after World War II because he was Jewish. Genia and Yelena simply phoned to wish me well. He was a writer for the satirical magazine *Krokodil*, which periodically aimed its darts at American reporters. My KGB "friend" asked me to meet him at our usual rendezvous near Pushkin Square. He was there the next morning with his girlfriend Alla. They met me bearing small gifts that I still possess: a painted lacquer box depicting a blond maiden holding a lamb, and an antique silver vodka cup. Calls came from friends at the U.S. embassy and from other correspondents offering help, condolences, congratulations, and invitations to dinners and a farewell party. I felt part of a big and caring family.

Later that week, when the packing was finished and the wooden crates were sent to customs for clearance and shipment to New York, I took a taxi to Red Square for a last look at the golden domes, the great towers, and the somber red brick walls. The long line of visitors to Lenin's tomb snaked across the cobblestones under a blue August sky. Militiamen in summer khaki directed traffic. As I stood quietly on the sidewalk in front of the GUM department store watching an enormous red flag fluttering over the old tsarist senate, now the offices of the chairman, I reflected on how much I had enjoyed working in Moscow. Despite the long hours, the harassment, the tension, and the official hostility, it had been a challenging assignment, fulfilling and rewarding. I thought about the stories I had covered and the first time I had seen the Soviet leaders shortly after my arrival for the UP in December 1955. At an Indian reception I found myself a few feet away from Nikita Khrushchev, Georgi Malenkov, Nikolai Bulganin, and V. M. Molotov. They had been only printed names until then, but here they were in the flesh and I could actually speak to them, ask questions, carry on a conversation. I was astonished that such powerful men were so accessible to an American reporter. Later I would discuss with Molotov my doctoral dissertation on the prerevolutionary *Pravda,* a Bolshevik newspaper published in 1912 on which he had played a leading role as an eighteen-year-old editor. I recalled the world championship hockey game at Lenin Stadium in twenty-five-below-zero temperature when a skillful Swedish team defeated the Russians to gain the cup. The Soviet goalie broke his stick over his knee to show his anger, while dozens of Soviet generals and marshals sitting in the front rows whistled disapproval of their own team. I remembered the tearful teenager, a member of the Young Communist League, telling me how she was heartbroken to learn, after the Twentieth Party Congress, that her idol Stalin was a monster who had destroyed millions of innocent people. Then there was the time I was walking down Pushkin Street and noticed a concert poster advertising the world premiere of Dmitri Shostako-vich's Fourth Symphony. I smelled a story because by 1962 he had already composed twelve symphonies. Pulling strings, I was able to obtain a ticket and found myself the only journalist in the hall sitting three rows in front of the composer who had come to hear his opus performed for the first time. Shostako-vich had finished the symphony in 1934, but fearing Stalin's harsh criticism, he quietly put it aside for almost thirty years. After the concert I asked him why the symphony could not have been performed when he wrote it. Cautious as ever, he gave me a tight-lipped smile and said, "Now I have a version I like."

Except for the final chapter, Moscow was fun with plenty of laughs to light up the serious nature of the assignment. Before I went there for the United Press, Henry Shapiro urged me to buy formal dress, white tie and tails, to be worn at the government's New Year's Day reception when the diplomatic corps and the foreign correspondents were invited to the Kremlin. Since my UP salary did not permit such an extrav-agance as buying a new suit for $175, I decided to try New York's legendary S. Klein department store, the forerunner of today's discount emporia. Much to my amazement, I found not one but three suits in my size, at the affordable price of $12.50, marked down from $50 and still bearing the John Wanamaker label, a store that had closed some five years earlier. During my three years with the UP, I never donned the tails, much to my disappointment. The Soviet leaders, instead of inviting the Moscow elite, opened the Kremlin's white marble St. George's Hall to thousands of children for a huge New Year's party. Prior to my departure from Moscow in 1958, I bequeathed the costume to Monsieur Dominique, the majordomo of a Western embassy. When I returned in 1960 to open the *Newsweek* bureau, I was surprised to find that he was still working there. He was as delighted to see me as I was to see him.

"Monsieur Bassow," he said, "I owe you money."

"What for?"

"For that suit you gave me. You know that it is very difficult to obtain formal wear in Russia, so I sold it to a Soviet *chef d'orchestre.*"

Dominique handed me one hundred rubles, about a hundred dollars.

"Next time you go to a concert at the Conservatory, observe the conductor. You will see your personal contribution to Soviet culture."

Then there were the modest and ephemeral triumphs, usually over the AP. In 1957, when the Soviets launched Laika the space dog into orbit, Roy Essoyan, my AP rival, and I were waiting for the first photos at the TASS office near Red Square. Agency cars, motors running, were outside. As soon as the clerk handed each of us a brown envelope with the photos, it was as if he had passed the baton to two runners in a relay. We raced to the cars, leaped inside, and sped across the edge of Red Square, up Gorki Street to the Central Telegraph. The AP car was ahead of me when we neared the building and stopped at the intersection to make a left turn on Ogarev Street. With both cars blocked by a red light, I jumped out and ran two hundred yards to Entrance 12 before Essoyan could see me. By the time he got to the Glavlit counter, my photo had already been deposited. Essoyan, a gracious loser, agreed that neither of us wanted to die of a heart attack for our employers. In the future we behaved like gentlemen and tossed a coin to determine who would hand in a photo first. Neither the UP nor the AP knew about this peace treaty. Ironically, the AP Laika photo was received in New York about one hour before the UP photo.

The most exciting aspect about the Moscow assignment was simply being there, to observe the momentous events and the principal actors. World personalities paraded through the Soviet capital: Marshal Tito, Premier Chou En-lai, Indonesian President Sukarno, Chancellor Konrad Adenauer, President Nasser, Vice President Nixon, and Mrs. Roosevelt. On a less exalted level, I had dinner with Elizabeth Taylor and her husband, Mike Todd; spent three weeks listening to Benny Goodman play my favorite swing music; heard William Saroyan wax nostalgic about his Armenian heritage; danced with

Shirley MacLaine in a Leningrad restaurant; shared a can of Chef Boyardee spaghetti with Truman Capote; and took tea with Cary Grant. With Daniel Schorr I attended a remarkable and private impromptu performance of Bach's double violin concerto presented by Isaac Stern and David Oistrakh in a classroom of the Moscow Conservatory.

The day of my departure was overcast; heavy clouds scurried across the sky, hinting that the brief Russian summer was nearing its end. My wife, Margit, and Fern had gone on ahead to the airport. I followed with the rest of the luggage in the UPI car lent by Henry Shapiro and arrived at Vnukovo Airport, where customs officials rushed me through without opening a single bag and without the body search to which they normally subject expelled correspondents. When I walked into the departure area, a crowd was waiting, friends from the United States and several other embassies and my press corps colleagues. It was good to see the familiar faces. We barely had time for a champagne toast drunk from paper cups. I clutched a few hands and walked slowly to the shuttle bus that was to take us to the plane. At the top of the aircraft ramp I turned to wave good-bye, not just to my friends, not just to Russia, but also to my career as a Moscow correspondent. I knew I would never return as a reporter.

Sunday, October 28, 1962, was cold and gray in Moscow, a fitting conclusion to a frightening week. The Soviet Union had placed long-range nuclear-tipped missiles in Cuba, threatening the security of the United States. President John F. Kennedy had demanded that they be withdrawn immediately, establishing a naval blockade of the island to ensure that no further Soviet supplies would be delivered. Nikita Khrushchev accused the United States of planning to invade Cuba, claiming that the missiles were intended only for self-defense. As tension heightened, the American correspondents in Moscow worked around the clock to fathom Soviet intentions, without success. In the streets of Moscow, however, everything seemed calm. Traffic was normal. People were at their jobs.

There were no signs of military activity. Although the press emphasized that this was a Cuba–United States confrontation, not a United States–USSR confrontation, people in Moscow reading between the lines and listening to the BBC and the Voice of America began to fear a nuclear war. Even the correspondents were worried for the safety of their families.

"I thought there was a distinct possibility that Moscow would come under attack and that my family and I would become victims," recalled Seymour Topping of the *Times*.

On that October Sunday, AP reporters Reinhold (Gus) Ensz, George Syvertsen, and bureau chief Preston Grover were in the agency office, monitoring the TASS teleprinter and the TV set for news on the Cuban situation. The two Soviet interpreters, as customary on Sunday afternoons, were off-duty.

Suddenly the regular TV program halted and Khrushchev appeared on the screen and began to read a message he had just transmitted to President Kennedy.

Syvertsen, who had studied Russian for one year and with the aid of a dictionary was able to read *Pravda* laboriously, began to type a rough translation. He did fairly well until Khrushchev announced the Soviet decision on the missiles. Syvertsen stopped typing and glanced at Grover in desperation, shouting:

"I don't know what he's saying! I don't understand whether he said 'in' or 'out'!"

Grover ran down the hall to ask *France-Soir*'s Russian-speaking correspondent Claude Day what Khrushchev said. The answer, she replied, is "out."

Across town at the UPI office, a similar scene was taking place, but with a happier result for the agency. When Khrushchev appeared on the TV screen, Lev Shtern, the Soviet interpreter, dictated a translation to correspondent Nicholas Daniloff, who took it down on a typewriter. Robert Korengold quickly wrote a story for transmittal to UPI in London.

The dramatic incident only confirmed the importance of a good working knowledge of Russian as part of a Moscow correspondent's professional equipment. Command of the language is especially critical for agency reporters, who must work quickly and against constant deadlines if they are to serve well their employers and thousands of newspaper, radio, and TV clients around the world. The Russian language opens doors to Soviet society and to news; ignorance keeps those doors shut. I cannot count the number of stories I developed simply because I could read, ask questions, and carry on an extended and complex conversation in Russian. For example, I once saw a poster announcing a presentation of *Porgy and Bess* by the graduating class of Moscow's Theatrical Arts Institute and decided to investigate. The director was delighted to see an American reporter and permitted me to attend the dress rehearsal. Hearing George Gershwin's "Summertime" sung in Russian by Russians in blackface was a strange but delightful experience. My contribution to the authenticity of the performance was a bottle of bourbon (full) to replace the bottle of vodka (empty) used as a prop in the early scenes. I told the director that the inhabitants of Catfish Row were not likely to be drinking vodka on a Saturday night. The story made a good offbeat feature for *Newsweek.* My first hint of the launching of *Sputnik I* came from a loudspeaker on Pushkin Street, when Moscow Radio proclaimed that there would soon be an important announcement. Without hesitation I raced to the Central Telegraph to phone the UP office and was positioned to file the first official account. In 1958, when American pianist Van Cliburn won the International Tchaikovsky Piano Competition, I broke the story almost twelve hours before anyone else after getting a tip from a friendly Russian member of the jury—who spoke no English. When the American Ballet Theater danced in Moscow, I was able to chat with the Bolshoi Theater's prima ballerina, Galina Ulanova, during intermission, the only correspondent who obtained her comments on the company's performance. None of the other reporters at the theater could speak Russian.

The list of opportunities was long, but the most important journalistic reward was to be able to meet Russians and learn about their lives and dreams. I remember Valya, an attractive, dark-haired woman I met at Benny Goodman's concert in the outdoor theater of Sochi, the resort town on the Black Sea coast. Under the spell of the music and the fragrant summer night, she told me that her dream was to stroll on such a night on a Paris boulevard, then sit at a sidewalk cafe and watch the elegant women passing by. A train engineer in the Moscow subway, she had little chance of ever seeing the Champs-Élysées. Raoul, a director of documentary films, a warm and charming man, was able to tell me he was angry at the father of the girl he wanted to marry. "He won't let her marry me, even though she loves me, because I am a Tatar," he complained. Alexander was an architect, working for Moscow's municipal government. A Jew, he rarely talked about his personal problems, but one night over herring, potatoes, and vodka at his kitchen table, together with two other Jewish friends, he finally revealed his bitterness at the anti-Semitism he had experienced. He was being blocked for promotion because he was Jewish, although he was a member of the Communist Party and a decorated war veteran. His friends had similar complaints. Without the Russian language I would have known nothing about this or much about how the system worked.

Sam Jaffe could speak only a few words of Russian, but in the four years he served as the ABC correspondent he knew more Russians, both official and unofficial, than probably any other American reporter in Moscow. A garrulous, friendly, brash, some would say foolhardy man, he would talk to anybody who would listen, usually about himself, treating all comers as if they were old buddies. As a thirty-one-year-old bachelor, Jaffe entertained lavishly in his apartment, inviting young people he met on the street, writers like Evgeny Yevtushenko; Nikita Khrushchev's personal interpreter, Victor Sukhodrev; and Soviet journalists and artists, including a daughter of a KGB officer. "We'd discuss politics and drink," recalled Jaffe. His parties entered the journalistic folklore of Moscow with their wild exuberance, drinking bouts, pretty girls, and the smashing of glasses in the old Russian tradition. Jaffe's bachelor party at the Aragvi, the famed Georgian restaurant, ended in disaster. One Soviet guest tried to swallow vodka from a flaming glass, scorched his throat, and was rushed to the hospital. Martin Page, a British correspondent, staggered into an open manhole outside the restaurant and broke his hip. But Jaffe recuperated from the binge in time to marry Jeane Georgeson, a horticulturist from New Zealand working as a nanny for a British family.

Jaffe's brazenness was legendary. At a Kremlin reception, for example, he was the only correspondent who had the guts to walk up to where all the Soviet cosmonauts were sitting and ask them to autograph his invitation card. They did. Once while he was driving with McGraw-Hill correspondent Stewart W. Ramsey in downtown Moscow, the car pulled up at a stoplight. A brown Pobeda sedan halted alongside.

Ramsey recalled, "The next thing Sam is shouting, 'Hey, General Loginov! Hey, General Loginov!' at a man in the other car. The man was startled. I said, 'Sam what the hell are you doing?'

"Sam said, 'That's General Loginov. He was head of the KGB at the UN.'

"But you're drawing attention to my car. Now it's going on a list of cars to be watched!"

Jaffe shrugged and grinned, but for Ramsey the incident was serious, revealing the "essence of Sam Jaffe—very emotional, very poor judgment."

His Moscow contacts, however, paid off for Jaffe and for ABC. The network was the first to televise live coverage from the Soviet Union, a United States–USSR track meet. He obtained the first exclusive interview with Mme. Nina Khrushchev for a documentary, "Soviet Woman." When Yale professor Frederick Barghoorn was arrested on a trumped-up charge of receiving secret government documents and released after President John F. Kennedy personally attested he was not a spy, a tip from a Soviet official enabled Jaffe to interview Barghoorn before he left.

But even Jaffe's contacts could not help him with certain sensitive stories. During elections for the Supreme Soviet, Russia's parliament, his crew filmed eighty-year-old President

Klimenti Y. Voroshilov drooling saliva as he cast his ballot. The omniscient Press Department warned Jaffe not to ship the film, but he defied the order and smuggled it out to New York. All in vain, however. James Hagerty, the president of ABC News, later informed Jaffe that ABC had received a blank reel. Jaffe was convinced that the Russians warned Hagerty not to use the film and he decided to kill the story.

One of Jaffe's acquaintances was Vyacheslav Kislov, a KGB lieutenant colonel to whom he had been introduced by a Soviet journalist working for Novosti. Jaffe later learned that Kislov worked in the section that kept track of foreigners living in Moscow, including the correspondents. Jaffe invited the Russian to his apartment for drinks. Kislov accepted. After exchanging amenities, the KGB officer accused Jaffe of working for the CIA.

"What makes you think that?"

"Why were you here for the Powers' trial?"

"CBS wanted me to help Kalb."

Kislov appeared skeptical, and he may have had his reasons. The unusual circumstances of Sam Jaffe's travel to Moscow and his relationship with Barbara Powers suggested that a larger, more powerful hand than CBS was involved. Jaffe told me that he did not know how, why, or who made these arrangements for the Powers trial, but incapable of keeping quiet, he often boasted about his contacts in the Soviet government and with the KGB.

Aggressive and at the same time unctuous, Jaffe was always seeking favors, interviews, and access—all legitimate journalistic enterprises. Many of his colleagues, however, felt that he was pushing too hard. At diplomatic receptions, for example, he was always the one who barged through the throng of reporters toward Khrushchev, shouting, "Nikita Sergeyevich! Nikita Sergeyevich!" as if they were old friends. After Jaffe left Moscow he worked for ABC in Vietnam and Washington but by then he was embroiled in a web of innuendos, rumors, and allegations that he had had connections with the KGB. He resigned from ABC in 1969 and spent the next fifteen years trying to clear his name. After publicly disclosing that he had kept the FBI informed about his KGB contacts at the United Nations, Jaffe was further enmeshed in the intelligence net when he was identified as a KGB agent by a Soviet defector. Jaffe claimed the allegation was false and spread by the FBI and CIA to undermine his professional credibility. Under a cloud, during those years he worked as a free-lance reporter, unable to obtain employment with a major news organization. The origin of the rumors—many of which are still classified "secret" by the FBI and the CIA—has never been entirely explained. In 1984, U.S. District Judge Barrington D. Parker issued an opinion stating that the FBI had no grounds to question Sam Jaffe's patriotism and that all the derogatory material against him in the government files came from discredited sources or was gossip or innuendo. In 1970 the CIA informed Jaffe that its own investigation had shown him to be a loyal citizen.

Perhaps the most accurate appraisal of Sam Jaffe has come from Ramsey, a close friend who observed him in Moscow for almost three years:

"I don't think that anybody who was as talkative and loudmouthed and was the center of attention as was Sam could have been very good as a spy. . . . He must have been the cleverest spy in the history of the world to do something like that, to constantly promote yourself, to be front and center stage, talking all the time about himself. . . . I don't understand what secrets he could have had."

Sam Jaffe died of lung cancer in January 1985, and as a former Marine Corps combat correspondent in Korea, was buried among the heroes at Arlington National Cemetery.

On the morning of October 14, 1964, Henry Shapiro was working in the UPI office when the phone rang. Raya, his housekeeper, announced that a visitor wanted to see him immediately on an urgent matter. Reluctant to return to his apartment, Shapiro asked her to tell the Russian he could not leave the office, a decision he was soon to regret. The man wanted to tip him on the biggest Moscow story in years: Nikita Khrushchev, apparently the most powerful man in the Soviet

Union, had just been forced to resign from his post as first secretary of the party and chairman of the Council of Ministers. If Shapiro had taken the time to see him, he would have had a world beat of eight hours.

Sam Jaffe also had received a phone call from Vyacheslav Kislov, his KGB contact.

"Sam," he said, "an old friend of yours is out."

"What do you mean?"

"Don't you know? An old friend of yours is out!"

"Khrushchev?"

"Yes."

"When will it be announced?"

"Soon." And Kislov hung up.

Mistrusting Kislov and worried that he was being used for some KGB purpose, Jaffe held up the story for several hours. Finally he went to see Shapiro, hoping to obtain confirmation, but the veteran correspondent told him he did not believe it. Shapiro sent a reporter to Red Square to look for Khrushchev's portraits, which together with those of other Soviet leaders had been displayed in downtown Moscow. They were gone. In the meantime, Victor Louis, a well-connected Soviet journalist who often served as the Kremlin's unofficial information link to the rest of the world, phoned the *London Evening News* at 11:40 A.M. that Khrushchev's portraits were missing from the street decorations being prepared to welcome the return of Soviet cosmonauts from a space mission. He also reported that the newspapers were not mentioning Khrushchev's name or publishing his photograph for the first time in almost ten years. Within a few hours the other correspondents began to get callbacks from their offices and phoned their sources trying to find out what was happening. They knew that something was brewing but were uncertain what it was. Soviet officials were unavailable or silent. Jaffe obtained additional confirmation from a reliable but unofficial source and broke the story with a phone call to New York at about 5:00 P.M. Shapiro, more conservative, filed about two hours later.

"My sources began to come through," he recalled. "They

didn't actually say what happened, but they didn't deny it."

A few minutes after midnight, the TASS English wire carried the official communiqué:

NIKITA S. KHRUSHCHEV HAS BEEN RELEASED FROM HIS DUTIES AS FIRST SECRETARY OF THE COMMUNIST PARTY OF THE SOVIET UNION CENTRAL COMMITTEE AND CHAIRMAN OF THE COUNCIL OF MINISTERS OF THE USSR. LEONID I. BREZHNEV HAS BEEN ELECTED FIRST SECRETARY OF THE CPSU CENTRAL COMMITTEE. ALEXEI N. KOSYGIN HAS BEEN APPOINTED CHAIRMAN OF THE COUNCIL OF MINISTERS.

The communiqué went on to say that Khrushchev had been relieved of his duties at his own request "in view of his advanced age and deterioration of health."

The correspondents finally had their story—officially. Around the world there was astonishment and disbelief at the rapidity of the change—without hints, leaks, or rumors. Suddenly the man who had steered his country away from the terror and repression of Stalinism, who had led it into the space age, who had moved the Soviet Union onto the world stage as the other superpower, had been unceremoniously dumped with an explanation that no one believed.

For Henry Shapiro, the transfer of power was a dramatic contrast with the events of March 1953 when Stalin died. He was the only American correspondent still in Moscow who was able to report the end of both the Stalin and the Khrushchev eras. In 1953 every word he wrote had to be carefully weighed, knowing that the censor was looking over his shoulder. In 1964 he could write freely, drawing on thirty years of experience and his vast knowledge of Soviet affairs. Shapiro not only scored a beat on the other print media but also wrote a perceptive and informed series of articles on what had occurred and why, winning an award from the Society of Professional Journalists. No other correspondent in Moscow could have matched that performance.

Sam Jaffe had his moment of glory. The parties, the drinking, the brashness had paid off. In less than a year, however, a few weeks before he was scheduled to leave Moscow to take charge of ABC's Hong Kong bureau, he was expelled. The action was not directed against him but against ABC for a broadcast by John Scali, its Washington correspondent, reporting that Leonid Brezhnev was ousting Alexei Kosygin from his post as premier. The report, which was false, was based on unidentified sources in Moscow.

In his innocence or ignorance, ABC News president Elmer Lowrer lamented, "To say the least, it is a surprise to us that our Moscow correspondent has been asked to leave because of a report we carried from Washington." He was unaware that the policy of holding the Moscow bureau responsible for any story that originates elsewhere in a news organization is one of the oldest traditions of the Press Department. Six months passed before ABC was able to obtain a visa for George Watson, Jaffe's successor.

The Khrushchev era introduced ten years of dramatic change in the status of foreign correspondents working in the USSR, but despite the improvements, the pressure, harassment, and surveillance of correspondents continued. In the four years following the termination of censorship, six American reporters, including Sam Jaffe, were expelled. I was the first. Then Adam Clymer of the *Baltimore Sun* was accused of pushing a policeman during a demonstration of Vietnamese and Chinese students in front of the U.S. embassy and was ordered out of the country. Frank Bourgholtzer of NBC was required to leave and the bureau closed because the network's TV special *The Death of Stalin* irked the Press Department. Stephen Rosenfeld, after barely a year as correspondent for the *Washington Post,* was expelled when the newspaper refused to halt publication of the "Penkovsky Papers," the memoirs of a convicted Soviet spy. The Press Department accused the *Post* of a "premeditated action in the worst traditions of the Cold War that cannot but harm Soviet-American relations." Similarly, Israel Shen. er of *Time* was expelled and the bureau closed for an article about Lenin that referred to a *ménage à trois* relationship with his revolutionary colleague Inessa Armand and his wife, Nadezhda K. Krupskaya. *Izvestia* accused *Time* of "touching with dirty fingers the memory of the founder of the Soviet state." The Press Department had made it abundantly clear that it would take extreme action against not only the correspondents but also their publications and networks if they stepped over the line.

Nikita Khrushchev's presence on the Soviet stage had a profound effect on the news and the coverage. He was articulate and accessible to American reporters at public events and diplomatic receptions, ranging from the opening night performance of Benny Goodman to a vodka-drenched party for Chou En-lai. His willingness—indeed, eagerness—to comment on foreign policy, space exploration, literature, modern art, corn crops, missiles, red tape or almost any other subject made good stories and often headlines. After Khrushchev's departure from the Kremlin, the Soviet Union became a much duller assignment for Western journalists.

The former first secretary quietly lived out his years in a government *dacha* on the outskirts of Moscow, puttering in his garden and playing with his grandchildren. When he died in September 1971, a one-sentence obituary in *Pravda* informed the Soviet people that the man who had shaped their destinies for over ten years had died at age seventy-eight. He was buried not under the Kremlin wall, together with Joseph Stalin, Jacob Sverdlov, Felix Dzerzhinsky, Mikhail Kalinin, and other heroes in the Soviet pantheon, but in a cemetery in the shadow of a monastery on the banks of the Moscow River.

How sadly prophetic proved the joke I sent to *Newsweek* about Nikita Khrushchev's fate. The world indeed found out what kind of man he was—when he died.

9

Détente and Dissidents

They put us in a position where they made adversaries out of us. . . . They forced you to see the dissidents because they wouldn't let you see anybody else.

George Krimsky
Associated Press
1974–77

Fear of expulsion was nowhere near as great as the fear they would pick you up and do something with you. . . . It's a tough thing to live with. . . . You get pushed and shoved. Sure it bothers you, but you go on anyway.

Hedrick Smith
The New York Times
1971–74

The four-day trial was over for Yuli M. Daniel, a poet-translator, and Andrei D. Sinyavsky, a popular lecturer at the Gorki Institute of World Literature. Accused of spreading propaganda aimed at "undermining and weakening Soviet power . . . disseminating slanderous material with the same intent of besmirching the Soviet state and system," the two forty-year-old members of the intelligentsia were sentenced respectively to five and seven years at hard labor for publishing their writings in the West. Both men stoutly proclaimed their innocence during the proceedings, which were barred to Western correspondents. Only relatives of the accused and invited guests were permitted inside the courtroom. When the verdict was announced and sentence passed by the judge, a mob of Komsomol bullies massed in the street in front of the Supreme Court building, shouting at the waiting reporters, pushing them, and demanding, "What are you doing here?" As the wives of both men emerged from the courthouse, no one could speak to them. The two women, in tears, kissed each other and walked off in opposite directions. A few moments later, a police van followed by a jeep drove from the rear of the courthouse, taking Daniel and Sinyavsky to prison. The final act of the drama was barely over when the agency correspondents rushed off to file their stories.

That day in February 1966 was a landmark, signaling the beginning of turmoil and convulsion in Soviet society that spawned a decade of dissent and dissidents. Although only a relatively small number of individuals became involved, their appearance as a highly visible and vocal group was to affect profoundly the professional and personal lives of the American correspondents. When the plight of the dissidents became intertwined with the plight of Soviet Jews seeking to emigrate, the threat to the personal safety of the reporters covering these stories reached levels unseen in the Soviet Union since the worst days of the Cold War.

The growth of the dissident movement began during a period of relative stability in the Soviet Union soon after Leonid Brezhnev ascended to supreme power. Under his rule the Soviets moved aggressively to "normalize" relations with the United States through the Strategic Arms Limitation Treaty (SALT), an agreement to stop the spread of nuclear weapons, a series of actions to stimulate trade, including the establishment of direct air service between New York and Moscow, the creation of a United States–USSR Trade and Economic Council, and the opening of a U.S. trade office in Moscow. These efforts resulted in a U.S.-Soviet summit meeting of President Nixon and Chairman Brezhnev in 1972, which launched a period of détente between the two superpowers.

Over the next few years, a torrent of tourists and official visitors from the West, especially from the United States, inundated the Soviet Union in unprecedented numbers: businessmen, tourists, students, academicians, scientists, and performing artists driven by curiosity, intellectual and artistic pursuits, or the desire to make money. Although this influx provided the Soviets with valuable foreign exchange, it also encouraged dissidents to reach out to this new and wider audience. The phenomenon itself can be traced directly to

Nikita Khrushchev's shattering of the Stalin legend, creating among many Soviet citizens skepticism about the system's infallibility and perfection. Stimulated by the increasing flow of information from the West through radio broadcasts, publications, and cultural exchanges; the failure of the Soviet economy to meet consumer needs; and continuing fetters on literature, art, and music, a small number of intellectuals began to ask the most potent question that could be directed at the Kremlin leadership: "Why?" The same question had been addressed to the tsarist autocracy by philosophers and writers of the nineteenth century such as Georgi Plekhanov, Nikolai Chernishevsky, and Alexander Herzen. Tsarist Russia punished its dissidents with imprisonment, exile, or both. Communist Russia did the same.

Following the trial of Yuli Daniel and Andrei Sinyavsky a new wave of dissent arose. A clandestine *samizdat* (self-publication) movement produced a steady stream of literary works, statements, and articles that circulated in Moscow, Leningrad, and other cities, criticizing the trials and the verdicts and calling for freedom of expression. A typewritten underground bimonthly, *Chronicle of Current Events,* appeared in 1968 with detailed accounts of arrests, trials, and prison conditions of dissidents. New arrests and new trials took place, the most notorious being that of, among others, Vladimir Bukovsky, Yuri T. Galanskov, and Aleksandr I. Ginzburg. They were accused of publishing illegal journals, violating currency regulations, and maintaining links with Russian émigré groups, and their vehement denials did not prevent them from being sentenced to long prison terms at hard labor. Western correspondents, although barred from the trials, obtained details from relatives and friends of the accused.

Dissidents, quickly sensing they could use the foreign press to communicate their views to the outside world and reach a sympathetic and influential audience, began to contact and cultivate American reporters. The AP and UPI, *The New York Times*, the *Washington Post*, the *Chicago Tribune*, and the networks began to receive the *Chronicle*. Phones almost never stopped ringing as mysterious and often unknown voices would ask for an immediate meeting to pass on "important information."

Initially the Press Department and the KGB did little to interfere with reporters who attempted to cover the dissidents. In 1967 and early 1968 the Soviets seemed uncertain about how to treat the nonconformists, perhaps believing that if they were ignored they would go away. Arresting them in large numbers would only turn them into martyrs in the eyes of the outside world, something the Kremlin did not want. As a result, the correspondents became increasingly bolder in covering the story. Almost every week they filed dispatches about *samizdat* publications, petitions, and protest letters to the Central Committee and to the Soviet government on such subjects as the revival of Stalinism and freedom of literary expression. A frightening incident, however, shattered the tranquillity of the correspondents. On Christmas Day 1967, the rear end of AP bureau chief Henry Bradsher's Volkswagen was demolished by a mysterious explosion minutes after he parked near the apartment house in which he lived. No one was hurt, but the blast shattered windows in neighboring buildings. There seemed to be no connection between the incident and AP coverage of dissidents, but the correspondents regarded this as a warning from the KGB.

By early 1968, the dissident movement, which was beginning to wane, received new impetus from the Ginzburg trial, which received wide publicity in the West. The response of the Soviets was to take a hard line against the correspondents covering the story. When Ludmilla Ginzburg, Aleksandr's wife, called a news conference in her apartment after the trial, the Press Department phoned all the Western news agencies and specials *after 10 P.M.*, warning them not to attend and reminding that it was illegal for correspondents to contact Soviet citizens without going through the Foreign Ministry. "Severe measures" would be taken against those who tried to attend the conference. Of the almost one hundred non-Communist correspondents in Moscow, eighteen of whom were Americans, only four decided to go: Robert Korengold, now with *Newsweek;* Raymond Anderson of *The New York Times;* Anatole Shub of the *Washington Post;* and Robert Evans of CBS News. The AP and UPI were conspicuously absent. A few other correspondents watched as the four reporters approached the line of KGB plainclothesmen who stood in the driveway, blocking access to the Ginzburg apartment. The newsmen turned back.

Robert Korengold did not consult *Newsweek* about covering the press conference but decided to go on his own. Raymond Anderson telexed New York asking whether he should attend, warning that the Russians might close the *Times* bureau. The reply was swift:

YOU COVER THE NEWS. WE'LL TAKE CARE OF THE CONSEQUENCES.

The cable from the *Times* became the unspoken mandate of most of the American correspondents as they tracked the story of the dissidents, setting the stage for confrontation, sometimes violent, with the Soviet authorities. For the next seven years, as reporters sought to convey to the American people the extraordinary blossoming of skepticism about the nature of Soviet society, the Kremlin attempted to block access to the people who wanted to tell the story, using strong-arm tactics and intimidation, harassment and blackmail to frighten the correspondents into silence. The effort failed. American and other Western correspondents, persistent, cunning, and often courageous, got the story out.

In early July 1968, Raymond Anderson obtained a copy of a sensational ten-thousand-word essay written by Dr. Andrei D. Sakharov, a pillar of the Soviet scientific establishment, a distinguished physicist, a member of the prestigious Academy of Sciences, and the "father" of the hydrogen bomb. The manuscript, which Sakharov sent unsolicited to a few members of the Central Committee, challenged the basis of Soviet society by calling for intellectual and scientific freedom, which he termed essential for the modernization of the country. He was harshly critical of many current Soviet policies, saying they could lead to thermonuclear war. Dissident Andrei Amalrik, an historian and writer, passed the essay to the *Times* correspondent through a mutual friend.

Anderson, forty-two, who had an unusually strong command of Russian, returned to his office to read the manuscript. He was astonished by the contents.

"I realized that if authentic, it was surely something devastating because of Sakharov's importance in the Soviet system," he told me.

But how was he to confirm that the manuscript was authentic? How did he know that it was not another provocation by the KGB? He had never met Andrei Sakharov and had no idea of his views.

After making a few discreet inquiries, Anderson was convinced that the document was genuine and decided to file a story summarizing the statement. The dispatch made the front page of the *Times* and headlines around the world. The full impact was felt when the story, despite Soviet attempts to jam the transmissions, was broadcast by the Voice of America, the BBC, and Radio Liberty, and millions of Soviet citizens learned what one of their most distinguished countrymen thought about their society. Anderson later translated the text and sent it to New York by undisclosed means. The *Times* published it in full.

"Then, of course," he recalled, "the fat was in the fire."

Since the Soviets have always dealt cautiously with the newspaper that publishes "All the News That's Fit to Print," there was no immediate reaction to Raymond Anderson's scoop. Not until October, when he and his wife departed for a vacation in Greece, did the USSR embassy in Washington inform the *Times* that Anderson's reentry visa was canceled "because he was dealing with matters unrelated to journalism." The reporter was permitted to return to Moscow to pack his bags, retrieve his two young children, and leave within seven days. Anderson was the first *Times* correspondent to be expelled since Welles Hangen in 1956. Although a State Department spokesman deplored "this action against a member of the American press who had been pursuing his normal journalistic duties," no retaliatory action was taken—a policy that was destined to change in a year.

In the meantime, two events occurred that profoundly affected the dissident movement: Israel's spectacular victory over Arab armies in the Six-Day War in mid-1967, and the Soviet Bloc invasion of Czechoslovakia in August 1968. The Israeli triumph sparked a surge of pride among Soviet Jews and resulted in an unprecedented demand for the right to emigrate to their homeland. The Kremlin's harsh response was to dismiss from their jobs those who requested exit visas and to send many to exile and prison. Small protest demonstrations, sit-ins in government offices, distribution of leaflets, and the attempted hijacking of an Aeroflot plane brought the plight of the Jews to the world's attention—through the foreign correspondents in Moscow.

The dissident movement was further reenergized when Soviet and other Warsaw Pact troops invaded and occupied Czechoslovakia, crushing a reform-minded government that promised liberty to its people. Viewing this as a move aimed not only at the Czechoslovak people but also against the aspirations for greater freedom within their own country, dissidents began a new series of protests, including a short-lived demonstration on Red Square by seven bold Russians in August 1968. The courageous attempt to brave the wrath of the regime in the shadow of the Kremlin was brutally disrupted by the KGB, inaugurating a trying period both for the dissident movement and for the American correspondents. To deal with the hazards of covering the dissidents and Jews seeking to emigrate, reporters developed unusual tactics for the normally competitive American news media.

When Robert Korengold, James Yuenger of the *Chicago Tribune,* Roger Leddington of the AP, or any other American correspondents set out to meet a dissident or a Jewish *refusenik* (those who were refused exit visas), they rarely ventured forth alone. Working in pairs, they met with their sources at a pre-arranged rendezvous established by complicated codes to thwart the KGB, a strategy that developed spontaneously. There was so much activity—so many rumors, so many phone calls from tipsters, and so much to be confirmed and verified—that in most cases two or more heads were far better than one. To spread the responsibility, the AP, UPI, Reuters, and AFP shared stories of dissidents by the simple expedient of telexing the news item across town. Correspondents exchanged information to an extent unknown in any other world capital. In addition, reporters felt that joint enterprises provided a measure of protection from the KGB, from "irate Soviet citizens," and from arrest and interrogation by police. The traditional feeling of Moscow correspondents that they were a beleaguered group confronting the repressive apparatus of the entire Soviet state cemented professional cooperation and mutual support. During his two years in Moscow, recalled James Yuenger, "It was a 'we' versus 'they' situation."

Some correspondents felt that an exclusive story was largely irrelevant in covering dissidents, human rights activists, and Jews who had been refused exit visas. When a reporter received a document from a dissident source, for example, he was expected to inform his colleagues and to help provide a translation for their common use. In the 1970s, nobody expected the dissidents to phone some twenty American correspondents and provide them each with information. Those correspondents who could understand Russian were expected to serve the rest—and they did.

"The five who knew Russian carried a lot of extra freight for the other correspondents," *Times* bureau chief Hedrick Smith told me. "They got a free piggyback."

All the Americans developed tricks to deceive KGB surveillance, not always successfully. One device, for example, was to use complicated codes to fix a time and place for meetings with dissidents, a system used by James Jackson, who worked for UPI from 1969 to 1972 and then for the *Chicago Tribune* from 1974 to 1976. A contact would begin a phone call by asking:

"Hello, Jeem, how is your wife?"

"She is fine," which meant they would meet in front of the Puppet Theater.

"She's not feeling well" meant the meeting would not take place.

"She's okay" meant they could meet at the toy store.

Setting the time was also complicated. Different codes were used to fix days and hours; a time announced on the phone could actually mean one or two hours later or an hour and a half earlier. Tuesday could mean Wednesday and Wednesday could mean Thursday.

During one exchange, Jackson recalled, both parties were so confused that he blurted out, "See you at the toy store in two hours." Fortunately, no KGB tails were visible. A few years later, after he had left Moscow for a London assignment, Jackson found out why. His contact, Leonid Tsitin, was revealed in the pages of *Izvestia* as a KGB informer assigned to penetrate the dissident movement.

Triumphs over the system, however, were not uncommon. On one Saturday afternoon, James Yuenger rolled out of the foreigners' housing compound on Sadovaya Samotechnaya Boulevard in his red Volkswagen for a rendezvous with a dissident. Three KGB Volgas picked him up immediately, but he managed to shake off two of them. The third stuck to him like a shadow.

Suddenly Yuenger's sixth sense showed him the way out. In Soviet society, he reasoned, nobody does anything blatantly wrong. What you do is stay out of trouble and avoid the authorities, so when he came to a one-way street, he sped into it the wrong way.

"You just don't do that in Soviet society. These guys were dumbfounded, and by the time they figured out what I had done and had come in after me, I had time to turn around in a very narrow street because I had this little VW and they had this big Volga. I went past them laughing my ass off. . . . I was three blocks away before they figured out what I had done.

"It was a great psychological triumph over the current Soviet mentality. I made my meeting. I got my story, and I hope they got demoted. It was the most brilliant move of my journalistic career."

*   *   *

At the beck and call of the dissidents, the American reporters often responded like firemen. When the alarm went off, they headed for the action. One afternoon, for example, Christopher Ogden, a twenty-seven-year-old UPI correspondent, got a phone tip that *refuseniks* were planning to demonstrate near the Ministry of Interior. He grabbed a camera, quickly rounded up UPI colleague Gordon Joseloff and John Shaw of *Time*, and drove to the site to observe what would occur. The entrance to the ministry was already under the surveillance of men in dark coats and wearing fedoras and carrying briefcases. Five Jews approaching from different directions converged on the doorway, turned abruptly, and unfurled hand-lettered banners inscribed, "Let us emigrate to Israel!"

"As soon as they did it," Ogden recalled, "the police leaped on them, and just as I started squeezing off the pictures, one plainclothes guy swung a briefcase at me. . . . [It] felt like it was loaded with bricks. It got me right in the stomach. Then a uniformed policeman grabbed me by the scruff of the neck and knocked my glasses off and started kicking me in the back and pushing me across the street. Since he was in uniform, I certainly wasn't going to struggle with him."

The policeman kept kneeing Christopher Ogden in the small of his back. Only the heavy overcoat he was wearing saved him from serious injury. The reporters and the demonstrators were hustled inside the entrance into a reception room, where Ogden successfully changed the roll in his camera, protected by a walking screen of demonstrators who understood what he was trying to do. The three correspondents were detained until a senior official in an electric green suit strode into the room, glared at them, and said with a hiss, "Journalists! American journalists!" and stalked out.

The reporters were released; the five Jews were held for several weeks and never seen again in Moscow. UPI photos were smuggled out of the country and made front pages around the world.

Physical harassment and intimidation of American correspondents quickly became an occupational hazard. James Peipert of the AP was attacked, his glasses broken by KGB thugs to prevent him from meeting with dissidents on a street corner. He was later held for several hours after dining with a Russian medical student. KGB agents grabbed Anthony Astrachan of the *Washington Post,* shoving him back into his car as he sought to talk to his dissident contact. Roger Leddington was detained by police after he had observed a sit-in by Jewish demonstrators at the Supreme Court building and refused permission to phone the U.S. embassy. Slashing car tires was a frequent and favorite pastime of the KGB. When Harry Trimborn of the *Los Angeles Times* met with film director Mikhail Kalik, who had applied for an exit visa, he found his car tires slashed and a warning scratched on the hood:

SO IT WILL BE FOR ALL OTHERS!

Despite the official existence of détente between the United States and the USSR in the early 1970s, incidents of physical violence and harassment of correspondents multiplied to such an extent that Moscow began to resemble a combat zone. Every time a reporter met a dissident or a would-be Jewish émigré or a Russian friend, an ugly encounter with the KGB was almost inevitable. How to deal with these attacks created a dilemma for the correspondents and their editors back home. The gut reaction was to fight back, but bravado would not avail against KGB bruisers. Shouting to the police for help—in Russian—sometimes embarrassed and distracted the thugs, who had nothing visible to distinguish them from ordinary Soviet citizens except their bulk. They could have been muggers, a rare phenomenon in the Soviet Union, but the presence of an indifferent uniformed policeman nearby was evidence that the attacks had official sanction. For some correspondents it was a wearying business; for others, an unusual journalistic challenge.

"We loved the dissident story," James Jackson told me, "because it was the only live story in town."

In addition to the physical harassment, the Americans were constantly vilified by the Soviet press, usually by name. The newspaper *Trud* demanded Anthony Astrachan's expulsion, charging that he engaged in "criminal and anti-Soviet activities." Roger Leddington, who was the lead man covering dissidents, was accused of transforming the Associated Press into "a transmittal point for anti-Soviet slander to the West." The Foreign Ministry even went so far as to inform the U.S. embassy that Gordon Joseloff would be expelled if he did not change his "provocative and hostile behavior." *Pravda,* in language reminiscent of the Cold War years, urged the Soviet people to increase their "vigilance" against Western influence. The newspaper denounced foreign correspondents who obtain "rumors and gossip" from the "dregs of society" for their "dirty anti-Soviet fabrications" and called them "enemies of the Soviet people." No names were mentioned, but the reporters assumed that anyone who covered the dissidents was on that list. *Izvestia,* however, was more specific, accusing five American and British correspondents of going far beyond the boundaries of their professional responsibilities. The newsmen had reported that thirty-nine Soviet Jews sent a letter to the Foreign Ministry stating that they were so eager to emigrate to Israel, they were ready to leave "on foot" if necessary. The *refuseniks* had complained that at an official news conference, a number of prominent Soviet Jews who announced that all Jews were happy in Russia gave only one side of the picture. *Izvestia* warned John Bausman, AP bureau chief; Bernard Gwertzman of *The New York Times;* Adam Kellet, Reuters bureau chief; Dennis Blakely of the BBC; and Frank Taylor of the *London Daily Telegraph* that they were in the Soviet Union to work as journalists, not to represent "international Zionism." The implication was clear: Stay away from the story or face retaliation or expulsion.

Since they were so dependent on each other, a symbiotic relationship soon developed between correspondent and dissident. The reporter needed the dissident for access to information, to news about arrests, harassment, petitions, and Soviet efforts to quash the movement, while the dissident needed the correspondent to relay his story to a sympathetic and hopefully influential audience in the West. Some dissidents felt that they acquired a certain immunity from persecution because Western correspondents gave them a degree of notoriety outside the Soviet Union. Even Andrei Sakharov, the most prominent dissident, did not hesitate to press reporters on behalf of a colleague. He frequently phoned the AP's George Krimsky, urging him to publicize the plight of a particular individual. Although it was difficult to refuse Sakharov, Krimsky informed him that he alone would decide whether the story should be reported and only on its merits.

"After a while it got extremely tiresome," Krimsky told me. "More than once I used to say to some of these dissidents, 'Now, hold it, wait a minute, you don't understand. I'm not a priest, I'm a journalist.' "

The coverage took an unusual twist when reporters began to get callbacks, not from editors in the United States but from dissidents in Moscow. Thanks to détente, the Kremlin had ceased jamming Western broadcasts, and millions of Soviet citizens could tune in to the Voice of America and hear what Western correspondents were reporting. Whenever there was a demonstration by Jews, a statement by dissidents, or a trial unreported in the Soviet press, Russians would learn about it from the VOA. Then the bureau phones would start ringing with calls from dissidents.

"It sometimes got to the ridiculous point," said Krimsky, "where you'd get a phone call from one of your sources, saying, 'Why didn't you say such-and-such in your story?' And I'd say, 'How the hell do you know what I said in my story?' And they'd say, 'Oh, I heard the VOA report,' or 'I heard the BBC report.' It was becoming like Washington."

Confronted with the persistence of American and other Western reporters in covering dissenters and Jews, the Kremlin began to use its ultimate weapon against correspondents: expulsion. Raymond Anderson was followed by Anatole Shub of the *Washington Post* in May 1969 for writing "slanderous articles" about the Soviet Union. In November, Aaron Einfrank, an American working for the *Toronto Daily Telegram*, was ordered to leave because of his "disparaging articles."

Three Americans were expelled within the next fifteen months for a variety of reasons: Stanley Cloud of *Time*, William Cole of CBS, and John Dornberg of *Newsweek*. The U.S. Department of State lodged formal protests with the Soviets over the expulsions and for the first time in the history of the U.S.-Soviet relations took retaliatory action. When Shub was expelled, the State Department informed the Soviet embassy in Washington that TASS correspondent Viktor Kopytin must leave the country within forty-eight hours, the same deadline allowed the American reporter. Carl Bartch, the department spokesman, said that the United States was "forced" to counter in this fashion because of the Soviet government's "unwillingness to tolerate the free exercise of journalism." Until then the State Department, following the advice of newspaper editors and TV news executives, had refrained from retaliating because such a response might imply that there existed a formal link between the press and the government. The United States did not want to imitate Soviet practices. Retaliation, however, was regarded less as an end in itself than as a means of forcing the Russians to think twice before getting rid of an American reporter.

In response to Stanley Cloud's expulsion, the United States ordered Boris M. Orekhov, *Pravda*'s New York correspondent, out of the country for undefined "activities incompatible with his status as a journalist"—almost the identical language favored by the Press Department. Leonid Zhegalov, the Washington correspondent for TASS, paid the penalty for Dornberg's departure and was forced to leave within three days. The Soviet news agency called the decision "arbitrary and unfounded," a term that could apply equally to John Dornberg's treatment.

The new U.S. policy worked effectively for almost seven years. No Americans were expelled, nor were any Russians, thus saving both sides the expense of moving families and their belongings back and forth across the Atlantic. But the standoff was to break down in 1977 with the departure of the AP's George Krimsky. The Soviets found it difficult to abandon a tactic they had first employed in 1923 against four of the first Americans to report from Moscow.

*   *   *

In early February 1974, Alexander Solzhenitsyn, author, Nobel laureate, and political and literary outcast of Soviet society, was on the phone speaking to Hedrick Smith of *The New York Times*.

"Come immediately!" he ordered.

Smith knew the writer was in trouble, but he had no indication of what was brewing. With Murray Seeger of the *Los Angeles Times* and BBC correspondent Erik de Mauny, Smith drove to Solzhenitsyn's apartment off Gorky Street, walking the last two blocks. The KGB stakeouts were in place: men lounging in doorways and sitting in parked Volga sedans and smoking long Russian cigarettes.

"It was like swimming through jellyfish in August, slimy and awful," recalled Smith.

The policemen at the door let them pass. Solzhenitsyn and his wife, Natalya, were waiting. The writer announced that he had finished the seventh and last section of *The Gulag Archipelago*. The preceding parts of this epic work on Stalin's labor camps had already been published in the West and had been harshly condemned by the Soviet government. The new segment described the lawlessness and corruption of the Brezhnev era. As Smith examined the manuscript, de Mauny asked Solzhenitsyn to read a passage for radio broadcast. Seated behind a table in his tiny study, with Natalya standing behind, her hands on his shoulders, he quietly began to read to the three reporters in a rich, chewy Russian, as if he were on the stage of a theater.

When Solzhenitsyn finished, he handed Smith the manuscript and bade the reporters farewell. His bag was packed. He was certain that he was going to be arrested. A trial, prison, perhaps exile lay ahead.

The correspondents faced a terrifying dilemma: They did not know what would happen when they walked out the door. In their hands was a manuscript, "anti-Soviet propaganda," which presumably they would smuggle out of the country to the West. Under Soviet law, their action was *prima facie* evidence for arrest. But nothing happened as the three newsmen left the apartment and walked down the stairway and through the KGB stakeouts. Unbelievably, no one stopped them. De Mauny and Smith spent the rest of the day translating the text, which Smith filed to the *Times* that night. Solzhenitsyn's fate was sealed the next morning when seven men broke into his apartment and arrested him on unspecified charges. For the next two days the three correspondents feared that they might join him in prison as accomplices, but on February 13 Solzhenitsyn and his wife were bundled onto a plane headed for West Germany and into forced exile.

For Smith, who was to win a Pulitzer Prize a year later for his Moscow reporting, it was a frightening experience but not entirely unexpected. When dealing with Alexander Solzhenitsyn, as the writer had warned him, "You're in a radioactive zone. You enter at your own peril."

Robert Kaiser of the *Washington Post* and friend of the author was out of the country and missed the Solzhenitsyn arrest and exile, one of the biggest stories of his Moscow assignment. When he caught up with him in West Germany, the Russian apologized for contacting his rival, Hedrick Smith.

"I phoned you but your maid told me you were skiing in France, so I had to call *The New York Times*."

The dissident and *refusenik* story stirred controversy within the ranks of the American correspondents unmatched by any other development in postwar Russia. Some reporters decided that overt dissent was a significant new force for change in Soviet society that merited close attention. Others believed that the phenomenon involved such a small group of people that it was of no great importance. Each opposing view was influenced by the needs of the readership and audience of each reporter's newspaper, magazine, or network. *The New York Times* and the *Washington Post* gave the story a good deal of attention, while the *Los Angeles Times* and the *Chicago Tribune* did not, although much depended on the personal interest of the individual reporter. The wire services fell somewhere in between because of the broad range of client newspapers and networks they serviced.

But some correspondents believed that a number of their colleagues were playing down the story, unwilling to risk expulsion or endanger their bureaus. Those who did not give total attention to the human rights issue were convinced that it was not the central story in Soviet society. Other important developments, they believed, should not be shunted aside if the reporting was to provide a balanced and comprehensive picture of life in the USSR.

For example, Charlotte Saikowski, then forty-three, correspondent of *The Christian Science Monitor* from 1968 to 1972, has conceded, "I don't think I would have wanted to jeopardize my stay in the Soviet Union by dwelling on the dissidents. You have to ask yourself, 'How often can I do this story?' It became a matter of judgment. It was a tough one to call."

Saikowski never hesitated to report other developments that the authorities found objectionable, such as the nationalist cultural dissent she uncovered on a visit to Lvov University in the Ukraine. Official displeasure with her reporting was frequently and publicly communicated in the pages of *Pravda*.

Within the AP in New York, some editors felt that the Moscow file was tilted toward the dissident story at the expense of broader and less political reporting. But at no time did the editors order the Moscow bureau to play it down. How the bureau handled the dissidents was left to the discretion of the bureau chief. At UPI, a target for criticism was Henry Shapiro, already nearing retirement after almost forty years in Moscow. Because of his long experience, he was at first skeptical of the dissidents who, he admitted, later became important information sources. Malcontents had been finding their way to his apartment for years, since he lived outside the foreign ghetto without a policeman at the door. Any Russian could walk up the two flights and ring his doorbell: KGB agents, provocateurs, would-be defectors, purveyors of secret documents, and unknowns with "secret" information. Once an elegantly dressed man walked in and offered him blueprints for a weapon that was "better than the atomic bomb" and asked to be driven immediately to the American embassy. Shapiro told him to deliver the papers himself and ordered him to leave. Claiming he would not sign off on a dispatch he could not confirm, Henry Shapiro simply did not trust the dissidents, and his reluctance to report their plight was seen by some correspondents as toadying to the Press Department. According to the reporters on his staff, however, he never interfered with their coverage of the dissidents but gave them free rein to follow the story wherever it led.

While dissidents made headlines during the early 1970s, American reporters scrambled to cover numerous other developments, particularly after the Nixon-Brezhnev summit and the expansion of détente between the United States and the USSR. Especially newsworthy was the vast influx of American corporate executives seeking to do business with the Soviets. Chase Bank opened a Moscow branch. Pepsi-Cola signed an agreement to build a bottling plant. The Cargill Company, one of the largest grain dealers in the United States, sent salesmen to sell the Russians wheat. Dr. Armand Hammer, playing on his Lenin connection, signed a contract to furnish scientific and technical information in exchange for oil, gas, and metals. Most of the businessmen treated American correspondents with the consideration usually accorded the media in the United States, while others irked the reporters by aping the secrecy and aloofness of their Soviet hosts. As one correspondent put it, "They discovered the SEC rules did not apply in Moscow. Not only did they not answer phone calls but, when confronted, refused to see American reporters."

"They decided that they liked the idea of being met at the airport where their private jets often came in, picked up in Chaika limos with curtains drawn, and whisked off to *dachas* for real serious business discussions. And no press, thank you!" recalled Axel Krause, correspondent for *Business Week* and the McGraw-Hill News Service from 1970 to 1974.

A blunter assessment came from James Jackson:

"American businessmen annoyed us more than the Russians did. They would come in here during the détente period and they'd be willing to overlook anything. We were the enemy because we were critical and skeptical. They were altogether too credulous for our stomachs. There was always a bitterness between the journalists and the businessmen."

Jackson was particularly contemptuous of one company trying to sell the Russians pipeline-laying equipment.

"They knew that slave labor was going to be used. And they would justify it by saying that it was easier on the slave to use the equipment than laying pipe by hand. Most of us found these people to be quite unpleasant representatives of American business."

After Donald Kendall, chairman of Pepsi-Cola, arrived in Moscow to close a bottling plant deal, he met Axel Krause for an interview that began at the Hotel National and continued in a black Chaika limousine as they drove out into the Moscow suburbs. When they arrived at a shabby residential building, Krause was astonished to learn that Kendall was going to have his portrait painted—a gift of the Soviet government.

"This," announced Kendall, "is the way they treat American businessmen."

Donald Kendall invited Krause to continue the interview during the sitting, but the accompanying protocol officer whispered to the executive that that was forbidden. Somewhat embarrassed, Kendall cut off the interview. Krause was hustled into another car and driven back to Moscow.

Axel Krause wrote a story on how American businessmen make deals in Moscow, underscoring the willingness of U.S. executives to operate in secrecy and enjoy the perquisites offered by the Soviets. When it appeared in *Business Week*, there was much unhappiness in some of the best-known boardrooms in the United States.

When Henry Shapiro retired as UPI bureau manager in 1973, he ended a career unique in the history of Moscow reportage. His long stint, with interruptions, spanned almost two thirds of the history of the Soviet Union. Purges, World War II, the Cold War, the Khrushchev era, de-Stalinization, Sputniks and cosmonauts, a Brezhnev decade, détente, dissidents—all were grist for his reporting. His knowledge of men and events was encyclopedic.

A short, round-faced man with bushy eyebrows and large moustache, Shapiro was in many ways the ideal Moscow correspondent. His Russian was fluent, and over the decades he had met and cultivated an extensive network of Russians, some of whom were friends of his wife, Ludmilla. Tireless and tenacious when in pursuit of a story, a demanding taskmaster for his reporters, including me, he was a fierce and intolerant competitor whose ambition always was to beat the Associated Press. And yet many of his colleagues, friends and rivals, envious and curious, wondered why he remained so long in the Soviet Union, whether he had been compromised in some way by the system. CBS correspondent Murray Fromson called Shapiro "a great puzzle."

Henry Shapiro has angrily denied that he had any special relationships with the Soviets, and there is no evidence that he did. The scoops and beats that he regularly obtained, in my judgment, were largely the results of longevity and hard work, not because the Press Department favored him above the other correspondents. As for his long tour of duty, he was more valuable to the UPI in Moscow than anywhere else in the world. And why should he leave? The perquisites were formidable: a car, a chauffeur, a rent-free apartment, a living allowance, an expense account, frequent vacations, and sabbaticals. Moreover, he was so specialized he probably could not have earned his pay in any other assignment—no secret within the UPI.

In Moscow, however, Henry Shapiro was usually but not always invincible. He understood that reporting in Russia was like detective work: Patiently putting the pieces together could give you the big picture. As an example, some of the correspondents were convinced that the Press Department was tipping Shapiro in advance on one of the hottest stories of the 1960s, the Soviet space program. Cosmonauts were launched regularly, executing increasingly complicated missions. And more often than not, Shapiro seemed to know in advance when they would be launched and when they would return to earth, providing UPI with numerous beats, much to the chagrin of the Associated Press. There was no secret to

Shapiro's success, only his intimate knowledge of how the system worked. Before a space launch, he knew that editors on Moscow's newspapers and magazines received an unmarked envelope containing photos and biographies of the cosmonauts that could be opened only if the launching was successful. Shapiro's journalist contacts alerted him to the arrival of the envelope on a Soviet editor's desk, and he was able to report that a launching was imminent. Meanwhile, Ludmilla Shapiro worked as diligently as her husband, accumulating an extensive clipping file on the space program that enabled her to spot references to "Cosmonaut X," a graduate of the Leningrad Advanced Fighters School, married and the father of two, who spoke to a regional Communist Party meeting. The designation X meant that this officer was a future cosmonaut preparing for his flight, usually the next launching. That was the way Henry Shapiro deduced that the Russians would launch the first multimanned capsule in October 1964, and he was correct.

"The Press Department never notified anybody, of course, and when I once called them, they answered, 'You know more about these things than we do,' " Shapiro told me.

For many years, Henry Shapiro was the guardian of the "camp" system, an arrangement launched by Henry Cassidy just before World War II to protect the Associated Press. When he arrived in Moscow in 1940, Cassidy found that Shapiro had set up a news pool under which the few resident correspondents were exchanging copy. Determined to give the UPI some serious competition, Cassidy lured several journalists to his side, dividing the press corps into two camps. The new system made it possible for reporters to deal with the difficulties of gathering and reporting news in Moscow, providing desperately needed allies and support systems. From 1949 to 1953, when only four Western agencies plus *The New York Times* were permitted correspondents, they divided naturally into two competing groups whose members worked together against the other camp. One of the main objectives was to allow one correspondent to get a night's sleep while the other ally was at the Central Telegraph waiting for the morning newspapers. Subsequently, with expansion of the press corps beginning in 1954, a small coterie of "specials" clustered around the rival UP and AP, relying on the agencies for "protection"—that is, assurance they would be informed about any breaking news. This was provided by around-the-clock staffing, or at least for sixteen hours a day, and access to the TASS wire. Over the decades, coalitions were established and remained together, passed on from one generation of reporters to the next. Around the AP and Reuters gravitated *The New York Times,* the *Baltimore Sun,* NBC, and others. The core of the other camp consisted of UPI and AFP, CBS, and the *Herald Tribune.*

Jerrold Schecter, *Time* correspondent from 1968 to 1970, has accused Henry Shapiro of devising and using the camp system as a means of controlling the correspondents, an unfair charge. If Shapiro was to be blamed, so should Eddy Gilmore, AP bureau chief during the Cold War who headed the other camp, with Harrison Salisbury and Andrew Steiger of Reuters as allies. Over the years, Shapiro wooed every newly arrived correspondent and tried to recruit him or her onto his team, offering to share his own vast knowledge of the Soviet Union as an inducement. Like other correspondents, when B. J. Cutler arrived in Moscow, he reluctantly joined the UP camp, although he did not entirely trust Shapiro to share all the news. Some reporters tried to stay neutral and work with both the AP and the UP, but Shapiro refused to cooperate. For him divided loyalty did not exist. Correspondents who did not buy into Henry Shapiro's arrangement risked his rejection and professional ostracism.

The camp system began to unravel after censorship was abolished and the Central Telegraph no longer served as the correspondents' club. Reporters still banded together, but allegiances were largely based on the location of newspaper and network bureaus. Both the AP and UPI moved to the foreign ghetto on Kutuzovski Prospekt. Reuters moved to Sadovaya Samotechnaya adjacent to *The New York Times* bureau. By the time Henry Shapiro left Moscow, the camp system was all but dead.

One of Shapiro's legacies was the dozens of young reporters he trained over the years. Usually they were eager, smart, and ambitious, but on arrival they were not versed in the complexities of Soviet history and politics. He taught them prudence and skepticism, the need to verify information, and awareness that they were awesomely ignorant about the country they were covering. Above all, he taught them to understand that the history of Russia did not begin the day they sat down at the typewriter in the UPI bureau.

"Henry's standards were that you had to be sure of what you were saying, but really sure because Moscow was filled with rumors and we had to check them and double-check them. . . . Accuracy and prudence were Henry's standards. . . . To meet Henry's standards and to beat the AP, that was my goal in life," recalled Robert Korengold, one of the ablest of Shapiro's staffers, who later won a Neiman Fellowship at Harvard.

Other reporters who worked for Shapiro admired his enormous knowledge and remarkable memory for names and dates. When working on a story, they would ask whether this was indeed an important decision by the Kremlin, and he would usually reply that the Russians had decreed something similar in 1962, and in 1959, and in 1938.

"Whenever anyone was tempted to write in a precedent-shattering manner, all you had to do was go in and talk to Henry and he could keep you straight," recalled Christopher Ogden, who worked in the UPI bureau from 1972 to 1974.

Henry Shapiro was secretive, guarding his sources, revealing little even to his own colleagues. In later years he worked alone covering the diplomatic dinners and receptions and the national day parties. He sent junior members of the bureau to cover press conferences and the comings and goings of distinguished visitors whom he later invited to dinner—or who, more often than not, invited him as the dean of the press corps and the legendary Soviet expert.

The difficult and bitter Cold War years spawned a rivalry between Henry Shapiro and Harrison Salisbury that has endured for decades, long after both men had left Moscow. Undoubtedly, Shapiro was jealous over Salisbury's reputation as a Russian expert because of his many years with the *Times*, his Pulitzer Prize, and numerous books on the Soviet Union. Shapiro never published a book and never won a Pulitzer. What probably galled him most was that, despite his longevity in the Soviet Union, he was far less known to the public than Salisbury. Furthermore, Shapiro was thin-skinned enough to take umbrage at what he considered to be a personal slight when Salisbury, in one of his books, described Shapiro's moustache as "Stalinesque." Actually, Shapiro's moustache bore no resemblance to Stalin's.

Indicative of the relationship, Henry Shapiro has even claimed—without apparent evidence—that Harrison Salisbury stole his copy during Nikita Khrushchev's visit to the United States in 1959. As he traveled across the United States, the UPI correspondent had numerous opportunities to chat with the Soviet leader, and since the other reporters knew no Russian, they tried to find out from him what Khrushchev had said.

"I gave them some things, but sometimes I didn't," he told me. "I kept things for myself, for UPI. Salisbury would then run down to the [local] UPI office, read my copy, and phone a story to *The New York Times*, and he put into his story that Khrushchev talked to him."

Ludmilla and Henry Shapiro retired to Madison, Wisconsin, where for a number of years he held a special position in the University's School of Journalism. Their tidy ranch house on Waukesha Street is filled with souvenirs of four decades: thousands of Russian books, handsome silver and brass samovars, icons, posters, rare volumes, and photographs. A farewell gift from Ilya Glazunov, the painter of the Soviet elite, hangs on a wall. It shows a youthful Ludmilla and Henry Shapiro sitting at a window overlooking the towers of the Kremlin, a far different view from what they saw from the UP apartment on Furmanova Street during the Cold War years: two police sedans parked in front of their doorway—day and night.

Reminiscing about the past, Henry Shapiro remembered only the most pleasant times:

"It's been a very interesting, sometimes fascinating experience. I've lived very well. I met good people, bad people. I don't think anyone in the United Press had more front-page stories than I did."

No other foreign assignment embraces a correspondent as totally as does Moscow and Russia, a universe uniquely different from anything experienced before. Many Americans have covered Paris, London, Rome, Tokyo, and New Delhi but have never found those capitals evoking an emotional response that goes deeper than the professional obligation to report. When Eugene Lyons was forced to leave Moscow in 1934, the sad farewell tugged at his heart. Many others, although departing under normal circumstances, have felt the same way. Their attachment is to the Russian people, the stoic, long-suffering people, who are trusting, warm, and outgoing when they permit themselves to be befriended. And then they are friends who are often loyal, intellectually stimulating, and passionately devoted to a journalist who has gained their confidence.

The attachment is strengthened between reporter and Russian to some extent because they share the same system of injustice, coercion, and arbitrary action from which there is no appeal. This helps to create a common bond and sympathy between them not easily defined. In Moscow a correspondent will often shed his professional role to become a helpful human being taking risks for a Russian friend. Axel Krause, for example, smuggled out of the country an article on trends in Soviet cybernetics written by a Jewish cyberneticist who had been banned from his profession. The article was published in the United States. Another correspondent offered to transmit to the West the unpublished poems of Osip Mandelstam, one of the most talented victims of Stalin's purges, but his widow finally decided that they must remain in the Soviet Union. Correspondents often bought clothes for infants, cameras for their parents, perfume, books, records, magazines, medicine, and other gifts, a normal part of human relationships, which in the ambience of the Soviet Union immediately became suspect by the authorities. Some of the actions were not without risk. Peter Osnos, correspondent of the *Washington Post* from 1974 to 1977, did not hesitate to send letters from his Russian friends to relatives outside the country through the U.S. embassy mail room. Correspondents have had the privilege of sending personal mail in this manner since the embassy opened its doors, but sending letters for Soviet citizens was forbidden. Although the letters were supposed to be submitted in open envelopes, the mail clerk often had no time to inspect them all. The letters were sent out of the country in the diplomatic pouch and mailed in Helsinki.

"But the real help you give people in the Soviet Union is simply the day-to-day stuff, going to see them, having a party, bringing food, and buying their paintings, even if you didn't think they were very good," said Axel Krause.

Almost every story covered by an American correspondent in the USSR provides insights into the nature of Soviet society and the character of the Russian people. Although every country is alike in this respect, a reporter working in Moscow must be able to extrapolate a generalization from a single incident, a larger picture from a few stones of the mosaic— and even then, only with caution.

Harry Trimborn, forty-one, of the *Los Angeles Times,* one of the ablest American reporters in the early 1970s, had that faculty. With fifteen years of experience, including an assignment in Vietnam, he brought to Moscow thorough professionalism and a thoughtful approach based on his study of history. For Trimborn, the funeral of Nikita Khrushchev in September 1971 revealed more about Soviet society than any other story he covered during his two years in Moscow. Like the other correspondents, he learned about Khrushchev's death through the grapevine and rushed to the hospital, where he was able to view the open casket in the Hall of Farewell. Khrushchev was dressed in a black suit, black tie, and white shirt. On a black velvet cloth lay his twenty-six decorations, the highest honors of the Soviet state. The only people present were members of his family; his wife, Nina; and the foreign press.

Trimborn was appalled by the way the Soviet government treated Khrushchev.

"Here was a man," he told me, "regardless of his faults, regardless of his mistakes—who was the leader of a powerful nation. He had reached the top. He had been a world figure and the Soviet media and the leadership, they treated him as if he were a nobody."

A few days later, under gray skies and a light rain, he attended Khrushchev's burial at the cemetery of the Novo-dyevichi Monastery, on the banks of the Moscow River, the final resting place of Anton Chekhov, Sergei Prokofiev, and Nadezhda Allilueva, Stalin's second wife. While over a thousand police and KGB agents surrounded the area, the family paid its last respects, ringed by a few close friends and foreign correspondents. For Trimborn, the funeral was more revealing of the system than anything he had experienced in the Soviet Union.

"It demonstrated the fear and lack of confidence and the sense of inferiority that permeates Soviet society—especially the government. They were, in effect, afraid of a dead man they had discredited years and years before. I mean, there was no sense of magnanimity there. . . . It left such a bad, bad taste in my mouth—and I just wrote up a storm about it," said Trimborn.

Harry Trimborn was angry enough to write a lead that he remembered fifteen years later:

Nikita Khrushchev was born a plumber and they buried him today as though he had never been anything else.

For Charlotte Saikowski, a chance encounter illuminated an aspect of Soviet life she had not suspected—that some Russians have an unrealistic and naïve view of their own society and their own freedom of action. One evening in 1972, she attended a public lecture to find out what the official line was on the Strategic Arms Limitation Treaty (SALT) signed in Moscow that day by President Nixon and Chairman Brezhnev. When she got into her Volga automobile after the lecture, two naval officers asked her for a ride. "Why not?" she thought, and she invited them in. They could not believe she was not a Russian, since her Russian was fluent, nor could they believe that she was an *Amerikanka* and a journalist. After she dropped off one officer, she drove the other across Moscow to the suburbs, all the time candidly discussing Stalin, Khrushchev, and political events in the Soviet Union.

"I was intrigued that a naval officer would be willing to talk about these things with an American correspondent in a car," Saikowski recalled.

When they arrived at the officer's apartment house, he invited her to continue the discussion upstairs. After she had determined that he was married, Saikowski accepted. It was already past 10:00 P.M. The officer's wife was dressed for bed when the guest arrived but quickly prepared tea and vodka.

Saikowski, impressed with the officer's gold braid, inquired about his rank.

"*Kapitan.*"

"*Kapitan* of what?"

"Atomic submarine."

Saikowski could not believe her ears.

"You must be kidding!"

"No, I was a captain in the Arctic, but now I work in the Atomic Institute in Moscow."

Charlotte Saikowski was astonished that a man with his background would invite an American journalist to his apartment, but the officer apparently felt no constraints. They drank tea and talked till almost midnight; then Saikowski departed. He accompanied her back to town to show her the route. Before getting out of the car, he asked her when she would return.

"I told him it's not very good for an American journalist to be acquainted with a captain of an atomic submarine, and frankly, it wasn't so good for him, either."

The officer seemed surprised.

"Really?" he asked, as if he could not believe what she was saying, and wondered why they could not continue the relationship.

Charlotte Saikowski never saw him again, but the encounter confirmed her impression that many seemingly sophisticated Russians comprehend neither the restraints imposed by a totalitarian regime on their actions nor the consequences that may result. They are like the peasants visiting Moscow who do not understand that they cannot cross Gorky Street against the lights, as they can the single road in their village. As Saikowski put it, "They don't seem to realize they can get hurt."

On a September evening in 1971, the Great Hall of the Moscow Conservatory was filled to capacity for an extraordinary concert, honoring on his sixty-fifth birthday Dmitri Shostakovich, a survivor of Stalin's harshest criticism and disfavor. Conducted by his son Maxim, the gala performance featured the father's stirring Leningrad Symphony, written during World War II as a musical challenge to the Nazi invaders. Soloist was Mstislav Rostropovich, one of the premier cellists in the world, who had angered the Kremlin when he publicly defended Alexander Solzhenitsyn and sheltered the writer at his country estate.

Present for the occasion was *Chicago Tribune* correspondent James Yuenger, who watched in astonishment as Solzhenitsyn, the nonperson, walked in with his wife. Tense whispers could be heard: "Solzhenitsyn—there's Solzhenitsyn." Heads turned, seeking the bearded face in the crowd. The white, high-ceilinged hall crackled with electricity. Maxim Shostakovich raised his baton, and the concert began.

"We reached the point in the concert," Yuenger recalled, "where you've got this hymn of defiance by a composer, which had been turned into a hymn of defiance by virtue of the presence of the others there against the Soviet regime. Things had turned. It was absolutely crazy and totally Russian."

When the concert ended, the audience rose in a thunderous ovation. Clearly, people were applauding not only the composer, the conductor, and the soloist, but also the dissident writer.

"I walked out of there about three feet off the ground," said Yuenger, "because I never, with the exception of the day my son was born, had such an emotional experience. . . . I think it was the greatest story I ever wrote in my life."

Years later, reflecting on what he experienced that night and what he observed during his Moscow assignment, Yuenger told me he discovered another aspect of Russia, "the sense of the nobility that can exist in a people, a sense of how people sometimes must compromise and yet can remain essentially honorable."

On August 1, 1975, an extraordinary assembly of presidents, prime ministers, premiers, and chancellors met in Helsinki to sign the Final Act of the Conference on Security and Cooperation in Europe. The agreement expressed principles for assuring permanent peace in Europe and confirmed as inviolable the national boundaries drawn up at the end of World War II. The thirty-five signatory countries included the United States, represented by President Gerald Ford, and the Soviet Union, in the person of General Secretary Leonid I. Brezhnev. They also pledged to expand cultural and economic relations, tourism, the freer flow of information, and to respect fundamental human freedoms. Appended to the Final Act of the conference were two "baskets," both strongly pressed by the United States, on human rights and working conditions of journalists. No one doubted that both were aimed directly at the Soviet Union.

When the act was signed, the Moscow correspondents had reason to rejoice. For the first time in its fifty-eight-year history the Soviet government had committed itself publicly to improve the environment in which foreign journalists worked, in effect recognizing the grievances voiced over the decades. The accommodations were considerable, including speedy decisions on visa applications, which would be reviewed "in a favorable spirit"; easing of travel restrictions; provision of greater access to officials; and the right to multiple entry and exit visas for resident correspondents. By signing the act, the USSR also agreed to "reaffirm that the legitimate pursuit of their professional activity will neither render journalists liable to expulsion nor otherwise penalize them. If an accredited journalist is expelled, he will be informed of the reason for this act and may submit an application for examination of his case."

On paper, at least, the Helsinki Accords could usher in a new era for the Moscow correspondents. The provisions in the "basket" represented a significant change in Soviet policy, especially the promise of multiple visas, which meant that the practice of denying a reporter reentry after a vacation or a brief assignment elsewhere would no longer be possible. This tactic had been used to bar Drew Middleton of the *Times* in 1947, Joseph Newman of the *Herald Tribune* in 1949, Daniel Schorr of CBS in 1957, and Raymond Anderson of the *Times* in 1968. Furthermore, a quick departure to a Helsinki hospital with an ailing child would not be delayed by bureaucratic red tape.

To test the new arrangement, four American correspondents applied for multiple visas within one week after the Helsinki Accords were signed, but their applications were rejected by the Press Department. Not until September did the Foreign Ministry agree to issue multiple visas, after negotiations with the American embassy on reciprocal arrangements for Soviet journalists in the United States. The Moscow press corps adopted a "wait and see" attitude on how the Helsinki Accords would be implemented, knowing that the Soviets would twist every clause to their advantage. The skepticism—and fears—were only too soon justified. Within months, the Kremlin made it clear that Russia was not going to be a workers' paradise for foreign correspondents.

10

The Helsinki Accords

After you've covered Moscow, you can cover anything.

James Jackson
UPI, 1969–72
Chicago Tribune, 1974–76

Everybody, when they left, took a piece of Russia with them, and left a piece of themselves behind.

Harry Dunphy
Associated Press
1977–79

AP correspondent George Krimsky handed his blue U.S. passport to the young soldier in the control booth at Moscow's Sheremetyevo Airport. With him was his wife, Paula, holding the hand of their eight-month-old daughter Alissa, who had taken her first steps that day. Krimsky, thirty-two, was abruptly ending a 2½-year assignment on a melancholy note. He was being expelled for unspecified espionage activities and currency violations, the first American correspondent forced to leave in seven years and the first since the Helsinki Accords were signed in 1975.

The soldier thumbed through the passport without looking up, carefully scrutinizing every page.

"This is irregular," he announced. "You cannot leave!"

"What's wrong?"

"Well, your passport says your name is Krimsky, and your exit visa says your name is Krinsky with an 'n.' Because your exit visa does not match your passport, you cannot leave. Step aside!"

Much to the soldier's astonishment, the two Americans burst into uproarious laughter.

"You'd better check with your superior," Krimsky advised him, grinning. The soldier wheeled around and marched to a nearby office. Two minutes later he returned, red-faced, stamped the passports, and said, "Go!"

"It was," recalled George Krimsky, "the ultimate bureaucratic irony."

The Helsinki Accords, designed to improve working conditions of foreign journalists in the Soviet Union, had been in place just over two years. During that time, the Soviet government had taken legal steps to carry out the treaty's requirements. In January 1976, the Foreign Ministry announced travel restrictions would be eased, eliminating the requirement that correspondents were obliged to request permission each time they sought to leave Moscow. Under the new regulations, they had only to advise the Foreign Ministry of their destination and the route to be taken, and if the areas were not closed to foreigners, they could proceed. Except for military zones, travel in the Moscow region was unrestricted, whereas previously reporters could travel only within a twenty-five-mile radius of the city without advance permission. Affected by the new rules were some 250 correspondents representing 180 news organizations from forty countries. Of these, twenty were Americans reporting for fourteen agencies, newspapers, magazines, and networks. In June, a government decree permitted correspondents to bypass the Press Department and deal directly with Soviet officials, a move that could profoundly affect the way journalists worked in the Soviet Union. If this policy were actually implemented, reporters would have access to an entire new world of hitherto inaccessible Soviet diplomats, government officials, ministries, scientific institutions, and the powerful bureaucrats who rule the USSR.

The changes were, indeed, for the better. In the late 1970s American correspondents traveled more widely and more freely than at any time since the early 1930s, when there were virtually no restrictions on the movement of foreign reporters. They fanned out to Murmansk, Irkutsk in eastern Siberia, the Caucasus, Latvia, Lithuania, Birobidzhan, the rarely visited Jewish Autonomous Republic, and the central Asian cities of Alma Ata and Ashkabad; they also took cruises down the Volga to Volgograd and crossed the USSR on the Trans-Siberian Railroad. Arranging trips through Intourist, they traveled in pairs, often with their wives. Local meetings and interviews were frequently made through the Novosti news agency, which many correspondents regarded as a thinly disguised arm of the KGB. Perhaps 40 percent of Soviet territory, however, was closed for military and security reasons to both journalists and diplomats. Border areas came under this category, as well as some of the major ports such as Vladivostok, the home base of the Soviet Pacific Fleet.

The Helsinki Accords, however, had little impact on deeply ingrained Soviet attitudes. Foreign journalists were still regarded as hostile, nosy probers seeking only to portray the negative aspects of life in the USSR. Moreover, the traditional suspicion that all correspondents were spies and therefore fit subjects for surveillance, provocations, and dirty tricks remained unchanged, especially within the KGB. As dissidents and *refuseniks* continued to stand up to Kremlin repression and, consequently, obtained publicity in the world news media, the Soviets constantly violated the spirit if not the letter of the Helsinki Accords. Physical surveillance continued, phones and walls still had ears, and reporters were continually harassed whenever they met with dissidents. Even during their travels, when they were under less stringent observation than in the capital, correspondents were detained by police, trailed by KGB agents, and made to understand that impromptu contacts with Soviet citizens were not favored by the authorities.

To set the tone for the post-Helsinki era, in May 1976 the weekly *Literary Gazette* launched an attack against American correspondents in an effort to discredit them and to warn Russians to stay away from foreign journalists. A publication of the Union of Soviet Writers and a favored vehicle for chastising correspondents, the newspaper accused George Krimsky, Christopher Wren of *The New York Times,* and *Newsweek*'s Alfred Friendly, Jr., of being members of "a vast network of agents in the world of journalism" serving the U.S. Central Intelligence Agency. The charges were based on disclosures in the *Columbia Journalism Review* linking a number of reporters, although not any of the three, to the CIA. In an unprecedented move for a foreign correspondent, Friendly decided to take legal action to force a retraction. With *Newsweek*'s approval, he filed a civil suit in the People's Court of the Dzerzhinsky district, where *Literary Gazette*'s offices were located, suing the newspaper for defamation.

"I was leaving in a few weeks," he told me, "and didn't want to return to Washington to look for a job with the Soviets saying I worked for the CIA. My interest was in making some noise to clear my name."

Under Soviet law, the burden of proof in a defamation case lies with the defendant, and *Literary Gazette* would have had to prove the *Newsweek* correspondent worked for the intelligence agency. A Soviet lawyer who often defended dissidents predicted that the court would not accept the case. The assessment was correct. When Alfred Friendly submitted his complaint, the judge said that he would convene the newspaper's editors to discuss the complaint, but then he stalled for time, knowing that the American was scheduled to finish his Moscow assignment in a few weeks. With the hearing in limbo, Friendly left the country but not before writing the judge requesting that the case go forward. He never received a reply.

As far as Friendly was concerned, his demands were satisfied, "If it ever came to trial, I would have lost. *Literary Gazette*'s charges would have been upheld. It was a gesture. I just didn't want to leave without making some kind of a ruckus."

The first victim of the new Soviet onslaught was George Krimsky, an aggressive, Russian-speaking reporter with many friends and contacts among the Moscow intelligentsia. He was especially close to Andrei Sakharov. As the AP's point man for dissident coverage, he annoyed the KGB, the Foreign Ministry, and the "journalists" at Novosti. What may have tipped the scales was a photo published in *Newsweek* in January 1977 showing historian Andrei Amalrik; Yuri Orlov, a founder of the Moscow chapter of Amnesty International and soon to be arrested; Valentin Turchin, a mathematician and human rights advocate; and other dissidents at a party. In the middle of the group sat George and Paula Krimsky, grinning at the camera. The photos were furnished by the AP to *Newsweek* in New York to illustrate a report on dissidents. Apparently no one at the magazine realized that the man wearing a turtleneck sweater was an American correspondent.

One month later, AP bureau chief David M. Mason was summoned to the Press Department and told that the Soviet government wanted George Krimsky recalled by the agency because he had violated currency regulations and engaged in espionage. Specifically, he was accused of attempting to recruit Soviet citizens by offering them scarce foreign goods such as tape recorders and records. If the Soviets thought that the Associated Press would quietly withdraw Krimsky, they must have been disappointed. Mason phoned AP New York, explaining the situation. The quick response: George Krimsky stays. When Mason communicated the message to deputy press chief Valentin A. Khazov, he was told that the American correspondent would be expelled. The Soviet decision created a furor in the United States. Keith Fuller, AP president, denounced the Soviet move as "a flagrant violation of the Helsinki Agreement as it pertains to news reporters carrying out their missions." In Washington, Secretary of State Cyrus Vance summoned Soviet Ambassador Anatoly Dobrynin to protest the expulsion, unusually high-level intervention on behalf of a reporter. The U.S. Senate passed a resolution condemning the Kremlin's action as a violation of the Helsinki Accords. More annoying for the Soviets than the angry newspaper editorials and the Senate speeches was a brief statement by the State Department announcing the expulsion of a TASS correspondent, Vladimir I. Alekseyev, who had been in Washington less than a year. The Soviet embassy called the expulsion "absolutely groundless" and a violation of the Helsinki Accords!

While George Krimsky was packing his bags, his apartment phone rang incessantly. *Literary Gazette* and *Izvestia* had published articles "unmasking" his nefarious activities and included his home phone number, information normally unavailable to their readers. The obvious intent was to encourage irate Soviet citizens to phone Krimsky to denounce him, but Paula kept a log of the hundreds of calls and found that 75 percent were supportive. A typical caller said, "I'm phoning from a pay phone. I haven't got much time, but I want you to know just don't think poorly of us because of this nonsense in the papers." (click) Many, however, were nasty. One man read a lengthy statement denouncing Krimsky and warning that "we do not tolerate spies." Every time Paula interrupted him, he had to start from the beginning. Another caller, a musician with a jazz combo, asked if Krimsky would render an important service to the Soviet jazz world by delivering a tape made by his group to Ray Coniff.

On the departure day, a large crowd of Krimsky's friends were at the airport to bid farewell: Western correspondents, diplomats, other foreigners, and a few brave Soviets. The KGB was also represented by men in fur hats wearing scarves that shielded their faces. The Krimskys pressed through the throng, touching outstretched hands, exchanging a few words, choking back tears. After a perfunctory baggage inspection, they were pushing through the turnstile when they heard a shout: "Wait! Wait!"

Turning around, George Krimsky saw Andrei Sakharov and his wife, Yelena Bonner, making their way through the crowd. They had come to say good-bye. Across the turnstile, Sakharov planted a kiss on Krimsky's mouth, Russian-style, and thrust an English edition of his book *My Country and the World* into his hands.

David Mason had a look of absolute horror on his face. He was so anxious for Krimsky to depart without incident, he had urged him to leave behind anything that would attract the attention of the Soviets. Mason feared that if Krimsky accepted the book he might not be permitted to depart.

"I looked at Dave and saw his expression, and I thought, this we don't need. We were so weakened by the whole experience, we were so drained by it that I couldn't muster the courage to accept the book," Krimsky recalled.

Krimsky thanked the scientist for the gift and suggested that he give it to Mason, who would arrange delivery. Sakharov looked crestfallen. He had presented the book with something of a flourish in front of an audience and the KGB, but Krimsky had backed off, something that Sakharov, who had risked so much in following his own sense of justice, of right and wrong, could not understand.

"I will regret my decision," George Krimsky told me, "till my dying day."

The book ultimately arrived in New York with a dedication to Alissa from her Grandpa Andrei.

George Krimsky's expulsion was a warning to the correspondents to cool down coverage of the dissidents, but the momentum was irreversible. With the election of Jimmy Carter as president of the United States and his elevation of human rights to the level of international policy, the Kremlin's treatment of dissidents quickly became an issue between the United States and the USSR. President Carter accused the Soviets of violating the Helsinki Accords and infuriated them even more when on February 5, 1977, the day after Krimsky was ordered to leave the Soviet Union, he sent a personal letter to Andrei Sakharov, which he received at the U.S. embassy. Denouncing the message as unacceptable interference in domestic Soviet affairs, the Kremlin swiftly replied by arresting the leading dissidents, including Yuri Orlov; Aleksandr Ginzburg; and Anatoly Scharansky, the spokesman for the dissident community. Police raided their apartments, where they found files documenting human rights violations in the USSR. Despite attacks by the Soviet press and complaints by the Foreign Ministry, the American correspondents energetically continued to report on the dissident movement.

Together with criticism of dissident coverage, the Soviets hurled their customary harpoons at the Americans because of other stories. For example, when Peter Osnos sent a dispatch to the *Washington Post* on Leonid Brezhnev's seventieth birthday festivities, he quoted a tribute from a Communist Party bureaucrat that seventy is only middle age in the Soviet Union. Osnos reminded the general secretary that if he had a really good memory, that kind of praise would give him a chill. Brezhnev himself had similarly toasted Nikita Khrushchev in June 1964 when he turned seventy—and four months later, Khrushchev was removed from his post. Within a week, Osnos was called to the Press Department and scolded for "systematically writing articles of a rudely anti-Soviet nature. . . . You attempt to create a feeling of enmity and disbelief toward our country . . . to worsen Soviet-American relations." Periodically accused of being a CIA agent, Osnos was convinced that he was being readied for some kind of major provocation. Fortunately, his father-in-law, Albert W. Sherer, a U.S. career diplomat and a former ambassador to Czechoslovakia, was appointed to the American delegation to the Helsinki Accords review conference. When he arrived in Belgrade for the meeting, he bluntly told the Soviets that working conditions of foreign journalists in Moscow was on his agenda. "And as you probably ought to know, my son-in-law is a correspondent in Moscow." As Peter Osnos had hoped, he left Moscow on schedule in 1977 on his own, standing up "without their foot in the back of my pants."

Robert Toth, forty-nine, of the *Los Angeles Times* was less fortunate. He, too, was able to leave standing up, but only after a frightening ordeal that sent a cold shiver through the entire Western press corps. An experienced foreign correspondent who had worked in London, covered the Near East, the U.S. State Department, and the White House under President Nixon, Toth's specialty was science reporting, a beat he had covered for three years for the *Herald Tribune*. His undergraduate engineering degree sparked an intense interest in subjects incomprehensible to most of the other American reporters. While they covered dissidents as a political story, Toth tapped them as sources for articles on Soviet science and technology because many had held scientific or engineering positions in major ministries and some of the most important research institutions in the USSR. He was especially close to Anatoly Scharansky, who had been fired from his position at the Institute for Gas and Oil Exploration when he applied for an exit visa to emigrate to Israel.

For three years, Toth traveled widely in the Soviet Union and wrote trenchant stories about his observations in Murmansk, central Asia, Siberia, Baku, and the Baltic states, never once incurring the wrath of the Press Department. One week before his scheduled departure in June 1977, at Scharansky's suggestion, Toth made an appointment with a parapsychologist named Valery G. Petukhov, who had wanted to present him with an English-language copy of research showing a physical basis for extrasensory perception. They met on a busy street, where the Russian handed Toth a package.

"As soon as I received the package, a car drove up and five goons jumped out and grabbed me. The scariest part was driving downtown the wrong way on one-way streets in that tiny Zhiguli sandwiched between two guys in the back. I was holding a jar that I had brought to buy some *smetana* [sour cream] to go with caviar. We were celebrating my child's graduation from eighth grade."

Toth was driven to a police station on Pushkin Street, where a senior KGB officer and a Foreign Ministry official soon appeared. After three hours of questioning, he was finally permitted to phone the U.S. embassy. A consular officer quickly arrived. Then an expert from the Academy of Science examined the package Toth had received and announced it contained research undertaken in a "closed," or secret institute. Toth was in serious trouble.

Robert Toth's ordeal began three days later in Lefortovo Prison, where he was interrogated for three hours in a small, airless room by two KGB officers in civilian clothes. An interpreter provided Toth with a translation of the questions. When the reporter began taking notes, one of the men scolded him, "This is not a press conference, Mr. Toth."

Only after the session was completed was the American reporter given permission to phone the U.S. embassy. The

Russians then told him he could leave but instructed him to return the following day, when the interrogation continued, focusing first on the science stories that Toth had been writing, then on his relations with Anatoly Scharansky.

"I was scared," he told me. "People at the embassy said I could conceivably get two years. . . . The kids were really scared. Paula wanted to chain herself to me so they wouldn't take me inside [Lefortovo]. I went in alone, without a translator or anybody from the embassy. There was no choice."

For the first time in his life, Toth took tranquilizers.

After two days of interrogation, Robert Toth was informed that he could leave the country. The KGB had obtained what it needed from him to build a case against Scharansky, who would be tried a year later on charges of treason. Toth was not expelled. He departed with his family a few days later. All his baggage, papers, notes, photos, and personal belongings passed through customs without inspection under the watchful gaze of the KGB agent who had presented him with the summons to Lefortovo.

Toth's detention was a warning to the Western journalists and their dissident contacts, signaling that they were at the mercy of the KGB, regardless of the Helsinki Accords. Furthermore, the Soviets made it clear that, whatever delicate negotiations were under way with the United States on arms control or trade, treatment of correspondents would be governed mainly by domestic political considerations, the traditional Kremlin policy. Said Toth, "It was a terrible message."

Why did the KGB pick on Robert Toth? After Anatoly Scharansky was released from a prison in 1986 and deported to Israel in exchange for five convicted Soviet Bloc spies, Toth interviewed him. They agreed that one of Toth's reports may have triggered the interrogation by disclosing a contradiction in the Kremlin's policy toward those Jews who were refused exist visas. The Soviets denied visas to many Jews, claiming that they had worked in military or "closed" establishments and had access to secret information. Yet when the Kremlin wanted to buy Western high-tech equipment, these "closed" operations suddenly became nonsecret. As an example, Toth cited the case of Scharansky, who was refused an exit visa on security grounds, but his institute was declassified in an attempt to obtain a British computer.

"So either they were lying or inadvertently publicizing where their secret organizations were. I said they can't have it both ways," explained Toth.

One day after that story was published in the *Los Angeles Times,* an angry IBM salesman phoned Toth to complain that his reporting was hurting business.

"That," said Robert Toth, "was one of my most disturbing experiences in Moscow."

Another victim was Emil Sveilis, who had opened a UPI bureau in Leningrad in 1976 and was greeted by the local TASS correspondent as the successor to John Reed. The warm welcome was brief. Reed's successor was subject to more severe harassment and physical violence than any other American reporting from the Soviet Union at that time. In fact, he is convinced that the KGB tried to kill him.

A hard-driving reporter, born in Latvia during World War II, Emil Sveilis escaped as a child with his mother to Sweden and lived there until 1953, when he was taken to the United States. After college in Pennsylvania, he joined UPI's Washington bureau and was subsequently assigned to the New York cable (foreign) desk and then to Montreal and Stockholm. Under a consular agreement with the Soviets, the U.S. permitted TASS to open a bureau in San Francisco in exchange for an American bureau in Leningrad. UPI decided to seize the opportunity, expecting to expand Soviet coverage and thus enhance the salability of the service.

When Sveilis saw his new apartment in the foreigners' ghetto, he was appalled. It had been unoccupied for four years; the windows were broken and the parquet floor had buckled under snow and ice. Mushrooms were growing in the bathroom. Sveilis painted the apartment, brought in Finnish furniture, and made it habitable by the time his wife and two children arrived. After much argument with the Soviets, he obtained a small office equipped with phones and a telex connected to Stockholm and Moscow. His initial story described the November 7 parade, with the first display of Soviet military hardware in several years. When news of Sveilis' arrival in Leningrad was broadcast on the Voice of America, local dissidents welcomed him. An instant celebrity, he was the only non-Soviet correspondent in the city.

Emil Sveilis immediately began to write the kind of stories the Soviets disliked, stories about everyday life in Leningrad. He was no Soviet expert, far from it, but he had a good eye for detail and simply wrote about the things he saw and did: how he tried to buy a coat hanger, make a spare key for the apartment, purchase gasoline for his Soviet car, and search for a pane of window glass.

"Since I was ignorant about the political repercussions," he told me, "I wrote about the dissidents, shortages, government foul-ups, just general Russian behavior, things I saw on the street like trucks on three wheels with cement blocks in the back to counterbalance the missing wheel."

Although UPI commended Sveilis on his reporting, the Soviets were less enthusiastic, especially about his stories on the dissident community. Then the KGB began a terrifying attempt to frighten him—and his wife, Charlotte—into silence.

In January 1977, Sveilis made an appointment to meet a dissident near the Astoria, Leningrad's best-known hotel. After parking his blue Zhiguli car near two militiamen on duty at the entrance, he walked to the meeting place. Sveilis waited for half an hour, but no one appeared. Returning to the car, he found that the steering wheel was not turning properly. Sensing that there might be trouble, he inspected the front tires and found that a wheel had been changed, carrying a totally bald tire secured with a single lug nut screwed on by one-quarter inch. Since his homeward route crossed four bridges and took four sharp turns, as soon as he would have turned the wheel, the pressure would have snapped off the nut and the car would have veered into the Neva River. He could easily have been killed. The warning was clear: Stay away from the dissidents. Undaunted, the UPI reporter continued to cover their activities. After the car incident, the beatings began, usually at night when he met dissidents in outlying neighborhoods. He was once attacked by a gang of five thugs. Three beat him on the stomach, back, and legs, where there would be no marks, while the others watched in silence.

"I had to struggle to get home," Sveilis recalled.

The KGB then turned to Charlotte Sveilis, who was employed as a clerk in the U.S. consulate. One afternoon, when she finished work, she took a taxi that had been ordered by the Soviet switchboard operator. After she got into the cab and gave the driver her address, she noticed that the doors had no handles. Her apprehension was confirmed when the car crossed Leningrad in the direction opposite from her destination. For the next 2½ hours, Mrs. Sveilis was a prisoner in the taxi, unable to escape or call for help. Finally the driver took her to a deserted dock area, where he parked the car and turned off the lights. He looked over his shoulder, smiled, and said in English, "Well?"

"Well what?" she replied. She did not know whether she would be raped, attacked, or killed.

The driver then drove around Leningrad for another forty-five minutes, picking up two men who sat down on either side of her without saying a word. Charlotte Sveilis was finally driven home at 10:00 P.M., having left the office at 5:30 P.M.

The kidnapping of Charlotte Sveilis was the first time the Soviets had harassed the spouse of an American correspondent in such a flagrant manner. When the news reached Moscow, the Western press corps was deeply disturbed. All the married reporters suddenly felt vulnerable. An angry U.S. embassy protest to the Foreign Ministry produced no response, but the KGB left Mrs. Sveilis in peace afterward.

Sveilis was not deterred by the pressures; they just made him angry. "In my mind," he recalled, "I was saying, I'll show you guys. It made me more determined. . . . If the Russians had left me alone, I would have caused them fewer problems. It became almost a game."

The game ended for Emil Sveilis in June 1978, when UPI decided to close the Leningrad bureau, concluding that it was too expensive to maintain and that many of the stories generated by Sveilis could have been handled by Moscow. Moreover, with the lifting of travel restrictions, UPI reporters could visit the Baltic republics—part of Sveilis' beat—as frequently as he could. With the growing importance of eastern and southern Africa for news stories, UPI would use the Leningrad budget to open a bureau in Nairobi.

The UPI correspondent was not sorry to leave. Toward the end of his tour, he was deeply worried that he might be forced to go through the same ordeal as Robert Toth.

"When my time was drawing to a close and knowing how much they disliked me, how nervous they were about me, I became completely paranoid. I wouldn't go anywhere, wouldn't do anything. I didn't stop filing, but I didn't write anything about sensitive matters. I just used the official stuff."

Ten years have passed since Emil Sveilis filed his last dispatch from Leningrad. Both AP and UPI have no interest in opening a bureau there, and it's doubtful if either agency ever will. In the meantime, TASS continues to operate a two-man bureau in San Francisco, probably one of the most desirable assignments in Soviet journalism.

Back in Moscow, the harassment continued, but in subtler and more sophisticated forms. In a burst of creative imagination, the State Radio and Television Committee (Gosteleradio) brought a civil suit against Harold Piper of the *Baltimore Sun* and Craig Whitney of *The New York Times* for "spreading slander injurious to the honor and dignity of the Television Committee in the foreign press." The basis for this unprecedented legal action was curious, indeed. A firebrand dissident named Zviad Gamsakhurdia had publicly exhorted his compatriots in the fiercely nationalistic republic of Georgia to reject Russification of their proud and ancient culture. Moreover, he dared proclaim that U.S. intervention would be welcome to help Georgia secede from the Soviet Union. This was strong stuff for the KGB. In April 1977, Gamsakhurdia was arrested. Thirteen months later, at a trial closed to the Western press, he was sentenced to three years in prison and two years of internal exile, a relatively mild sentence. Shortly thereafter, Gamsakhurdia appeared on national television in a 3½-minute "interview," astonishing everyone who knew him by recanting all his previous views. Intrigued by the reversal, Whitney and Piper flew to Tbilisi, Georgia's capital, to try to find out what really happened. They interviewed Soviet newspaper editors about the trial, members of Gamsakhurdia's family, and his friends. Their conclusion: There was insufficient evidence to determine that he had or had not genuinely recanted. This balanced evaluation irked the Soviets because when the correspondents' dispatches were published, they were immediately broadcast by the Voice of America. Millions of Russians for the first time heard a report on the story that was not the official party line, a development, said Whitney, that "forced the official hand against us."

Responding to a summons, Harold Piper and Craig Whitney, accompanied by U.S. Consul Richard T. Carter, were led into the chambers of Judge Lev Y. Almazov on June 28, 1978. The judge read Gosteleradio's complaint, which demanded a published retraction of the articles. He set July 5 as the trial date and ordered that a written response and a list of witnesses be submitted by the defense on June 30. With that statement, the judge walked out of the room, leaving behind copies of the complaint for Harold Piper and Craig Whitney to acknowledge by signing a receipt. After arguing with the court clerk, Piper and Whitney declined to sign but instead wrote their own statements, saying they were refusing to acknowledge the complaint and were not obligating themselves to appear at the trial. On June 30, the Americans returned to court to inform Judge Almazov that they had not had sufficient time to determine their course of action and presented no list of witnesses. Almazov granted them an extension to July 3 to submit arguments, two days before the trial date.

In the meantime, the U.S. government forcefully signaled its displeasure to the Soviets. President Carter canceled the sale of a Univac computer to TASS. Secretary of State Cyrus Vance summoned Ambassador Anatoly Dobrynin to his office to read him a stern lecture on the unfavorable impact such a trial would have on American public opinion and U.S.-Soviet relations. Furthermore, three Soviet correspondents were called into the State Department for a "review" of their accreditation, implying that if any action was taken against Harold Piper and Craig Whitney, they could start packing. Four other Soviet journalists were called to the White House for a meeting with Deputy Press Secretary Walter Wurfel. The message to the Kremlin was clear: The United States was taking a dim view of this unusual Soviet tactic to intimidate American reporters.

With both Harold Piper and Craig Whitney out of the country on vacation, the trial was held on July 18. Zviad Gamsakhurdia appeared briefly to repeat his earlier recantation. The two Americans were found guilty *in absentia,* ordered to publish retractions in the Soviet press and in their newspapers, and fined 2,289.07 rubles (about thirty-five hundred dollars). A. M. Rosenthal, executive editor of the *Times,* had already decided that the newspaper would pay the fine under protest. Neither newspaper published a retraction.

In retrospect, Whitney said he believed that Gamsakhurdia had actually recanted, despite what his friends and relatives thought.

"It's clear that the guy had confessed because he did so again at our trial," he said. "I suppose in one sense, you could argue the Soviets were right in that case to sue us given that the articles were wrong.

"It was a stressful experience because we didn't know exactly which way it would turn out—maybe we'd end up in jail, but we got through it."

When the incident was closed, a Press Department official told the two reporters that they were spared expulsion because they had paid their fines, and "in the interest of developing Soviet-American relations" were being let off with a warning.

The warning did not deter the American correspondents from tenaciously covering the story of the dissidents or other sensitive, newsworthy developments. Proof of their professional effectiveness was the ongoing criticism by the Soviet press of their efforts following the Piper-Whitney trial. *Pravda* sharply attacked Robin Knight, a British citizen working for *U.S. News & World Report,* for an article on racism in the Soviet Union. Seven months later, Knight was drugged and his wife sexually molested on a tourist trip to Tashkent. Soon afterward, the newspaper *Sovietskaya Rossiya* accused Kevin Klose of the *Washington Post* of having "close contacts" with U.S. intelligence following publication of a story on Soviet oil production. Anthony Austin, a Russian-speaking correspondent of *The New York Times,* was castigated by *Literary Gazette* for a magazine piece on his four years in the Soviet Union. In May 1982, Ann Garrels of ABC News was deprived of her accreditation and ordered to leave the Soviet Union. She had recently been rebuked by *Literary Gazette* for suggesting official complicity in the theft of her purse while visiting Russian friends in Kiev. *Newsweek*'s Andrew Nagorski was expelled in August, charged with impersonating a Soviet editor during a trip to Siberia. Harassment continued to be an occupational hazard in covering Russia. The Soviets hoped that by using these tactics they could intimidate reporters and consequently influence the coverage. For the most part they were wrong. Despite the Kremlin's efforts, few correspondents were cowed.

During the trying years of the 1970s, as in the past, the U.S. embassy served as a bastion of support, underscoring an affinity between reporters and diplomats unmatched anywhere else in the world. Ever since 1934, when the embassy first opened its doors, there has been a closeness in personal and official relationships between the two professions engendered by a hostile society that regards members of both as spies. In addition, Moscow's ideological and geographic isolation from Europe, coupled with the tiny number of diplomats and journalists (there were probably less than 150 in residence through the mid-1960s) and restrictions on social intercourse with the Soviets brought the American community even closer together. Joseph E. Davies, a Democratic politician who served as President Roosevelt's envoy from 1936 to 1938, courted the journalists, often relying on them for advice, much to the annoyance of his own staff. When he brought his yacht into

Leningrad harbor, he invited the Americans to a "press party," which produced no news, but everybody had a grand time. During the purges of the 1930s, Davies often interceded, unsuccessfully, on behalf of Soviet citizens working for reporters. He was able to obtain an exit visa for Edmund Stevens' Russian-born wife, Nina, directly from Maxim Litvinov by asking for a final favor at a farewell party prior to his departure from Moscow.

During the early days of World War II, with the Germans nearing Moscow, Ambassador Laurence Steinhardt ordered all American correspondents to have a bag packed and to be prepared to leave Moscow on three hours' notice. He even set up an evacuation tent city outside the capital for Americans. The encampment was never used, since the Soviets ordered the entire foreign colony moved to Kuibyshev. In return for the embassy's solicitude, when correspondents were finally permitted to visit the battlefields, they frequently described what they had seen to the American military attachés. Sometimes their views were not appreciated. On his return from Stalingrad, convinced that the Red Army would crush the Germans and go on to defeat Hitler, Henry Shapiro sought to share his observations with a U.S. military attaché—who refused to see him.

"What does Shapiro know about these things?" he asked another American correspondent.

In the Cold War years, the embassy served as a haven for the four American correspondents married to Russians who were forced to remain in Moscow, offering sympathy for their plight but little else. During the height of press attacks against reporters as spies in 1952, embassy officials warned both Henry Shapiro and Harrison Salisbury that they might serve as the accused in a show trial on the scale of the great extravaganzas of the 1930s. Joseph Stalin's death in March 1953 may have spared them.

When Charles E. Bohlen arrived in 1953 as the U.S. envoy, he ran a hospitable embassy as far as the correspondents were concerned. Not only did he inaugurate a weekly briefing for American reporters but also a Sunday night poker game, frequently held in the small salon at Spaso House. Bohlen further endeared himself to the reporters by giving them limited but welcome access to the embassy commissary, the result of an encounter with B. J. Cutler.

At an embassy party he asked Cutler, who had just arrived, how he was getting along.

"I'm starving to death," Cutler replied without blinking, "I'm six feet tall, weigh 128 pounds, and could be a credible famine victim."

"Don't you have access to the commissary?" asked the ambassador.

"No, sir, they beat us away with sticks," replied Cutler.

Ambassador Bohlen immediately turned to Rollie White, his administrative officer, and instructed him to admit the correspondents. Rations were limited, but access to American canned goods and staples made a big difference in family diets.

"My dying-swan act made it possible," recalled Cutler, "but Henry Shapiro was first on line the first day the commissary opened. Nina Stevens was right behind him."

In addition to being a home away from home, the embassy provided correspondents with a range of services not available to U.S. citizens in any other foreign country. For example, in addition to the privilege of sending and receiving mail through the diplomatic pouch, an embassy physician—a military officer—was available to American reporters and their families. Many a child had a splinter removed, cuts stitched, or colds treated by the doctor, with medicine provided at government expense. During one cutback period in late 1972, the commissary officer barred reporters from buying fresh milk delivered from Helsinki. He was overruled by the doctor, who said that American children must not be deprived of Finnish milk because "Russian milk is so lousy."

Thanksgiving dinner in the spacious white-walled dining room/salon of Spaso House, the residence of United States ambassadors since the 1930s, more than anything else epitomized the closeness of the American community in Moscow. Under the great crystal chandeliers, an eye-boggling assortment of delicacies flown in from military commissaries in West Germany were displayed on a buffet table thirty feet long: luscious stuffed turkeys, bowls of cranberry sauce, candied sweet potatoes, green salads, mounds of assorted fruit unavailable in Moscow, bananas, oranges, tangerines, pineapples, grapefruit—and pumpkin pies. For many years, most of the guests were diplomats and correspondents, their wives and children and occasionally a handful of Soviets. These were augmented by American businessmen beginning in the 1970s and 1980s. I attended four Thanksgiving dinners, each time departing with a sense that I was leaving a tiny island of security and returning to a cold and hostile world.

Ambassador Charles Bohlen's weekly off-the-record briefing for reporters has become a Moscow tradition, but its value always depended on who was doing the briefing. As a rule, ambassadors did not reveal information that was not already known to the correspondents. More experienced diplomats like Bohlen, his successors Llewellyn E. Thompson, Walter Stoessel, and, more recently, Arthur A. Hartman, an appointee of President Reagan, were helpful in evaluating Soviet policies or would comment—without attribution—on their significance. Thompson, normally extremely cautious, once deliberately leaked a story to the American correspondents about bread riots in the southern city of Novocherkassk. Although the story was confirmed by Soviet journalists, not a single American newspaper or agency correspondent reported the riots for fear of expulsion. Bohlen, an articulate man with a gift for the colorful phrase, in a moment of candor told reporters why it was so difficult to understand "what's going on inside the Kremlin."

"It's like watching ten men wrestling under a rug. All you know is that there's a lot of action going on there, but you don't know who's on top—or who's on bottom."

Some ambassadors tried to obtain information from the correspondents during the briefing, but reporters were reluctant to respond. Nobody wanted to share news or views with the competition present. The briefings were occasionally so boring and uninformative that correspondents considered them a waste of time. At one meeting with Ambassador Jacob Beam, who had served in the embassy previously, Edmund Stevens fell asleep and began to snore—until Beam paused and the snoring reverberated through the office. The laughter of the reporters awakened Stevens.

Why the KGB repeatedly used enticements and traps to obtain information on these meetings was difficult to understand.

At a lower level, correspondents often sought the assessments of the agricultural attachés, who traveled widely in the grain-producing regions of the country and who were exceptionally well informed about crop conditions, grain production, breeding experiments, and Soviet agricultural policy. Fred Coleman of *Newsweek,* however, found that the Chinese embassy was the best source on wheat crop projections, usually coming within one percentage point of the official result. The big mystery in Moscow was how the Chinese could predict the harvest with such accuracy since, during the 1970s, the Soviets severely restricted the travel of Peking's diplomats. The joke around town was that the Chinese planted some sample seeds in the embassy garden and based their forecasts on how well they grew.

On economic and business stories, reporters often turned to specialists in the American embassy who followed the ups and downs of the Soviet economy. These were career foreign service officers who read the industry newspapers and journals, the scholarly studies, the heavy (and usually boring) professional publications, who regularly visited the shops and markets to note prices of food and merchandise, and who met with American executives doing business with the Soviets. When rehearsals began for the big military parade on November 7, tanks, missile launchers, self-propelled cannons, and other equipment would rumble down Gorky Street and along the embankments. Then the correspondents would turn to the military attachés, who monitored this activity for information on anything new that might be unveiled on Red Square. On the day itself, the reporters would ask the air attachés if there were new aircraft models in the flyovers.

Despite their occasional utility as sources of specialized

information, embassy officials usually possessed less knowledge about Soviet life than the reporters did. The American correspondents had greater contact with Soviet citizens, traveled more widely, and were under less surveillance. Only during World War II, when Averell Harriman was U.S. ambassador, was the embassy better informed about political developments than the press corps was. During the Cold War years both diplomats and correspondents were reduced to almost total isolation, and therefore total ignorance, about the events of Stalin's final years. Beginning with the Khrushchev era, the information balance began to shift to the correspondents and has remained there ever since.

A healthy skepticism by the correspondents was always essential in dealing with the American embassy. Despite what the Soviets believed, the reporters were not agents of the U.S. government, nor were they puppets who transmitted without question the official Washington line. For example, in October 1970 a light aircraft with two U.S. generals aboard flew along the Soviet border from a Turkish base and landed accidentally at a Soviet airfield. The Americans were held in custody for over two weeks before being released. As the embassy explained it, they had mistaken the Soviet airfield for a Turkish airfield. Harry Trimborn of the *Los Angeles Times* expressed his doubts to Boris Klosson, a senior embassy official, as to whether the incursion was due to pilot error. He asked Klosson how the pilot could fail to see the difference between a Turkish town with a small population and a very large Soviet city with an enormous population as described in the *Encyclopaedia Britannica*.

Snapped Klosson, "I don't care what the encyclopedia says—they made a mistake."

With the U-2 flight in mind, Trimborn remained unconvinced and made that point in his story.

Nor was the embassy always helpful, as James Gallegher of the *Chicago Tribune* discovered. Before departing on a trip organized by the Press Department to Uzbekistan in central Asia, the first such trip since the Soviet invasion of Afghanistan, he obtained from an embassy official the name and telephone number of a local contact, a woman in Tashkent. When some of the correspondents called on her, she announced that she had been an information source for many of their colleagues over the years, and since "I knew you were going to ask me a lot of questions about Afghanistan, for the last few days I've been listening to the Voice of America so I'd have something to tell you."

In the cautious interplay between the ambassador and correspondents, the reporters occasionally permitted themselves to be used. One of the experts in this game was Malcolm Toon, who served from 1977 to 1979. An outspoken, acerbic career diplomat, he was appointed by President Gerald Ford and found himself out of tune with the administration of Jimmy Carter. When Toon's cables were ignored by the White House and the State Department, he voiced to correspondents frankly and *on* the record, although without attribution, his concern about U.S. policy toward the Kremlin, giving them a more realistic appraisal of Soviet intentions than the somewhat rosier views entertained by Secretary of State Cyrus Vance. The combined power of *The New York Times*, the *Washington Post*, *Newsweek*, *Time*, the wire services, and the networks to place before Congress and the U.S. public some of Ambassador Toon's thoughts was awesome.

"Congress would look up and call the State Department or the White House and say, 'What's happening there?' That's how Toon got attention," recalled Fred Coleman, *Newsweek* bureau chief from 1976 to 1979.

During the period of extreme harassment, when American correspondents were subjected to almost daily arrests, beatings, and intimidation, the embassy probably delivered more protests, verbal and written, to the Soviet government than at any time in the over forty years of United States-USSR diplomatic relations. Whenever a reporter was arrested or detained, an embassy official rushed to see him, often in vain. For example, in 1970, four Americans covered a protest by two Italians who chained themselves to a department store railing and tried to distribute leaflets urging the release of dissidents. KGB agents shoved the reporters into an office and held them for several hours. U.S. Consul William Farrand argued with police outside the door but was not permitted to enter. The Americans were finally released to file their stories, but a quickly delivered U.S. protest note to the Foreign Ministry was just as quickly rejected. A few months later, when James Peipert of the AP and Andrew Waller of Reuters were summoned to KGB headquarters for questioning in connection with the arrest of dissident philologist Vladimir I. Bukovsky, the embassy sent an official to accompany them. Through its spokesman in Washington, the State Department reinforced the embassy action with a protest to the Soviet ambassador. Although the protests, the notes, and official announcements seemed to have little impact on the Russians, the correspondents were gratified that their government was standing behind them.

"It's extremely important for the correspondents to know that there's an American government out there helping you," Fred Coleman has observed.

"There are physical dangers involved in the Moscow assignment, though limited. Chances are if you end up in a Soviet jail, you're going to be pretty well treated. I would rather be in jail in Moscow than in Uganda. Nevertheless, the only protection you have as a journalist without diplomatic immunity is the amount of pressure the American government is willing to exert on a reciprocal basis.

"So if the Soviets hassle an American correspondent in Moscow, it's useful to know that the administration in Washington is willing to do something in return, that tells them that if you throw this guy out, we'll throw out three correspondents. That works."

James Gallegher's Volvo station wagon pulled up in front of the customs post on the Soviet-Finnish border. The Galleghers had just returned from a vacation/shopping trip in Helsinki, and the car was loaded with food. A stern-faced woman inspected the cargo and trumpeted, "Fruit! Fruit not allowed!" Only bananas could be legally brought into the Soviet Union by private individuals, she explained. When the fruit was off-loaded, she saw three small, anxious faces in the back of the car.

"Is this fruit for children to eat on trip to Moscow?" she asked.

"Yes," replied Gallegher.

"Put back in car," she ordered. "Soviet Union does not deprive children of fruit."

Gallegher, correspondent for the *Chicago Tribune*, drove off with a new insight into the Soviet mentality. Like a good reporter, he filed the incident away for future use.

Unlike the families of correspondents in Paris, London, and Tokyo, children and wives were always more than just dependents in Moscow. Serving as connections with Soviet society, they gave reporters insights into the nonpolitical side of Russian life, into the world of babies and mothers, schools, games, shopping, clothes, diapers, grandmothers, and parenthood. They established contacts and evoked perceptions that enriched the reporters' output. When Gallegher took his three boys to Gorky Park for an afternoon of ice skating, they played with Russian children while he chatted with the parents. Harry Dunphy of the AP often took his kids to the circus or the puppet theater, where he met doting Russian papas and mamas and their little ones. Over the decades, many children of American correspondents went to Russian schools, acquiring fluency in Russian and a kindling of interest in Soviet affairs. Others went to summer camp with Russian children and came home with stories about their friends and their lives.

When I first wheeled my two-month-old daughter in a blue plaid stroller near Red Square, within minutes we were stopped by an anxious grandmother who warned that if Fern continued to lie on her stomach, she would surely choke to death. A well-dressed man wanted to know where he could buy a similar stroller. He was disappointed when I told him that I had bought it in New York. Having Fern in Moscow gave me material for at least one UPI story a month. A feature on my unsuccessful search for diapers earned worldwide play and plaudits from editors in New York.

If the children were old enough to understand, their

parents educated them about the country they were living in, the do's and don'ts of a totalitarian society. For many of the youngsters, surveillance became a game. The Sveilis boys, Kurt, seven, and Jon, nine, sitting in the backseat of the family car, recorded the license numbers of the KGB vehicles that followed them. The same numbers appeared over and over again. Ultimately, Sveilis was able to report that he had been followed forty-eight times during his twenty-two-month tour. The children of CBS correspondent Murray Fromson used mimicry to signal which of his dissident contacts was on the phone. If ballet dancer Valery Panov was on the line, Fromson's daughter Lisa would hold her arms above her head; if it was dissident Pyotr Yakir, she would pretend to swing a badminton racket, playing his favorite sport. Fromson filmed one of her performances for broadcast on CBS television.

Over the years, about two hundred children of American correspondents lived in Moscow, ranging from infants to teenagers. Some children enrolled in Soviet kindergarten and grade schools, while others attended the Anglo-American school staffed by professional teachers brought in from abroad. The Sveilis boys attended an "international" school with eleven other pupils taught by two teachers in the basement of the American consulate in Leningrad. Some children had access to better facilities. Edmund Stevens' daughter Anastasia was admitted to the Bolshoi Ballet School and graduated as an accomplished performer. My daughter, then three, attended a Moscow kindergarten and learned the most important lesson on the first day: Unless she brought her own toilet paper, like the other children, she would be obliged to use the official newspaper of the Communist Party of the USSR.

Life in Moscow was not easy for the children. In the 1950s and 1960s, many families were lodged in hotel rooms equipped with hot plates and imported refrigerators. Over time they moved into apartments furnished with Danish or Finnish furniture where they lived comfortably, enjoying the amenities of imported food and Soviet culture, such as the circus, the puppet theater, ice skating, and the loving care of

Russian *babushkas* (grannies). Whether American children could play with Russian friends and schoolmates often depended on the state of relations between the United States and the USSR. Correspondents with children tried to be good parents and responsible professionals, but because of the work load the parental side sometimes suffered. A reporter often spent ten to fourteen hours a day on the job with no time off, a hostage to the news, little changed from the era of Walter Duranty and Eugene Lyons. What time remained was devoted to the family.

"Looking back on it," recalled Robert Toth, "you weren't spending enough time with the kids. It's a seven-day-a-week job. You're always in the office looking at TASS. Even when you go out to dinner parties, someone has your number to call in case anything broke. Sure you had kids, but it cost."

A price was also paid by the married couples. The strain of living in a hostile environment; the surveillance; the long winter that began in mid-October and ended in May; a grim, dreary city; the language barrier; and the lengthy absence of a husband could wreak havoc on a marriage. Some wives, after a few months in Moscow, packed their bags and returned to England or Germany with the children to wait for the end of the spouse's tour. Many marriages ended in divorce, usually after the couple left Moscow. At the same time, other reporters felt that their marriages were strengthened when both partners responded to the challenge and the opportunity to discover a strange and fascinating society, a rich culture, and a diverse people. A number of wives had prepared themselves for the assignment by studying Russian. Susan Osnos shared Russian lessons with her husband at the University of Michigan, while others studied the language when they arrived in Moscow. Each followed a different path, depending on personal interests. Evelyn Milks, wife of the AP bureau chief, ignored the Soviet Union. After she had been installed in the AP apartment, she hunted out other wives and played interminable bridge games for the 3½ years of her husband's tour. She could hardly wait to leave. Heidi Whitney, on the other hand, traveled widely with her husband and saw almost as much of the Soviet Union as he did. Carol Cutler, wife of the *Herald Tribune* correspondent, organized his office, kept his files, and became totally involved in his work. Paula Krimsky picked up Russian quickly and made her own Russian women friends whom she would see frequently, including the wives of dissidents. She also kept up with Moscow's turbulent art world, regularly visiting the museums, going to the theater, and attending concerts. Ludmilla Shapiro, who during the war tracked the course of battle in the UP bureau at the Metropole, continued to assist her husband until his retirement, a valuable collaborator with literary and family connections among the Moscow intelligentsia. The other Russian wife, Nina Stevens, was less interested in working with her husband than in buying icons and dissident art and selling both in the United States.

Axel Krause has described covering Moscow as a cooperative family effort unique among journalism assignments. Unlike reporting from another world capital, Moscow involved wives and children. "And when your wife is sharing your reporting assignment with you, I think you become a better correspondent. . . . Because we shared the involvement, our marriage was strengthened. We functioned as a team."

The second decade of Leonid Brezhnev's regime was marked by a vast increase in Soviet military power and by growing and grave economic problems. Production fell short of planned goals in agriculture, heavy industry, transport, housing, and consumer goods. Meat supplies were so low that in May 1976 meatless Thursdays were proclaimed for Moscow. Brezhnev's relentless military buildup stirred a counterbuildup in the United States, but the 1979 invasion of Afghanistan effectively terminated the remnants of détente and provoked angry reactions in the West and in the Moslem world. At home, despite the KGB, the social fabric began to unravel: Corruption reached into the upper levels of the government and the party, even to the family of Brezhnev himself; alcoholism, a national scandal and the traditional Russian scourge, became even more widespread. Absenteeism; waste; crime; black-

marketeering; the nagging, draining war; and plunging productivity all gnawed away at Soviet pride and confidence.

For American correspondents, the Brezhnev era presented
a rich menu of stories, not always easily accessible but available
to the aggressive and resourceful reporter. Exploiting the new
opportunities offered by the Helsinki Accords, even though
hindered by official reluctance to abide by their spirit, the
correspondents pried open some of the hitherto unexplored
aspects of Soviet life. And there were more correspondents
than ever before to do the prying. From 1972 to 1982 the
number of American correspondents had increased from
eighteen to twenty-five (including TV technicians), a new
high, representing seventeen newspapers, radio and TV networks, magazines, and agencies. Many of them discovered
what William Henry Chamberlin had learned fifty years
earlier: Only through travel, by escaping from Moscow, was it
possible to understand the Soviet Union. See the USSR in all
its diversity, from the permafrost regions of the Arctic to the
subtropical climes of Georgia on the Black Sea, from the
central Asian cities of Tashkent, Bokhara, and legendary
Samarkand to the Baltic ports of Riga and Tallinn. Be
prepared for adventures, the unexpected, the fortuitous
encounter with Soviets who had never seen a foreigner, much
less an American, willing, even eager to talk about life, and
then move on, never to meet again. Be ready to pick up the
little mosaic stones that help portray the Big Picture and to
save strings for future stories.

James Gallegher was an energetic traveler, probably more
than the accounting department at the *Chicago Tribune* would
have preferred. His frequent traveling companion was Robert
Gillette of the *Los Angeles Times*.

"We were illiterate in an understandable way," recalled
Gallegher, "but we did all right."

On a trip to central Asia, for example, the two reporters
were grounded at a small airport when fog blanketed their
scheduled stop at Kazan. Within a short time, every aircraft
headed for that city landed at the airport, discharging hundreds of passengers. Gallegher and Gillette spent twenty-four

hours talking to people and taking notes. They met soldiers just discharged from the army; they played tabletop soccer with a variety of garrulous opponents. They encountered a man who was so drunk he could hardly stand erect. When they told him they were Americans, he started telling them how much he loved America. But when he confided that he worked at a submarine installation near Arkhangelsk, his comrades dragged him away.

Said Gallegher with a smile, "That night alone was worth five years of seeing what the country was like."

On the same trip, Gillette and Gallegher picked up a hitchhiker on the road to the Kazan airport, a young man who talked candidly about the sex life of Soviet youth, including his own. At the airport they saw customs guards order the young man off the line at the security checkpoint and feared that he was being detained because they had given him a ride. When they boarded the plane, they found the Russian already seated and chuckling to himself. It seemed that in his travels he had acquired a foil-wrapped condom made in the United States. When the security guard inspected his baggage, the suspicious-looking item was discovered and opened. The inspector thought the package was an explosive device.

Even officially sponsored trips could yield unexpected results. When Emil Sveilis visited Murmansk, he was probably the first American reporter to see the gravesites of Allied servicemen killed during the perilous wartime run to the Arctic port. In May the snow was still seven feet deep, but a shovel crew had uncovered all forty-two graves and placed fresh flowers on each. Sveilis had also requested interviews with veterans of World War II who had survived the German attacks. Murmansk municipal officials had rounded up a dozen old men who were unusually candid about what they had seen. One veteran described the German bombing attacks, but continuing his narrative, he went on to describe how many Russians had collaborated with the invaders.

"They blew up trains right here in the port," he said. "Right on those tracks over there seventeen freight cars loaded with ammunition exploded and the whole port went up in flames."

Embarrassed by the veteran's candor, the interpreter and officials from the mayor's office tried to hush him, questioning his memory.

"Oh, shut up," insisted the old man, "I know what I'm talking about."

The other veterans shouted agreement: "Yes, our people collaborated with the Germans!"

Emil Sveilis had his story.

Taking risks has been a traditional occupational hazard for Moscow correspondents. Either the risk involved filing a story without being able to obtain official confirmation or in filing a story the Soviets regarded as unfavorable. During the Brezhnev era, except for a few reporters on their second tour, many correspondents were on the scene who had never felt the heavy hand of Glavlit, working as they had in Washington, London, or Paris. As a result, risk-taking became more common, especially in covering the dissidents and using them as valuable sources of unofficial information on Soviet society.

For example, James Yuenger had to make a risky choice one night. He had met a dissident source for what was described as "an important story" that turned out to be so routine that Yuenger could not use it. Undiscouraged, the dissident told him about "Abel, *shpion*," the spy who was exchanged for U-2 pilot Francis Gary Powers. Rudolf Abel was dead. Yuenger's Russian was not good enough to understand the cause of Abel's demise, so the dissident drew a sketch of lungs and covered them with little pencil marks. Rudolf Abel had died of cancer—a big story, but should Yuenger go with it?

The choice for James Yuenger was one that a Moscow correspondent often confronted. He had a story, not world-shaking, but of more than passing interest in the United States. To obtain confirmation was impossible. Although Abel was a longtime underground KGB agent in the United States and convicted for espionage, it was unlikely that the Soviet government would comment on the news. Should he take the risk of moving the story? In Moscow, such a working style is an invitation to all kinds of trouble, but Yuenger wrote of Rudolf

Abel's death because the details were convincing and he believed the dissident obtained the information from a reliable source. He dispatched the story to Chicago at 5:00 A.M., knowing it was exclusive.

"The sixth sense that you develop in Moscow with your antennae waving decided me to go with it," recalled Yuenger.

Two days later, Rudolf Abel's death was confirmed by an obituary notice in *Pravda,* but for James Yuenger, they were "forty-eight sweat-drenched hours."

Should a correspondent file a story that he knows will offend the Soviets and risk a reprimand or worse from the Press Department? The decision is not easy. For example, in the mid-1970s, a group of Jewish women seeking to emigrate announced that since they and their husbands could not obtain exit visas, they wanted to send their children to Israel alone. They recalled that Jewish women in Nazi death camps sometimes threw their babies over the fence, hoping the infants would be found and saved from certain death. Several correspondents discussed whether they should include the analogy in their stories, knowing that the Soviets would be furious, as they usually are, over any comparison with the Nazis. They decided to include the reference to the camps. As expected, the Press Department reacted by summoning the correspondents for a severe scolding, but nothing more. To teach the correspondents a lesson, the Soviets would have been obliged to expel the five who filed the story—a move that would have produced immediate retaliation and severe political repercussions, a price the Kremlin was not prepared to pay. The lesson was clear: Reporters could find a measure of safety—in numbers.

On the other hand, a correspondent would occasionally forgo a story because of the obvious risks. For example, one reporter who traveled widely, had always wanted to do a piece about the adulation of Lenin, founder of the Soviet state. The material was visible everywhere in the Soviet Union: millions of volumes of his collected works; cities, towns, streets, and factories bearing his name; statues showing him pointing symbolically toward the future; and portraits, usually tailored

to conform to a specific environment. In a kindergarten or
school, Lenin, who was childless, is shown beaming at children.
On a Ukrainian collective farm, he is depicted as a farmer; in
the Donbas, he is portrayed as a miner; at the headquarters of
the State Bank in Moscow, his portrait depicts him as a banker,
gold chain and all, the chairman of the board; in central Asia,
his eyes are slanted like those of most of the people in that
region. Tempting as it was, the Lenin cult story would invite
immediate expulsion—and this particular correspondent decided not to take the risk.

Risk applied to almost any story that had some zest in it.
Peter Osnos, for example, obtained a document from a
Russian acquaintance that showed that the Ministry of Milk
and Meat Production had reduced the meat content of
sausages.

"I don't know what they were substituting—leftovers, maybe
tails," recalled Osnos.

Osnos knew the document was not secret but was certainly
confidential and not one that the ministry would normally
make public. He filed the story to the *Washington Post,* where
it was treated routinely, but it was broadcast by the Voice of
America and heard by millions of Soviet citizens. Peter Osnos
became an overnight celebrity everywhere in the Soviet Union.
Oddly enough, his risk turned out to be no risk: the Press
Department ignored the story.

Over time, every reporter developed his or her own style of
operation. Much depended on personality, on maturity, on
how well he or she understood the Soviets, on training,
experience, and special interests. The ultimate test was what
came out of the typewriter, or the telex. Language fluency,
energy levels, charm, resourcefulness, humor, and patience all
played a role, but what was paramount was a reporter's inner
drive. These qualities are no different for Moscow than for
any other major reporting assignment, but reporting on the
Russians requires greater sensitivity, greater awareness of the
impact of a phrase or a paragraph than in any other world
capital. The differences are in the modes of operation re-

quired to thread a story together, the faculty of observation and of placing facts in an historical context.

The guiding principle for Dusko Doder, whose Moscow stint totaled more than seven years, first with UPI and then as correspondent for the *Washington Post,* was simple and straightforward:

"I tell these people that I don't like them. I tell them in the most brutal way and at the same time I try to be fair and try to understand their point of view. My job is not to fight, my job is to understand."

Robert Toth used his engineering training to focus on a hitherto neglected aspect of Soviet activity: scientific and technological developments. His predecessor in the *Los Angeles Times* bureau, Murray Seeger, wrote extensively about the Soviet economy. Craig Whitney sought to report on why the Russians behave the way they do, digging into the historical, psychological, and social influences that have shaped Soviet society, in the tradition of Walter Duranty and *Harper's* editor John Fischer, who wrote *Why They Behave Like Russians.* And George Krimsky set himself the supreme challenge: He sought to "get underneath the skin, into the souls of the Soviets." Like Walter Cronkite thirty years earlier, he wanted to give the Russians a chance to tell their side of the story. He succeeded only too well, since he got into the souls of the wrong people—his dissident friends—and under the skin of the KGB.

After almost five years James Gallegher learned how to deal with the Russians on their level, to play the game the way they did. One day he was driving his son and a young Russian girl through Moscow, took a turn, and found himself speeding down a one-way street—the wrong way. Two policemen stopped him. The terrified girl slumped down in her seat, pale and trembling. One policeman asked, "Why are you going down the street the wrong way?" Without hesitation Gallegher replied, "I guess because I'm stupid."

The policeman laughed, "*Khorosho.* Okay, stupid, get out of here!"

Gallegher explained, "Russia is a country full of peasants, and if you look down your nose at them or give the impression you're doing that . . . they get upset. . . . You just have to be at their level. . . . That's one of the most important things I learned over there. You also have to be as sly as they are."

The old Russian proverb "Save every piece of string, it may be useful on the road" applies to correspondents as well as to travelers. Every bit of information, a clipping or paragraph from *Pravda,* a casual conversaion in the Moscow subway, a statistic on refrigerator production from an economic journal, a poster announcing a series of public lectures or a new play, publication of the collected works of a classic author, a joke— all are material for a present or future story. The key to comprehensive reporting was always the clipping file from the Soviet press and magazines and notes compiled by reporters waiting for a news peg. A good example: James Gallegher, Gene Randall of NBC, and ABC cameraman Richard Townsend were waiting one morning in the spring of 1982 on Kutuzovski Prospekt outside the apartment building where a number of Politburo members lived. Rumors about Brezhnev's ill health had been circulating in Moscow for months, and they wanted to catch a glimpse of the ailing general secretary on his way to the polls to vote in the elections to the Supreme Soviet, the nominal parliament. They spotted another man and his wife waiting there who looked familiar, but they could not place the man. Suddenly they realized they were looking at Yuri Andropov, head of the KGB, a frail, sick man, bent over as if he had forgotten to take the hanger out of his coat. A few months later, when Andropov was chosen to succeed Brezhnev, among some of the implausible things written about him was that he was an ardent tennis player. But the correspondents who had seen him knew that he barely had the strength to lift a racket, much less hit the ball over the net. Yuri Andropov's frailty, noted in a reporter's file, was later used to confirm that he was an interim leader destined to hold office briefly, which turned out to be the case.

One of the biggest stories of 1978 was the discovery that Soviet soldiers had tunneled under a street to the U.S. embassy to install listening devices and intercept communications. Apparently a cat-and-mouse game had been played over several months while the Soviets extended the tunnel and the Americans bricked it up. The Soviet moles then dismantled the bricks and dug a little further until the Americans sealed it again. Finally the Russians got too close to the outer wall of the embassy building, resulting in a face-to-face confrontation between a Soviet digger and a U.S. Marine.

"You're interfering with communications of the Soviet government!" shouted the Russian.

"You're goddamn right I am!" shouted the Marine.

The embassy kept the story quiet. Not a word was leaked to the American correspondents, but as a collector of strings, an AP correspondent found out about the tunnel from the "nanny network" composed of young girls, usually French, Danish, Swedish, and English, who worked for the families of foreigners. Many of them dated members of the Marine detachment, which provided security to the embassy, creating a network for gossip and inside information. The nannies often reported back to the correspondents what they had heard or overheard. The girl who worked for the AP correspondent told him about the tunnel, and he broke the story by obtaining confirmation from an embassy official.

The same network produced another big story a few months later. One evening while a nanny was visiting her Marine boyfriend, she overheard one embassy official whisper to another, "They've got him! They've got him!" The girl mentioned this to an AP reporter, who phoned the embassy spokesman and asked whether an American diplomat had been kidnapped. The official said no, but the correspondent knew something was amiss. He realized he would get no additional information from the embassy until he could ask a specific question. A few unofficial inquiries disclosed that Francis Jay Crawford, a representative of International Harvester Company, had been arrested. The correspondent phoned the official again and asked, "What can you tell me about Jay Crawford?"

Now the official could be more forthcoming. "Okay, I'm glad you asked me that because I am authorized to state that. . . ."

Crawford had been arrested by the KGB on charges of currency violations, but it became clear almost immediately that he was being held hostage for two convicted KGB spies imprisoned in the United States. He was freed after sixteen days in exchange for the two men and deported.

The Brezhnev era ended on November 10, 1982, with a TASS communiqué announcing the death of the general secretary. After lying in state under chandeliers draped with black crepe in the Hall of Columns, where other mourners had sobbed at the biers of Lenin and Stalin, Leonid I. Brezhnev was buried under the Kremlin wall facing Red Square. Two days later, Yuri V. Andropov, who until 1982 had headed the KGB for fifteen years, the man directly responsible for the harassment of the foreign correspondents, was chosen general secretary, hardly a good omen for the long-suffering reporters.

11

Transition: From Brezhnev to Gorbachev and Glasnost

Anybody who comes here and says they can't find anything to write about is an idiot. Good stories—they fall out of the trees.

> Howard Tyner
> UPI, 1975–77
> *Chicago Tribune*, 1982–85

Moscow is a city rich in rumor and impoverished in hard data, and those who report on the political scene there struggle perpetually to distinguish between fact, educated speculation, planted rumor, and just plain rumor.

> Serge Schmemann
> UPI, *The New York Times*
> 1980–86

Gaunt, stooped, and ailing at sixty-eight, Yuri Andropov was clearly a transitional leader, but before he died, he set in motion the first serious effort to overhaul the system of political and economic governance established by Joseph Stalin. Facing Andropov were formidable problems, but the fundamental challenge was how to pull the Soviet Union out of the morass that was curtailing economic vitality and growth.

"I do not have the recipe for their solution," he candidly announced. "It is up to all of us to find answers to them."

After years of semitorpor, Moscow had become an exciting news story again as Andropov tackled falling productivity, waste, overcentralization of economic decision-making, and the reluctance of Soviet workers to exert themselves for the Motherland and communism. Correspondents reported his declaration of war on absenteeism and corruption, which often took the form of police raids on bars, cinemas, restaurants, and public baths to nab truant workers and thirsty citizens drinking to excess. They described Andropov's new measures to raise productivity by providing workers with wage and bonus incentives, as well as his far-reaching reform in July 1983 giving greater authority over budgeting, investments, wages, and bonuses to selected industries, such as transportation, machine building, and electrical equipment manufacture. Equally important, Andropov began a quiet and bloodless purge of the bureaucracy, weeding out those who stood in the way of reform and change, advancing younger people who shared his views. Although thwarted by ill health from making more than a beginning, he started the process of generational change that would eventually bring his young protégé Mikhail Gorbachev to power.

At the same time, relations with the United States reached a new high in hostility and confrontation fired by continuing American support for the Afghan anti-Soviet resistance, the crushing of Poland's Solidarity movement, the Reagan administration's massive military buildup, and the modernization of NATO's defenses. The impasse in negotiations to control nuclear weapons contributed to mutual distrust and fear. When President Ronald Reagan described the Soviet Union as an "evil empire," the Kremlin launched a venomous propaganda campaign against the United States that caused shudders among the American correspondents in Moscow. The downing of a Korean Air Lines 747 aircraft with 269 passengers and crew in 1983 by a Soviet fighter was probably the most dramatic incident of the Andropov era, convincing many Americans and a good part of the world that the Soviet military establishment was trigger-happy, reckless, and irresponsible.

After Andropov's death in February 1984, another aging leader was elevated to power: Konstantin U. Chernenko, seventy-two, a party hack with no commanding qualities other than his thirty-year association with Leonid Brezhnev. The candidate of the Old Guard, he was also an interim leader, the oldest man ever to achieve the office of general secretary in Soviet history. Never having administered a region or a ministry, a farm or a factory, Chernenko owed his upward climb in the party bureaucracy entirely to Brezhnev. During Chernenko's tenure, he continued Andropov's drive against corruption and for labor discipline, although at a slower pace. But the country was still mired in the state of domestic paralysis that characterized the Brezhnev regime. Konstantin Chernenko's one significant initiative in foreign affairs was to resume the dialogue with the United States that had been broken off in December 1979 when Soviet troops invaded Afghanistan. At a meeting between Foreign Minister Andrei Gromyko and Secretary of State George Shultz in Geneva in January 1985, the two superpowers agreed to resume substantive negotiations on strategic and medium-range nuclear weapons and President Reagan's Strategic Defense Initiative. In September Gromyko met President Reagan at the White House, the first high-level Soviet to confer with the president since he assumed office in 1981. The confrontational cycle between Washington and Moscow had come to an end.

Konstantin U. Chernenko, barely thirteen months in office, died in March 1985, succeeded by Mikhail S. Gorbachev, who was waiting in the wings, the rising star in the Kremlin's political constellation. The announcement of the new general secretary's appointment came within four hours of Chernenko's death, the speediest transition in Soviet history.

Until then, for correspondents on the scene, the biggest game in town had been to ferret out the state of health of the nation's principal leader, no easy task in a society where only the inner few are privy to such information. When Andropov was weakened by kidney failure, reporters lined the sidewalks of Kutuzovksi Prospekt in the morning, hoping to catch a glimpse of his limousine en route to the office. When he disappeared from public view for almost six months, failing to attend important events and to meet with visiting foreign dignitaries, the Press Department announced that he was only suffering from a cold. On the night of February 9, Dusko Doder, acting on a hunch that Andropov had died, drove through the deserted streets of Moscow looking for confirming clues. He found them: lights ablaze at the Ministry of Defense, the headquarters of the General Staff, and the KGB. Patrols were guarding access streets to the Central Committee building, just as they did when Brezhnev died. At 11:35 P.M., Radio Moscow dropped without any explanation a scheduled jazz concert, substituting classical music. For Doder, the evidence was in hand: Yuri Andropov was dead. He filed the story—his alone—to the *Washington Post* in the predawn hours, while all the other American correspondents were asleep.

In Washington, *Post* editors decided to run Doder's dispatch on page one even though the White House, the State Department, and the CIA had not received any similar reports. At a State Department dinner that night, Soviet Ambassador Anatoly Dobrynin laughingly dismissed the story, while Undersecretary of State Lawrence Eagleburger, after checking, called it "bullshit." *Post* editors, unwilling to stand behind their correspondent, softened the language and moved the article to page twenty-eight.

The official announcement on Soviet TV came shortly thereafter: Yuri V. Andropov had died at 5:35 P.M. on February 9, a few hours before Dusko Doder picked up the trail.

Doder was astonished to learn from the *Post*'s daily play cable, which describes how major stories were used, that he was not on the front page.

"I was kind of mad," Doder told me, "I asked what the hell happened. How was it possible? Then I got involved in the follow-up work. . . ."

With Konstantin Chernenko, the correspondents faced a different problem: He was slowly wasting away in full public view. At meetings and on TV, he appeared thinner, his speech slurred, his movements painfully slow; he was incapable of standing at a rostrum for long periods. To track Chernenko's declining health, Robert B. Cullen of *Newsweek* found himself counting the number of times the general secretary gasped for breath in one minute. The Soviet people watched their leader, obliged by duty to make a spectacle of himself. Merciful death came on March 10, clearing the way for Gorbachev.

The ascent to power of Mikhail Gorbachev, fifty-four, inaugurated one of the most momentous periods in Soviet history, with the potential to shape the destiny of the USSR in a way radically different from anything experienced since the 1917 Revolution. After three old men holding supreme authority had died within twenty-eight months, they were succeeded by the first member of a new generation, unburdened by the trauma of Stalin's purges, unmarked by World War II, without responsibility for the economic stagnation and the errors of the past, a dynamic, educated, "modern" man with the courage to face problems and, without fear, to propose far-reaching, innovative solutions.

The Gorbachev era was barely two years old, but by mid-1987 it was already clear to the Western correspondents that the new general secretary intended to stamp his own imprint on Soviet society. After the tedium of the Brezhnev years and covering the deathwatches for Yuri Andropov and Konstantin Chernenko, the correspondents had a truly exciting and significant story to cover. Mikhail Gorbachev was proclaiming not only that the USSR had to "carry out profound transformations in the economy and in the entire system of social relations" but also that it had no other choice if it was to maintain its position as a superpower.

"We have forgotten how to work," he said. At the same time, he lashed out against government and party bureaucrats, warning those who obstructed efforts to revitalize the economy, increase productivity, and eliminate corruption and privilege to "get out of the way!" Attacking alcoholism as a "national evil," Gorbachev increased vodka prices, closed distilleries, limited sales of liquor to certain hours, and began a vast educational campaign on the dangers of drink.

The correspondents saw a dynamic, active leader barnstorming the vast country, not unlike the energetic Nikita Khrushchev of twenty-five years earlier. Mikhail Gorbachev traveled widely to sell his policies, meeting with workers in factories, talking to crowds in the streets, exhorting them to work harder, to speak up, to tell the leadership about the country's problems. To reach a wider audience with his message, Gorbachev appeared frequently on national television. And towering above all was the Kremlin's new policy of "openness (*glasnost*) and honesty," a phrase not often pronounced in the public discourse of the Soviet Union.

As the general secretary's words and actions slowly began to penetrate the system, Western correspondents reported on interesting new developments, especially in the intellectual world. Old Guard cultural watchdogs who had used their power to quash innovation and nonconformity in the arts were eased out of key positions in the writers' and filmmakers' unions, replaced by more tolerant officials. Books by long-banned authors began to appear in bookstores. A novel by Anatoly Rybakov on the tribulations of a Moscow family under Joseph Stalin received approval for publication. The press began to publish critical articles and letters on mismanagement and waste; it even attacked the practice of using anonymous informants to denounce neighbors, a custom that had not disappeared with the death of Stalin. When a passenger liner and freighter collided in the Black Sea causing four hundred deaths, the accident was made public immediately by the Soviet press, an extraordinary break with past practices when such disasters were hushed up. More significant, in December 1986, the press reported riots in the streets of Alma-Ata, capital of the central Asian republic of Kazakhstan, spurred no doubt by the replacement of the top local party leader by an ethnic Russian. Nothing similar had been seen in a Soviet newspaper since veiled references to peasant uprisings against Stalin's forced collectivation in the 1930s.

In response to the nuclear accident at Chernobyl, however, the Soviets reverted to form. At first they denied that anything significant had occurred, then grudgingly acknowledged that there had been a serious mishap while criticizing Western news media for wild and exaggerated reports on casualties. Mikhail Gorbachev himself remained aloof until almost three weeks after the disaster, when he appeared on television to explain what had happened. Eventually the Kremlin produced a remarkable amount of information, in contrast to its silence about the earthquake in Ashkabad (1948) that caused great material damage and took hundreds of lives.

In November 1984 I returned to Moscow, my first trip to the Soviet Union since I had been expelled in August 1962. After checking in at the Hotel National, I made the UPI bureau in the foreign compound on Kutuzovski Prospekt my first stop. Having once lived in the same building, I returned with some curiosity. Little had changed in the intervening period. On that cold, gray morning, it looked as seedy and run down as it did on the day I left. The yellow bricks, large gaps between them, still looked ready to drop to the ground. The muddy, unpaved parking lot was filled with Volvos, Volgas, Zhigulis, and Mercedes-Benz cars. Inside the booth at the driveway entrance stood a militiaman peering at everyone who came and went. A creaky elevator with flapping doors took me to the UPI office where Jack Redden, the bureau manager, met me.

The bureau was no different from any UPI bureau anywhere else in the world: a large newsroom with cluttered desks; electric clocks on the wall showing Washington, Greenwich mean, and Moscow time; battered filing cabinets; and photos of Politburo members. A kitchen, darkroom, and a closet that served as an audio transmission booth rounded out the facilities. Most impressive—and new to me—was the wire room, UPI's link with the outside world. In addition to the TASS printers spewing copy in English and Russian, two UPI transmitters provided direct connections to Helsinki and London. Another machine brought in the UPI newswire, the identical service distributed to agency clients in Europe. No longer were the correspondents, as we were in the 1950s, dependent on the BBC for the latest news. Speedy access to information about developments outside the Soviet Union, almost instant contact with the home office, and the ability to carry on a dialogue with other bureaus on an uncensored telex line had finally broken down the sense of isolation imposed on generations of Moscow correspondents.

That day, Jack Redden was suffering from a severe head cold, not something to be trifled with in a Moscow winter. He found some medication in the office, but instructions were in Finnish, a language no one in the bureau could understand. I watched as he sat at the telex and typed a service message to UPI's Helsinki bureau requesting information about the product. When the response clicked out on the machine, the news was good:

MOST POPULAR COLD REMEDY IN FINLAND. TAKE TWO TABLETS THEN ONE TABLET EVERY FOUR HOURS. HOPE YOU FEEL BETTER.

The entire exchange took exactly eight minutes.

While this message was not as historic as Alexander Graham Bell's "MR. WATSON, COME HERE. I WANT YOU!," for me it was mind-boggling. Working conditions for the correspondents had indeed changed since I toiled in the UPI bureau almost thirty years earlier. At that time, such a message was virtually impossible to transmit. Glavlit would not have passed it, probably convinced that the Finnish text was some sort of secret code, nor would UPI have countenanced a transmission of such a frivolous nature. But with the telex and without censorship, there was no problem. At the Associated Press bureau, also located in the Kutuzovski compound, the equipment was similar, but with the addition of word processors left over from the 1980 Olympic Games. The mode of operations of the two American wire services had been transformed.

Another striking contrast: When I arrived in Moscow to work for the UP at the end of 1955, the entire American press corps consisted of ten reporters, all males. Nearly thirty years later, the number had more than tripled, but almost one fourth were female. Three of the four staffers in the AP and one stringer were women. Roxinne Ervasti, thirty-four, of Park Rapids, Minnesota, on her first foreign assignment, was bureau chief. At UPI, two of the four correspondents were women.

Women journalists were rarely seen in Russia in the early years, the most prominent being Anna Louise Strong, who reported for INS from 1922 to 1925 before turning pro-Soviet, much to the consternation of her anti-Communist editor-in-chief, William Randolph Hearst. Strong, born in Friend, Iowa, had been a member of the Quaker Relief Mission during the famine years of the early 1920s. After she left INS, she worked as a free-lance reporter, contributing articles to *Harper's,* the *Nation,* *Atlantic,* and the American Communist newspaper, the *Daily Worker.* She also wrote a number of laudatory books about Russia and the Chinese Communists. In 1930 Anna Louise Strong helped establish *Moscow News,* an English-language newspaper financed by the Soviet government, and served as its editor until 1936. It is still being published.

In the days following the Nazi invasion, *Life* photographer Margaret Bourke-White broadcast briefly for CBS before returning to the United States. The *New York Herald Tribune* sent star reporter Marguerite Higgins to Moscow in 1955 to reopen the bureau closed with the departure of Joseph Newman in 1949. Before she left Helsinki for Moscow, she wrote to a friend in the U.S. State Department stating that in the event of arrest in the Soviet Union "this letter constitutes advance denial of any injurious utterances whatsoever against the United States that might be attributed to or actually delivered by me as a result of duress or torture." Although Higgins was not subjected to torture, she decided that the assignment was not to her liking. She quickly left to write a book about her experience. In July 1956, Henry Shapiro hired as a UP stringer Colette Schwarzenbach, a young woman from New York who taught at the Anglo-American School. Speaking fluent Russian, she quickly learned the trade and wrote some of the finest feature stories emanating from Moscow at that time. But before her by-line appeared on UP copy, Shapiro gave her a *nom de plume,* something unusual in the United Press. Although Colette was of Swiss-German origin, he wanted to avoid giving the impression that UP Moscow was staffed entirely by Jews. As a result, her copy was transmitted under the name Colette Blackmoore.

The first truly professional female reporter assigned to Moscow was Aline Mosby, then thirty-seven, who worked in the UPI bureau from 1959 to 1961. An agency veteran with almost twenty years' experience, she was best known for her coverage of the Hollywood film industry. A slight, red-haired woman from Missoula, Montana, she was a tenacious reporter who, in addition to the usual political fare, wrote superb feature stories about everyday life in Moscow. Considered something of an oddity by the Soviets, she wrote about cats and dogs, going to the hairdresser, fashions, food, shopping, housekeeping—about the things that happened to her.

One personal experience she did not write about began at the Praga restaurant, where she met two young men for lunch, ostensibly students. Her drink contained a potion that left her shaken and dazed. She stumbled out of the restaurant into the arms of a policeman and passed out. The next thing she knew, she was lying in her bed with the U.S. embassy doctor and Henry Shapiro standing over her. That day *Izvestia* published a long article describing how Mosby had been arrested by police for drunken behavior and taken to a cooling-off station where she spent the night. A photo showed her stretched out on a cot, her mouth open, staring at the ceiling. *Izvestia* described her as a typical American correspondent, an alcoholic abusing the hospitality of the Soviet people, trafficking in "degenerate art." When the Western reporters saw the story, they immediately guessed what had occurred. They were horrified, not only because a hardworking colleague and friend had been mistreated but also because they knew that they were potential victims. The correspondents would have reported the incident if Henry Shapiro had not phoned each one and urged them not to file, arguing that Mosby would suffer and might even be expelled. Privately he was convinced that the UPI bureau might be closed if the story was transmitted. Although many reporters, including me, had reservations, they decided to go along with Shapiro's request. The story was killed and the world was none the wiser—temporarily. The incident became known when *Izvestia* reached subscribers abroad, but by then the news was stale, of interest only to journalists and specialists on Soviet affairs.

The conspiracy resembled the Press Department's successful effort in 1933 to blackmail that generation of Western reporters into refuting the story about the man-made famine instigated by Joseph Stalin when he forced collectivization of agriculture on a resisting peasantry. The difference was that in 1961 the correspondents censored themselves.

Aline Mosby remained in Moscow, churning out bright, readable copy. The incident in no way changed her attitude or colored her reporting on the Soviet Union, although some of the correspondents thought it would.

"Why should it?" she asked. "I'm a journalist and I write down the middle of the line. I try never to use loaded words or write on one side or another. It's not my position to express opinions or to color anything. I merely report what is happening. That's what journalism is supposed to be."

Aline Mosby's assignment did not herald a breakthrough for women correspondents. In the twenty years after her departure, less than a half dozen female reporters were sent to Moscow, most of them in the wire services. They ranged from novices on their first overseas assignments to reporters with up to fifteen years of experience. The Soviets, unaccustomed to the presence of women in the press corps, were uncertain how to treat them. Sometimes their femininity was respected; at other times it was ignored.

Like their male counterparts, women were subjected to provocations, attacks, and other unpleasant experiences. Charlotte Saikowski traveled extensively and alone while she was in the Soviet Union, always subjected to surveillance, often to harassment. During a trip to central Asia, she was arrested for taking "insulting" photos in a marketplace. The Novosti guide refused to intervene on her behalf. At the police station, Saikowski declined to sign the customary statement describing the incident and was released. Subsequently, a visit to a clinic, which she had not requested, was arranged. She was ordered to don a white gown and cap and surrender her purse containing her passport and address book because of "germs." Everything was eventually returned, but obviously closely inspected.

Angered at her treatment, Saikowski returned to her hotel in Tashkent and phoned the U.S. embassy in Moscow from the Intourist phone in the lobby, where everyone could hear her.

She explained to an embassy official how she was being treated, knowing full well that there were other listeners on the line.

"The KGB is giving me a hard time and I don't understand it," she said.

After the phone call, the harassment on that trip stopped.

Ann Garrels, twenty-seven, the ABC correspondent from 1979 to 1982, was less fortunate than Charlotte Saikowski. A probing, innovative reporter who spoke fluent Russian and sought to film the unofficial side of Soviet life, she frequently ran afoul of the KGB, the police, and the passions of Russian men. One night, while she was phoning a friend from a telephone booth on the outskirts of Moscow, a man shoved his way in and tried to tear off her clothes. She screamed for help while fending off her attacker. The Russian fled. Even the militiaman at the entrance to the Kutuzovksi compound flirted with her. Eventually he asked her to meet him after duty so he could show her a restored Russian church. She agreed to a relatively safe daytime rendezvous, but he never appeared.

One of the Soviet chauffeurs assigned to the ABC bureau for the 1980 Olympics asked Ann Garrels for a private meeting in her office and immediately propositioned her.

"You must be joking," she said with a laugh. "I don't know whether you've been put up to this by your government, but you're on the wrong track.

"And if we were to have this affair," she asked, "how do you propose we have it? I live in an apartment that's bugged and you live at home with eight million other people. You don't even have your own room. . . ."

"Well," replied the chauffeur, "I have a friend who is divorced and he says we can have his apartment on Tuesdays and Thursdays from two to three."

"And does he change the sheets, too?"

The embarrassed Russian turned and left, but Garrels was

never certain whether he was pursuing her on KGB orders or exercising a little private initiative.

During a visit to Kiev to attend the fiftieth wedding anniversary of two Russian friends, Garrels had her purse snatched by two men on a public square, obviously KGB agents. Although the purse was returned by the Kiev police, Garrels phoned the U.S. embassy about the mugging, and the embassy informed the other correspondents. This time there was no self-censorship. The story went out on the wires. Shortly afterward, *Literary Gazette* began attacking Garrels, accusing her of spying for the CIA and fabricating lies about the Soviet Union.

A more frightening experience for Ann Garrels occurred on a rainy night in 1982 as she drove back from the suburbs where she was covering a story. Driving the office Volvo, she hit two drunks who were stumbling across Leninski Highway. One man later died, the other survived. With a police investigation under way, Garrels was ordered not to leave Moscow. Although she was cleared and the case dropped, the Foreign Ministry refused to provide her with the legal documents, claiming this was contrary to Soviet law. Although Garrels wanted to continue working in Moscow, ABC in New York, she claimed, was not supportive and let her know she would have to relinquish the post. ABC executives believed that the experience had so unnerved her that another assignment was mandatory. The Soviets accelerated the departure by asking her to turn in her credentials. Whether she was expelled or withdrawn was unclear, but she departed with regrets.

"I was not going to fulfill my Five Year Plan," she said. "I really loved it there."

Like the other women reporters, Roxinne Ervasti worked harder than in any other assignment of her career.

"I don't want to count the hours I work a week," she told me, "but I would say I usually put in a fifteen-hour day."

But this was nothing new. Aline Mosby had also put in her hundred hours a week in the early 1960s. Women were never spoiled or treated differently from their male colleagues by their bureau chiefs in Moscow or their editors in New York. They watched the wires and monitored TV newscasts; if they could read Russian, they read the newspapers and the magazines; they made the diplomatic rounds, wrote features, carried cameras, traveled whenever feasible, saw films and plays, went to concerts, and attended receptions. Like physicians, they were always on call. Everything they saw and heard and experienced was part of the job.

Roxinne Ervasti saw herself simply as a "wire service person who has been promoted to a position of responsibility." She was only aware of being a woman when, as AP bureau chief, she found herself dealing with Soviet officials, who were invariably men. For the Press Department, dealing with a large number of women could not have been easy, but the feminine presence evoked some remnants of prerevolutionary gallantry, even to the extent of saying "Good morning, dear," and kissing a woman's hand. When Ann Garrels first arrived, Press Department officials patronizingly suggested that she ought to specialize in "women's stories."

"When they found out I wasn't, they were outraged and sort of said, 'How could you do this to us?' "

Alison Smale, who reported from Moscow for the AP from 1983 to 1986, found that a woman had certain advantages over a man in getting to know people.

"They feel slightly less that a woman represents the official face of the United States," she told me. "With Soviet men, that may start up a conversation."

Since so few Soviet women work as journalists, the Russians had a natural curiosity about a female foreigner in the profession. This made "woman to woman" rapport easier.

AP staffer Louise Branson agreed with Smale:

"I think that Russians are more likely to be forthcoming with a woman because they're unused to dealing with women correspondents. I think they tend to see you more as a person."

In 1984, the Foreign Ministry had to deal with an unprecedented problem when Carol Williams, twenty-nine, a new AP correspondent, arrived in Moscow. She was the first married woman the ninety-two-year-old agency had ever sent abroad with a husband. Kenneth Olsen was her dependent, in the same position as all the female spouses who had preceded him to Moscow over the last seven decades. Barred from working as a reporter by the Press Department, Olsen was able to string for *Newsweek*, take photos, and write free-lance articles; he even worked part-time as an office manager.

Within a few months, a second female correspondent arrived, also with a nonworking spouse, to head the *Washington Post* bureau. She was Celestine Bohlen, daughter of the former ambassador, who as a little girl stiffened with fear when first presented to Nikita Khrushchev at a Spaso House reception. In early 1985, Joyce Barnathan became head of the *Newsweek* bureau, the first woman ever to serve in Moscow as chief for a major American magazine. Her husband, reporter Steven Strasser, had no accreditation, but the Soviets soon issued credentials permitting him also to file for the weekly. Philip Taubman and Felicity Barringer, another husband-and-wife team, began reporting for the *Times,* at the end of 1986. The policy of having a married couple working for the same publication was a change from the late 1960s, when Anthony Astrachan was assigned to Moscow by the *Washington Post.* Accompanied by his wife, *Post* reporter Susan Jacoby, Astrachan expected that the newspaper would welcome having an experienced reporter as a stringer in Moscow. The *Post* agreed to use her stories but refused to permit her to apply for Soviet accreditation, nor was she allowed a joint by-line even though she worked with her husband on stories published in the newspaper.

Male colleagues in the American press corps were not immune to muted feelings of chauvinism. For years they had built their tidy little men's club on the fraternal sentiments shared by reporters everywhere, cemented by the unique risks of the Moscow assignment. The sudden appearance of women, while completely accepted—indeed, welcomed— could not produce an immediate and complete change in attitudes. Some women complained that the support system enjoyed by the males was not extended to their female colleagues. And this was not limited to sharing the risks of covering dissidents. The weekly poker game, for example, was an all-male event, as were the intimate dinners for visiting newspaper and network executives, usually followed by cognac and cigars.

Said one female correspondent with a sigh, "I think in a year or two I'll have the kind of background and relationship that, if I want to go to the Thursday night poker game—they'll let me."

Edmund Stevens sat at the kitchen table in his Moscow mansion drinking vodka, nibbling on herring and black bread, and talking about the past. Fifty years earlier, he had arrived in Russia after graduating from Columbia University, a twenty-four-year-old idealist with vaguely leftist sentiments seeking to do something with his life. When I saw him in November 1984, he was still living there, part journalist, part legend, and a large part mystery.

During the intervening years, he first worked for a Soviet publishing house as a translator and editor. In 1935 he married Nina Bondarenko, daughter of a cossack from the Orenburg region, and enjoyed marital bliss in a communal apartment with three other families, without bath or toilet. Stevens still remembers the terror in the building during the Stalin purges, when doorbells rang at 2:00 A.M. and entire families disappeared into the night. Fired from his job a year later, Stevens was hired by the American-Russian Chamber of Commerce to write a monthly bulletin and began to string for the *Manchester Guardian* and the London *Daily Herald*. These accreditations provided him with official status, a residence permit, and a press card. He eked out a living by also serving as the local agent of the Cunard Lines, booking Soviets to the United States. In 1939 Stevens arranged the trip of the famed Red Army chorus to the New York World's Fair, but just as the group reached London, the outbreak of war in Europe forced it to return to Moscow. Before leaving for the United States with his wife and young son in 1939, Stevens achieved what no other Western correspondent had been able to do before—or since—in Russia. He bought a house that was to remain his personal property for almost thirty years. The house, actually a luxurious log cabin in traditional Russian style, had been rented by Joseph Barnes, the *Herald Tribune* correspondent, from its Russian owner. Stevens paid twenty thousand dollars for his abode, which eventually provided him with a life-style unknown to any other American in Moscow. After depositing his family in New York, Stevens returned to Europe as a war correspondent for *The Christian Science Monitor,* covering the Soviet-Finnish War from the Finnish side and the desert battles in Libya with General Montgomery, even entering Tripoli eight hours ahead of the British Eighth Army in January 1943.

"We signed the register at the Grand Hotel, then went out to the suburbs to meet Monty," he recalled.

When Averell Harriman came to Moscow in 1942 as U.S. ambassador, Stevens accompanied him for a brief visit, then returned a year later. While the other correspondents stayed at the Hotel Metropole, Edmund Stevens enjoyed the comforts of his own house, which had been occupied during his absence by Nina's family. One of the few Americans who could speak Russian, he produced some of the best reporting of the combat on the Eastern Front. During one battlefield foray following the liberation of Minsk, Stevens recalled, he helped round up some German prisoners "who came out of the woods waving a white flag."

Edmund Stevens returned to the Soviet Union with his wife and their two children in 1946, although Nina had been reluctant to leave the United States for the uncertainties of life in postwar Moscow. Unlike the other Russian wives of American reporters, Nina had obtained American citizenship, and when Stevens was assigned to Rome in 1949, she left with him. A harshly critical series on life under Stalin that he wrote for the *Monitor*—"Russia Un-Censored"—won a Pulitzer Prize in 1950. He returned in 1956 and has remained in Moscow ever since, working for various American and European publications and for AVCO, an American film distributor. Ed Stevens probably had better connections and knew more Soviets than

Henry Shapiro, many of Stevens' acquaintances dating back to the war. Among them were some of Russia's most distinguished writers, including Ilya Ehrenburg, Valentin Katayev, Konstantin Simonov, Alexei Tolstoi, and Konstantin Fedin. Stevens always seemed to be unusually well informed but was far from communicative or as gregarious as most of the other American correspondents. During the Glavlit period, he rarely showed up at the Central Telegraph to pool stories, although he seldom missed a Kremlin reception or a briefing at the U.S. embassy.

As we sat in the kitchen, I could see that Stevens had aged considerably since I had last seen him in 1962. His eyes were half closed and his head was bent forward on his chest, the result of an arthritic condition. He was always a mumbler, and his speech was even more indistinct and difficult to understand. An elaborately carved cuckoo clock punctuated our conversation with brief serenades on the quarter hour.

I asked him why he had stayed so long in the Soviet Union, longer than any American reporter since the Revolution, and why he still remained, even though his reporting activities had dwindled.

"Well, there were different reasons at different times," he replied. "For one thing, we had a house here. We had a life that was fairly well organized. There were also certain conveniences. It's easier here to organize your life than in New York, unless you are extremely rich. My son, who lives in Long Island, is an architect who is quite well off. But what do they have? A cleaning woman. Here we have a driver, a cook, a maid. Communications are no problem. You can get out as often as you want. I go to London two or three times a year and to the States at least once."

Stevens apparently did not mind living in a Communist society, enjoying the best of the two worlds. Some of his colleagues, however, have harbored doubts about his reasons. They wondered how his daughter Anastasia had managed to gain admission to the Bolshoi Ballet School when even talented Russian children were turned away. They speculated on Nina's ability to send underground art out of the country for exhibition and sale in New York. They could not understand why, when the log cabin was demolished by the Moscow municipality to make way for a housing development, Stevens was given a three-story mansion that formerly served as the embassy for an African country. Nor did they comprehend why, during all his years in Moscow, Stevens, unlike most correspondents, was rarely attacked by the Soviet press. True, some professional jealousy existed over Stevens' ability to fill his house with Soviet writers, artists, musicians, and other intelligentsia every time he gave a party. When Stasia was married to an Italian count, the entire Bolshoi Ballet attended the wedding reception in her father's mansion.

Despite the lack of proof, several correspondents over the years believed that Edmund Stevens had in some way compromised himself with the Soviets and had worked out an arrangement that would permit him to stay, in exchange for . . . what? No one knew.

Stevens, of course, vehemently denied that his reporting favored the regime or that he was given special treatment.

"I've never given them [the Soviets] reason to believe that I was contrary to an improvement in relations between the two countries. I don't think that constitutes either a crime or treason or anything else. I have openly criticized many aspects of Soviet foreign and internal policies. On the other hand, I've never written anything with deliberate malice or venom.

"Do you have any ground for suspecting I am playing a cover-up or doing a double role? After all, in any society regardless of the overall framework, one's position is determined by personal contacts. I don't do anything like Valentin Zorin [a Soviet journalist], who goes around photographing garbage dumps in the States and turns up the obvious absurdities he finds there.

"On the other hand, I've accepted this system as it is here as an accomplished fact and something we have to deal with. There are obviously lots of things we don't like about it, but that in itself is irrelevant. The main thing in all this is to promote better understanding at whatever possible levels are available to us. I haven't gone around with a chip on my shoulder."

Stevens explained how it was possible to beat the system by

knowing Soviet laws. When the Moscow municipal administration, for example, wanted to demolish his house, it was
obliged by law to replace it with equivalent space. That turned
out to be the mansion (to which Stevens had added a garage
and garden), located in the historic Arbat district, less than a
mile from the Kremlin. Richly decorated with antiques, icons,
tapestries, and dissident art, the house is a veritable museum.
The study is lined with books, memorabilia, and photos,
including a framed cover of the *London Illustrated News* showing a young, handsome Edmund Stevens in war correspondent uniform chatting with General Wavell at Tobruk.

In mid-1987, Edmund Stevens, now seventy-seven, was still
in Moscow, working on his memoirs, living out his years in the
mansion. He was still being invited to diplomatic receptions
and to briefings at the Foreign Ministry as a correspondent
accredited to *Newsday* and the *London Evening News,* but he
does not file as frequently as he once did.

Edmund Stevens will probably end his days in Moscow,
proof enough, as he told me with a wry smile, that he "got
stuck with the story."

The beige Volvo station wagon darted in and out of traffic
through central Moscow while Meade Jergenson, the twenty-
eight-year-old Cable News Network cameraman, aimed
through the windshield at the Volga fifty feet ahead—a chase
straight out of TV's *Miami Vice,* except that both cars stopped
for red lights. The quarry in the Volga sedan was Svetlana
Allilueva Stalin and her fourteen-year-old daughter Olga,
recently returned to Moscow after eighteen years in the
United States and England.

On a monitor in the CNN bureau, I watched the unedited
tape of that chase and the encounters with Allilueva when she
first arrived in Moscow—an astonishing sight. Coverage of her
return was a good example of the dramatic changes in
television operations that had occurred since Irving Levine
first aimed his 16mm silent camera at Nikita Khrushchev in
1955.

CNN correspondent Stuart Loory had been tipped that

Svetlana was staying at the VIP Hotel Sovietskaya and sent his crewmen, Tyrone Edwards and Jergenson, to flush her out. After waiting several hours in front of the entrance, they spotted a woman in a pink coat with a tall young girl waiting for a car. Jergenson approached her and boldly asked in English, "Are you Svetlana?"

The woman, surprised and obviously shocked, answered in Russian, "Who?"

Jergenson turned to the girl. "Are you Olga?"

The girl looked away without responding while Edwards was shooting through the window of the Volvo. When the woman and the girl got into the chauffeured car and whisked away, the CNN Volvo tailed them to a dead-end alley off Gorky Street, where it was blocked from following by an angry KGB agent. The footage was remarkable, but CNN Washington was not certain that the pair was the mother and daughter. Loory sent Meade Jergenson to London that very day with the tape for positive identification. Jubilation in the London bureau! Jergenson had indeed cornered the quarry. Millions of American viewers could see Svetlana Allilueva on CNN that same night. The following day, the "specials" and the agency correspondents organized a stakeout to corner her for a statement. Robert B. Cullen of *Newsweek* tried to speak to her, but two KGB agents pushed him away. Her only response was, "No comment!" Efforts to interview her were fruitless until the third day, when the CNN crew caught her as she took a stroll with her KGB guard. She shouted obscenities in English at them, which were bleeped when the tape was telecast in the United States:

"Why did you come back?"

"None of your fucking business! Piss off!"

As Edwards walked backward, shooting all the time, Svetlana advanced toward the camera and announced, "I will talk when I'm ready. In a special place, not on the street."

A few days later, she held a press conference at the Foreign Ministry, denouncing the West and accusing her American friends and advisers of using her and her father's name as a "sensational commodity" and her former American husband, architect William Wesley Peters, of marrying her for her money.

"I was not free there [in the West] for a single day," she declared. But in a dramatic turnabout, she left the Soviet Union with Olga in April 1986 and returned to the United States, stating that her family had "rejected us" and "we see no reason to stay."

CNN's coverage of Svetlana Allilueva's return to the Soviet Union was a remarkable achievement, showing that some news stories could be reported in Moscow just as they would be in Washington or New York. A tip came to the news desk; a crew was assigned to cover; the reporter staked out the target and either got on-camera comment or an on-camera "No comment." The Svetlana footage was no different from that of Lieutenant Colonel Oliver North, the staff officer of the U.S. National Security Council involved in the Iranian/ Contra arms deal. His initial appearance on television was limited to getting in and out of cars, and his reply to reporters' questions was a tight-lipped "No comment," minus the obscenities.

Stuart Loory, the fifty-two-year-old CNN bureau chief, was unusual among the American correspondents, having previously served in Moscow for the *New York Herald Tribune* from 1964 until the newspaper's demise two years later. After a distinguished career in print journalism, which included a stint as managing editor of the *Chicago Sun-Times*, White House correspondent for the *Los Angeles Times*, and science writer for *The New York Times*, he joined CNN as vice president and managing editor based in Washington. When CNN decided to open a Moscow bureau in 1983, Loory requested the assignment—and obtained it.

Looking back to when he was a *Herald Tribune* correspondent, Loory concluded that Moscow was becoming increasingly open, making it an easier place to work.

"For example, obviously you still cannot call the Kremlin and speak to any kind of briefing officer or official and get background information on what General Secretary Chernenko is going to say to the Supreme Soviet, but there are many stories you can do now in 1984, with official help, that one was not able to do before," he said.

As examples, Loory cited his filmed reports on two child musical prodigies, a pianist and a violinist, who performed in concerts at the Conservatory before a CNN crew and a live audience.

"It took us a year to set that story up, but we finally found someone in the bureaucracy who was willing to help us."

For his television assignment, Loory quickly found a greater spirit of understanding and cooperation on the part of Soviet officials than he did during his stint with the *Herald Tribune*. The official who headed the foreign department of the Gosteleradio, the Soviet TV and radio agency, promised him all the help he needed except for one thing: dissidents. There, he was told, you are on your own.

In the 1960s, recalled Loory, the conversation would have been different. The official would have said, "We will give you all the help you want, but I warn you that we don't have any dissidents here. However, if we catch you talking to them, you're liable to expulsion!"

Deputy chairman of Gosteleradio Henrikas Yushkaizichus once asked to see "negative" stories that Stuart Loory had been shipping to New York. The CNN correspondent agreed and showed him an interview he did with a militant *refusenik* in the CNN apartment. Afterward Yushkaizichus remarked, "Well, there are lots of people around here who may think that's negative, but I don't think that's negative because it shows an American audience that you can have a dissident in your apartment and you can interview him. And Americans think that the KGB follows the dissidents all the time."

Like the news agencies, the networks imported modern technology and endowed their bureaus with state-of-the-art video-cameras, editing, and monitoring equipment. Freed from the earlier dependence on traditional 16mm cameras, a correspondent could now produce a completely edited story within minutes after returning to the office with the tapes. The report could then either be transmitted by Gosteleradio via satellite for a fee ranging from a thousand to three thousand dollars, depending on length; shipped out via air freight; or hand-carried out by a staffer, a spouse, or a friendly tourist. There were still hitches in the system, however. Stuart Loory once shipped out an interview with Andrei Sakharov via air freight. When it arrived in London, the cassette and the container were badly battered, but the tape was rewound and usable.

"When they saw the story was about Sakharov, they took a sledgehammer to the cassette . . . and that was as close to any harassment [as] I've come," said Loory.

A major breakthrough for the American networks occurred when they were permitted to bring their own crews to Moscow, thus eliminating their dependence on Novosti. For several years the Soviet agency had insisted on providing, at an added fee, a "coordinator" for the team of technicians required to cover a TV story. The "coordinator" was the political watchdog for the KGB whose responsibility was to prevent "negative" coverage. Novosti's ability to sabotage what the Soviets considered an unfavorable story and its plain incompetence was legendary. When John Chancellor of NBC, after much travail, finally interviewed Georgi Arbatov, head of the Institute for the Study of the United States and Canada, he asked some tough questions about the state of Soviet-American relations. On returning to New York, he found that the Novosti cameraman had focused not on Arbatov's face but on his belt buckle. The tape was unusable. Novosti crews had strict orders never to shoot anything old—houses, people, streets—for fear that viewers would get a "negative view" of the Soviet Union. A Novosti cameraman working for CBS correspondent Murray Fromson shot two thousand feet of a news conference with General Secretary Brezhnev prior to his visit to the United States. For some unknown reason, every single frame was out of focus. The agency still had the gall to send CBS a bill for its "services."

Yet it was still possible to produce TV stories on life outside the officially sanctioned arena. For example, Ann Garrels,

Kevin Klose of the *Los Angeles Times,* and David Satter of the *Financial Times* of London flew to Donetsk to do a story on a coal miner who was committed to a psychiatric clinic because he exposed unsafe conditions in a mine. Barred from the mine itself, the reporters were arrested for standing on the sidewalk at the entrance, but were taken inside.

"We ended up having a full interview with the mine director on the very subject we wanted to talk about—on camera," said Garrels with a laugh.

The full impact of Mikhail Gorbachev's *glasnost* policy on TV reporting remains to be seen, but modest changes in official treatment of network journalists occurred after the Chernobyl disaster. For example, following a stonewalling press conference by the head of the USSR's atomic energy agency, Stuart Loory complained to a Novosti acquaintance that the story was worthless and asked for a one-on-one interview. Within an hour, it was arranged. But *glasnost* has already produced an unprecedented and richer source of TV stories for American networks than had been available before, the kind of information that correspondents could not obtain themselves. They found this material in the growing number of muckraking national television reports on the ills of Soviet society. An example was a remarkable series on corrupt officials in Rostov accused of selling meat on the black market. TV correspondents traced the "pyramid of corruption" to the Ministry of Trade in Moscow. When the culprits were tried, Soviet TV cameras were in the courtroom. Loory taped the footage off the screen and used the material for several CNN stories.

A dramatic live transmission to CBS in New York on December 28, 1986, may have heralded changes that can only be surmised. Andrei Sakharov, freed by the general secretary from his Gorky exile a few days before Christmas 1986, returned to Moscow. One day, the Kremlin's most outspoken critic was a prisoner, living in a city closed to foreigners, without a telephone, and with his mail scrutinized by the KGB. A week later he was addressing millions of American TV viewers on the CBS program *Face the Nation.* Using the satellite transmission facilities of the Soviet government, he vowed to continue his struggle for the liberation of all "prisoners of conscience" like himself.

American network correspondents in Moscow were asking what Sakharov's unimpeded access to the airwaves meant for them. Would they be able to interview other dissidents openly and transmit those interviews by satellite? Would they be able to report visually the stagnation in the economy, the shortages, the corruption, the backwardness in technology, the rural poverty that Mikhail Gorbachev himself has publicly disclosed? Would the correspondents have access to Soviet officials and other sources who can provide the information that would make this unprecedented reporting possible—and credible? If they could, TV coverage of the Soviet Union will have taken a quantum leap forward toward helping the American public understand the nature of the Soviet system. If they cannot, Mikhail Gorbachev's *glasnost* will remain just another slogan, like Nikita Khrushchev's vow to overtake and surpass the United States in the production of milk, meat, and eggs by 1958.

When I returned to Moscow at the end of 1984, I was struck by the dramatic changes in working conditions that had occurred since my expulsion in 1962. "Continuity and change," the hallmarks of Russian and Soviet history, were clearly evident in the way the Kremlin had dealt with foreign correspondents over the previous two decades. Through crude intimidation and threats, the Soviets were still attempting to control reporters and reporting. KGB agents continued to slash tires when correspondents sought out the few dissidents remaining in Moscow. Apartments of several reporters were burglarized to signal that no place was off-limits to the KGB. In an ominous development, in December 1982, barely a month after Yuri Andropov assumed supreme power, Walter Wisniewski, UPI bureau chief, and Robert Gillette were interrogated by criminal investigators about stories they had written almost a year earlier on Jewish *refusenik* scientists. Wisniewski, in a stance that sounded like a reaffirmation of press freedom under the First Amendment to the U.S. Constitution, refused to reveal his sources. Alison Smale of the AP was interrogated by the KGB and accused of assisting a Russian who was planning to flee across the border, a felony both for the Soviet and for the correspondent, who by law was obliged to report the incident to the police. Her name had been found in the would-be defector's address book. Smale denied the charge, saying that the Russian only talked about his hopes to leave, never about his plans.

One of the more grotesque and distasteful attempts at intimidation was mounted against *Newsweek* bureau chief Robert B. Cullen in May 1984, when he was summoned to the Press Department and told that a Russian woman had accused him of infecting her with a venereal disease. Cullen, thirty-five, married and the father of a three-year-old boy, was almost too shocked to deny the allegation, but he flew to Frankfurt that same afternoon for a physical examination. The doctor, a specialist, pronounced him in perfect health and signed a statement to that effect, which Cullen immediately dispatched to the Foreign Ministry with a copy to the U.S. embassy in Moscow. With the approval of his editors in New York, he returned to his post. Cullen never heard about the incident again.

And yet changes were also evident, though, like most changes in the Soviet Union, they were gradual. One of the most significant was the greater access to midlevel officials in government agencies and specialized institutes. The ban on such access was lifted by a government decree in 1982, but the bureaucratic consciousness needed time to adjust to the new policy. Many officials continued to refer queries to the Press Department, even though they were authorized to respond themselves. Robert Cullen tried to meet the Moscow-based official in charge of game preserves to arrange a visit to a site in the Ukraine that was the habitat of a rare breed of horse. The official stalled him off for three months, first claiming he was ill, then referring him to another department, then falling ill again. After further delay, Cullen finally was permitted to meet the official, but by then the free-lance American photographer whose pictures of horses had inspired the story had sold them to another publication. Cullen never made his trip to the preserve. On another level, correspondents were given increased access to Soviet journalists and institute heads who were sufficiently senior to serve on the leading bodies of the Communist Party, including the Central Committee, and even members of the Secretariat. They were able to meet regularly with such influential individuals as Valentin Falin, the head of Novosti and a former ambassador to West Germany; Aleksandr Bovin, of *Izvestia;* Fyodor Burlatsky, director of the Institute of the World Socialist System; and Georgi Arbatov. Although these men and lower-ranking officials who were authorized to see foreign correspondents had their own agendas, the dialogue was usually useful.

Although correspondents did not have daily contact with their Soviet acquaintances, they could meet with them periodically to discuss the Kremlin's policies and political trends, to learn about their thinking. For the Soviets, such dialogue was also valuable, since it provided a new source of information beyond what came over the TASS restricted wire. A knowledge of Russian was indispensable for these exchanges, since few Soviets spoke English, and the presence of an interpreter inhibited the candor of the discussion.

At press conferences, very senior officials began to meet with reporters. One of the most remarkable was a wideranging session conducted in 1986 during the Twenty-seventh Party Congress by Politburo member Geidar A. Alieyev, a first deputy premier, who exhibited humor, energy, and a willingness to take on all questions. He responded candidly when asked about the Soviet Union's black market, admitting that it did exist and that salesclerks "sometimes hold back goods to sell them later at a higher price." When asked about his salary, he said with a chuckle that it was not a general practice to "count the money in someone else's pocket." Not since the days of Nikita Khrushchev's appearances at embassy receptions was it possible to ask such questions of a Politburo member.

Indicative of the growing accessibility of official and unofficial Soviet information sources was a remarkable book by Dusko Doder published in 1986. *Whispers and Shadows* described with fascinating and authoritative detail the behind-the-scenes power struggle between Yuri Andropov and Konstantin Chernenko, between the Old Guard and the "modernists," between those Soviet leaders who fear change and those represented by Mikhail Gorbachev who recognize the urgent need for economic and social reform and who, despite the risks, are ready to carry them out. Doder was even able to learn in advance the date of a critical meeting of the Central Committee at which an ailing Brezhnev was to appear, information known only to the innermost Kremlin circles. Such a book could not have been written about the transfer of power from Stalin to Georgi Malenkov to Nikita Khrushchev, nor from Khrushchev to Leonid Brezhnev.

What had also changed was the sophistication of the Press Department, which for decades had served as a barrier to information sought by the correspondents. In 1984, a new Foreign Ministry spokesman, Vladimir B. Lomeiko, began to hold frequent press conferences on current issues. Unlike briefings at the White House or the State Department, which take place at the same time every day, Lomeiko's sessions were convened at any time and were usually limited to a single subject. Questions on other issues were not accepted. Sometimes the subject of the briefing was not even announced in advance and correspondents were obliged to appear if only because they could not risk missing out on an important story. The reporters welcomed the opportunity mainly because it offered an improvement over the old system of phoning the Press Department for comment or reaction, usually not forthcoming, on a specific news development. The press conference, at the very least, provided a chance to talk to a human being face-to-face. Moreover, by careful monitoring, a skilled correspondent could track the nuances and emphases in the Kremlin's foreign and domestic policies.

Why did the Soviets inaugurate the briefings after so many years? They probably felt they were not getting their message across to the rest of the world through the usual means: *Pravda* editorials and statements from TASS. Younger officials who had served in the West and observed the usefulness of the press conference in focusing journalistic attention on an issue may have been behind the new policy.

I attended a briefing at the Foreign Ministry press center on November 31, 1984, when over two hundred reporters crowded into a teak-paneled room to hear Vladimir Lomeiko read a statement on talks in Moscow between the United States and the Soviet Union on nonproliferation of nuclear weapons. After answering six questions relating to the discussions, Lomeiko terminated the conference by thanking everyone and wishing all present a pleasant weekend. Since the statement had already been moved by TASS and Lomeiko's replies were not enlightening, it was not exactly an earth-shaking story. But not all Press Department briefings were as uneventful. In early 1984, when rumors about the failing health of Andrei Sakharov were rampant in Moscow, Leonid Zamyatin, a Soviet spokesman, assured the correspondents that the scientist was in excellent physical condition. Unble to contain himself, Charles Lambroschini, correspondent of the Paris newspaper *Le Figaro,* confronted Zamyatin.

"You informed us that Mr. Andropov had a cold and later we learned that it wasn't true. You said the KAL plane was headed toward the Sea of Japan [after it had been shot down] and now we know differently. Why should we believe you now?"

"Next question," sniffed Zamyatin, obviously embarrassed. "Your question is without tact."

At another press conference, Nicholas Daniloff, who had left UPI and returned to Moscow in 1981 for *U.S. News & World Report,* rose to defend two colleagues, *Times* reporter Serge Schmemann and Donald Kimelman of the *Philadelphia Inquirer.* The newspaper *Sovietskaya Rossiya* had viciously attacked Kimelman as an alcoholic whose reports condoned genocide and who associated with criminals and renegades. Schmemann, like other Western correspondents in Moscow, received research material prepared by the United States–

funded Radio Liberty, which broadcasts to the Soviet Union. The newspaper criticized him for using this information in his dispatches. Stirred by the harsh attacks, Daniloff angrily told the Press Department officials that the correspondents deserved the right of reply.

"I said that if the Soviet leaders want a civilized relationship with the rest of the world, they ought to treat correspondents in the same way."

The other Western correspondents applauded Daniloff. It was the first time that anyone had publicly complained about the treatment of journalists by the Soviet press. What no one could foresee was that more ominous developments were in store for American reporters than mere attacks by Soviet newspapers.

On a quiet Saturday afternoon, the next-to-last day of August 1986, Nicholas Daniloff, fifty-two, who was preparing to leave Moscow at the end of a 5½-year assignment for *U.S. News & World Report*, decided to see a Russian acquaintance to bid farewell. He had met Mikhail (Misha) Luzin in the central Asian city of Frunze in 1982 and kept in touch with him over the years. Luzin was an attractive, outgoing, nonpolitical man in his midtwenties, interested in science fiction, and the two arranged to meet in a park in the Lenin Hills near Moscow University, where Napoleon had his first view of the city in 1812. After a brief conversation, Daniloff presented Misha with a farewell gift, two of Stephen King's novels. In return, the Russian gave him a sealed packet that he said contained clippings from Frunze newspapers. They parted, walking in different directions. A few minutes later, a van braked to a halt alongside Nicholas Daniloff; half a dozen men leaped out, grabbed him, slipped handcuffs over his wrists, and hustled him into the vehicle. Squeezed into a seat, two men on either side, he found himself facing a movie camera as the van sped across Moscow. The camera turned as one of the men fished out Daniloff's wallet and found his press card.

"*Bozhe moi!*" he cried in feigned surprise, "My God—a foreigner!"

Nicholas Daniloff was taken to Lefortovo Prison, the KGB's maximum-security installation, where the packet was opened. His friend Misha's farewell gift consisted of two maps marked "Secret."

Daniloff's interrogator, a KGB colonel named Valery Sergadeyev, who opened the packet, announced that the American was being held on suspicion of espionage. Conviction, under Soviet law, was punishable by death.

Thus began Nicholas Daniloff's ordeal, one that would transform him from a relatively unknown journalist into a world figure, a pawn in the summitry game of the United States and the USSR, and a frightening example for American reporters working in Moscow.

For the next thirteen days, Daniloff was held in a cell of eight by twelve feet, which he shared with a Soviet physicist, an obvious informer, named Stanislav Zenin, forty-four, who claimed that he had been arrested for leaving classified documents in unguarded locations. To prevent suicide, the reporter's belt was taken away, his shoelaces cut in half, and at night he was forced to surrender his eyeglasses, ostensibly to prevent him from slitting his wrists. Food was delivered through an opening in the metal door. During Daniloff's imprisonment, he was interrogated daily by the suave, dark-haired Sergadeyev. Using the "good cop," "bad cop" technique, the KGB officer tried to force Daniloff to admit that he had been spying for the CIA while posing as a correspondent.

"I am not a spy," Nicholas Daniloff insisted. "I am only a journalist trying to do my job."

Frequent visits from his wife, Ruth, his link with the outside world, helped sustain Nicholas Daniloff's morale. From her he learned of the outcry his arrest had precipitated, that Secretary of State George Shultz had declared that he was being held hostage and demanded his immediate release. Despite assurances from President Reagan in a personal letter to General Secretary Gorbachev that Nicholas Daniloff was not a spy, the Soviets refused to yield. The reason for their refusal quickly became clear. They were seeking an exchange for Gennadi F. Zakharov, a Soviet employee of the United Nations who had been arrested by the FBI as he handed an envelope containing a thousand dollars to a Guyanese student attending college in New York. The payment was for classified documents relating to military aircraft engines. The student was working with the FBI to trap Zakharov, who was not protected by diplomatic immunity.

Nicholas Daniloff's arrest was not the first time an American journalist had been incarcerated and charged with espionage. Anna Louise Strong, the former INS correspondent, was arrested in Moscow in February 1949 en route to China as a "notorious intelligence agent" and deported to the United States. Her real crime was her public support for Marshal Tito, who had defied Stalin and broken away from the Kremlin-controlled Eastern European bloc. Robert Toth, although interrogated in Lefortovo after receiving so-called secret documents, was never held overnight and he left the USSR when the interrogation was terminated. The trial of U-2 pilot Francis Gary Powers and his subsequent sentence to ten years' imprisonment could not have been far from Daniloff's thoughts as he tried to sleep under a light that burned all night.

In the course of the interrogation, Colonel Sergadeyev accused Daniloff of delivering to the U.S. embassy a letter he had found in his mailbox in January 1985 addressed to Ambassador Arthur A. Hartman. Paul M. Stombaugh, a diplomat who was subsequently expelled for espionage, opened the letter and found another envelope, addressed to William Casey, director of the CIA. The letter came from Father Roman, a Russian who claimed he was a priest but whom Daniloff considered a KGB *agent provocateur*. When Stombaugh tried to contact Father Roman, he said that he had obtained his address through "the journalist," meaning Daniloff, a reference that would not help the prisoner's case.

Intensive questioning of Nicholas Daniloff continued day after day, relieved by time out for exercise in a wire cage on the prison roof. The American reporter replied truthfully because he felt he had nothing to hide, but he also believed he "was digging his own grave" each time he opened his mouth.

Visits from Ruth and *U.S. News* publisher Morton Zuckerman bolstered his sagging morale.

On Friday, September 12, Daniloff was summoned to the interrogation room, where Colonel Sergadeyev and an unknown official were waiting. Speaking formally, the official announced:

"*Gospodin* [Mr.] Daniloff, a political decision was made at three o'clock this afternoon to release you tonight. We would like you to call the chargé d'affaires at the American embassy, who will outline the conditions."

Daniloff phoned Richard Combs to learn that he was being released to the custody of the Ambassador Arthur Hartman but would not be permitted to leave the Soviet Union pending final adjudication of his case. A few hours later, Ruth Daniloff and the American official arrived in the ambassador's limousine to pick up her husband and drive to the embassy. In New York, Gennadi Zakharov left a federal prison and was remanded to the custody of the Soviet ambassador to the United States. The dénouement came after Secretary of State George Shultz and Soviet Foreign Minister Eduard Shevarnadze finally agreed on an arrangement that would free both men and pave the way to the delayed summit meeting between Mikhail Gorbachev and Ronald Reagan.

After seventeen days as a guest in a spare embassy apartment, Nicholas Daniloff was finally a free man. With Ruth, he flew to Frankfurt and then to Washington for a joyful reunion with their two children and a welcome at the White House from President Reagan. The following day, Gennadi Zakharov flew to Moscow. Plans for the long-awaited summit—scheduled for Reykjavik—were announced within twenty-four hours. As part of the deal, Yuri Orlov, sixty-two, former chairman of the Helsinki Watch Committee, a watchdog group organized by Moscow dissidents in 1976 and disbanded by the KGB soon after, was released from exile in Siberia and permitted to emigrate to the United States with his wife, Irina Valitova.

A few hours before leaving Moscow, Daniloff visited the tomb of Alexander Frolov, his great-great grandfather, one of the rebel aristocrats who had planned the assassination of Tsar Nicholas I in 1825. Daniloff, who was writing a book about his ancestor, feared he would never see the grave again.

After Ruth and Nicholas Daniloff returned to the United States, they settled into a house in Chester, Vermont, where he was writing a book about Alexander Frolov and his own experience. In retrospect, Daniloff believed, he should have behaved differently during his imprisonment and been less forthcoming with his answers. However, he neither received nor was able to receive advice from the embassy, and since he was innocent, he had decided to respond fully to his KGB interrogator.

"I should have been more obstructive," he said, "and played for time, not dismissed the translator, but to go through the Russian to English to Russian . . . to try to avoid signing anything. . . . I was surprised how much they knew about me. They opened a file on me in 1961."

While Daniloff was happy to be free, there was a great sense of loss. As Ruth told me, "Nick spent twenty years of his life covering the Soviet Union. Now he feels he'll never go back. He's been cut off. There is sadness and anger in him."

The arrest and imprisonment of Nicholas Daniloff cast a chill over the entire Western press corps in Moscow. Clearly, the KGB could snatch any correspondent as a hostage when the need arose. As he pointed out at a press conference after he was freed from Lefortovo, what happened to him could have happened to any of his colleagues.

"Why not Serge Schmemann?" he asked.

Was Nicholas Daniloff chosen as the victim because he was a serious, hardworking reporter whose fluent Russian provided access to Soviets not available to non-Russian speakers? Was he singled out because of his White Russian ancestry, because his father fled Russia after the Revolution and his grandfather had served on the General Staff of the tsarist armies? Or did he make himself vulnerable by accepting the fatal packet from Misha or by delivering the letter from Father Roman to the U.S. embassy?

Faced with similar situations, correspondents react differently. In 1961, on an official trip to central Asia, I met Vladimir Sokolov, an agricultural engineer who worked on a state farm near the town of Mari. I gave him my *Newsweek* business card and invited him to phone when he came to Moscow, expecting never to hear from him again. About six months later, the office phone rang. Vladimir Sokolov was on the line. He was in Moscow on business and wanted to see me. We arranged to meet in the most public place I could think of: Pushkin Square in broad daylight. I arrived early, surveyed the doorways around the square, the shrubbery and the parked cars, but saw nothing suspicious. At the appointed time, Sokolov appeared, carrying a large cardboard box. We shook hands, chatted about how happy we were to see each other again, and talked about our families. Suddenly he thrust the box at me, saying, "Here is a present."

My antennae were out. I suspected the worst: a setup for the KGB. God knows what was in that carton: secret documents, maps, photos. I looked into the man's face. He was smiling, his eyes were friendly. He struck me as someone who couldn't possibly be devious or do something mean and underhanded. I said to myself, "The hell with it. He's probably just a kindhearted, generous Russian, like most of them," and accepted the carton.

"Open it!" he urged, smiling.

I carefully removed the string and pulled open the top. Inside were the most beautiful peaches I had ever seen in the Soviet Union, fat, fuzzy, and delectable.

"They are from our farm. I wanted you to have some," said Vladimir Sokolov proudly.

Perhaps I took a risk, but for me the greater risk was to yield to the system that systematically sought to maintain barriers between correspondents and the people, to cut us off from human contacts, from the Russians who are the flesh and blood of Moscow reporting. I could have walked away and left Sokolov standing there wondering about this rude American reporter, but I did not.

At one time or another almost every correspondent in

Moscow is offered a packet, an envelope, or a bulging briefcase by a Russian. Almost invariably the proffered parcel is rejected. A man who would not identify himself once phoned Christopher Ogden to ask for a meeting near the Ukraine Hotel, saying he had something "interesting" to show him. When the UPI reporter appeared, the Russian offered him an envelope that he said contained Soviet plans for cross-border raids into China. Ogden told the Russian that since they were such important documents, he should take them immediately to the Foreign Ministry, pointing at the skyscraper building on the other side of the Moscow River. The Russian was puzzled by the refusal and persisted in offering the packet. Ogden again refused. Shrugging his shoulders, the man strode away, immediately joined by three stone-faced bystanders. The KGB provocation had failed. In a variation from the direct approach, another agency reporter found a tightly wrapped roll of papers in his mailbox marked "for the U.S. embassy." Assuming that this was a KGB trick, he left the papers in the box, drove to the U.S. embassy immediately, and discussed a course of action with an official. He decided to leave the roll in the box, unopened. A few days later the papers disappeared, probably retrieved by the KGB.

What did the Daniloff affair mean for Western journalists, particularly for the Americans working in Moscow? The overriding significance was that despite *glasnost,* the slow opening up of Soviet society under Mikhail Gorbachev, reporting from Moscow is still a hazardous occupation. The American correspondent must understand that despite the veneer of a civilized society operating under stipulated rules, the Soviet system is arbitrary and the authorities ruthless. A correspondent runs a risk every time he or she walks out of the bureau to cover a story. By being cautious, by not taking chances, by not irritating the authorities, the dangers can be minimized, but the price is high: shortchanging the reader and the viewer who rely on the reporters to transmit the whole picture in a balanced, objective fashion.

The Moscow correspondents interpreted the Nicholas

Daniloff case—no matter what the ostensible political goal, that is, the freeing of Gennadi Zakharov—as a message to discourage unofficial contacts: "Stay away from the Mishas!" To the Soviet people, the message was that foreign journalists are spies and should be distrusted and avoided. Yet these contacts and information sources are essential to the reporters, who must place the official data in perspective. If Gorbachev urges Soviet citizens to drink less and work harder, a correspondent will not find the man-in-the-street reaction in *Pravda* but will have to dig it out from the factory workers who are at the receiving end of the exhortation. That is what the system is trying to prevent.

"And that," Nicholas Daniloff told me, "is destructive of the journalism process, which is to talk to people in authority and then to people who have unofficial views."

The effectiveness of the warnings remains to be seen. Several Moscow correspondents have told me that by the beginning of 1987, the Daniloff case had already receded into history, overtaken by a stream of new developments: the freeing of Andrei Sakharov and other leading dissidents; the scheduled publication of hitherto banned writings, such as Boris Pasternak's *Dr. Zhivago;* and dynamic efforts of Mikhail Gorbachev to restructure the party, the government, and the economy. The correspondents saw no long-lasting impact of the Daniloff arrest on their working modes. "We knew it was a one-shot affair that shook everybody up," said one agency journalist, "but we all continued to carry on as we did before."

In his first speech to the Central Committee session that elected him general secretary in March 1985, Mikhail Gorbachev laid down a basic and somewhat startling principle of his tenure, the concept of *glasnost* or openness. He reasoned:

"The better people are informed, the more consciously they will act, the more actively they will support the party, its plans, and its programmatic goals."

Gorbachev sees candor as essential to the radical reform he believes necessary for revitalizing the Soviet Union's stagnant economy, recasting its social system, and moving the country forward to a modern, technological society. In his speech he criticized those in the party who would, for whatever reasons, cover up mistakes and failures, the traditional Kremlin reflex when something goes wrong.

"You sometimes hear it said that we should speak more carefully about our shortcomings," he said. "There can be only one, Leninist, answer to this: Communists always and in all circumstances need the truth." The party, he added, should always be "calling things by their proper name."

The Chernobyl nuclear accident in 1986 showed that cover-up habits were still deeply ingrained. The Soviet government refused to acknowledge the extent of the damage, not just to an anxious world, but also to its Soviet people. Eventually the authorities produced a torrent of information, but coverage of Chernobyl by Soviet newspapers and television came in for unprecedented and scathing self-criticism. For example, *Literary Gazette,* a favorite Kremlin vehicle for attacks on American correspondents, commented that some reporting was "so falsely cheerful and cap-throwing that it was as if we were hearing not about a shared misfortune but about an alarm drill or a mock competition of fire brigades."

The Chernobyl experience may have encouraged more provocative comments from the two leading Soviet newspapers on the need to disclose intraparty debate and decision-making, a subject rarely discussed previously. *Pravda* even urged that reasons for dismissal of officials be made public.

"After all," the newspaper argued, "publicly significant information cannot be the privilege of only a narrow circle of 'the chosen' or of the 'ordained' among us."

Izvestia attacked those who refuse to communicate to the public decisions already made because they are not "prepared to lose this prestigious, in their eyes, privilege of unaccountability."

Moscow correspondents were further startled to read on the front page of *Pravda* that the KGB had dismissed several officials for harassing a journalist—a Soviet—for exposing corruption in a Ukrainian coal mine. The reporter, who worked for *Soviet Miner,* was arrested, his apartment searched, and his notes and papers confiscated. A few days after *Pravda* had published several articles describing the reporter's difficulties, Viktor Chebrikov, the KGB chief, announced that the officials responsible for such "unlawful actions" had been punished and that steps were being taken "to ensure the strict observance of the law in the activities of the state security organs." Public admission of KGB abuse was a rare event in Soviet history, and although the victim was a Soviet journalist, some foreign correspondents amused themselves by playing "what if . . ." "What if" the Soviets applied *Pravda*'s defense of press freedom to foreign correspondents? The conclusion: It's not likely!

Although it may be premature to predict the impact of the new *glasnost* policy on the way Western correspondents will be able to cover the news, if the Soviet press carries out the Gorbachev injunction on openness and accountability and communicates to the people what he has called "the bitter truth," the impact could be significant. The press, which has always revealed much to the perceptive American correspondent, has already become a more truthful mirror of Soviet society. It could evolve into an increasingly valuable source of information about the economy, decision-making, and how the Kremlin leadership is dealing with the awesome challenges that lie ahead. Andrei Sakharov, on his return to Moscow from his exile in Gorky, remarked that "the sort of articles that are now appearing read like some of the declarations from dissidents that were issued in the 1970s and for which many of my friends were jailed." Such openness in print and in public discourse cannot but reflect an openness in internal party discussions among the elite, much of which will filter out to the American correspondents as Soviet journalists, editors, and members of the intelligentsia prove less reluctant to talk about the issues raised publicly by Mikhail Gorbachev.

Like all change in Soviet society, the process will be slow, uneven, encountering stubborn internal opposition, overt and hidden. Ingrained attitudes on the need for secrecy will not be quickly altered. Gorbachev himself has admitted that the changes he envisages will not occur overnight. As he told a meeting of writers in June 1986:

"Generations must pass for us really to change. Generations must pass."

A beginning has been made, but working conditions for correspondents may never match those of the early and simpler days of Soviet Russia when George Seldes climbed the stairs at Lubyanka to interview a senior CHEKA official, when Walter Duranty's access to party leaders was such that he could chart the fall of Leon Trotsky, and when Albert Rhys Williams, onetime correspondent of the *New York Evening Post*, could open the door of his room at the Hotel National and find a neighbor inquiring whether he might come in for a "conversation."

The neighbor was Vladimir Ilych Lenin, head of the new Soviet state.

12

One Helluva Story

If you don't get into trouble with them to some extent, if your relationship with them is entirely placid, then it probably means that you're not doing a good job.

Robert B. Cullen
Newsweek, 1982–85

We live in a world in which, figuratively speaking, various telescopes are aimed at the Soviet Union, and there are not a few of them, big and small, from close up and from a distance. They watch for some sort of crack to appear in the Soviet leadership.

Andrei A. Gromyko
president of the USSR
1985

In mid-1987, nearly seven decades after the Bolsheviks seized power, the number of Americans in the Moscow press corps had attained an historic high. With the opening of four new bureaus (*The Wall Street Journal, Dallas Morning News,* Mutual Broadcasting System, *Newsday*) during the previous four years, twenty-two news organizations and networks were represented by forty-two journalists and TV technicians, more than one tenth of the three-hundred-odd American correspondents who have reported from Moscow since 1921. The Americans constituted the largest contingent in the Western press corps, twice the number of West Germans and three times the British. But compared to the Americans assigned to Paris or London during that period, numbering in the thousands, the count is small.

Over the years, an extraordinary variety of journalists covered the Soviet Union, with different educational backgrounds, professional experience, and political persuasions. They were educated at Harvard, the University of Illinois,

City College of New York, Oxford, Brown University, the University of Michigan, and the University of Paris. Some never went to college. As reporters, they had covered City Hall, science, sports, the theater, education, the police beat, the Normandy landings, war in the Pacific, fighting in Vietnam and Korea, and politics in London and Tokyo. Their personal views spanned the political spectrum from pro-Communist to anti-Soviet. When they arrived in Moscow, they ranged in age from the mid-twenties to the mid-fifties, with and without families, and with and without pets. Their preparation for the assignment ranged from three words of Russian to total idiomatic fluency, from having read John Gunther's *Inside Russia Today* to a Ph.D. in Russian history. Some were brilliant journalists who reported on Soviet life and politics with great insight and understanding. Others were mediocre time-servers who did little but the routine filing that permitted their newspapers to retain the franchise. The vast majority, however, were hardworking, conscientious, intrepid journalists seeking to push back the limits of what could be reported under difficult conditions.

Richard Growald, as correspondent and editor for UPI from the 1960s to the 1980s, has observed many reporters in action at the White House, at the U.S. State Department, and in Moscow, where he served on frequent short assignments. He told me, "I never saw a higher caliber of reporting than what was available from the Americans in Moscow."

Growald's enthusiasm was not always borne out by the record. The American press corps had its share of ill-prepared journalists whose inadequacies were masked by the system of mutual support and self-protection that prevailed in Moscow during the period of censorship. Assignments were often based not on language skills, knowledge of the Soviet Union, or any special qualities that could enhance the reporting but, especially in the wire services, on purely economic consider-ations: proximity to Moscow, thus saving on travel costs; whether the individual had a family, thus saving on living allowances; or youth and inexperience, thus saving on salary. INS sent Charles Klensch to Moscow in 1954 because he knew no Russian and was such an obscure reporter in the Denver bureau that Barry Faris, the agency's editor, was convinced that the Press Department would find no reason to reject a visa application. And he was correct. B. J. Cutler, who reopened the *Herald Tribune* bureau in 1956, was taken off the city desk and sent to Moscow, his first trip outside the United States. As if to underscore how editors' attitudes have not changed, thirty years later the *Chicago Tribune* assigned to Moscow Thom Shanker, a reporter whose professional experience was limited to writing think pieces on arms control and a stint covering City Hall politics. In 1986 the *Philadelphia Inquirer* dispatched Steve Goldstein to the Moscow post after he had distinguished himself as a sportswriter. Unlike Cutler, however, Shanker and Goldstein had brief training in the Russian language. Cutler's intrinsic talents and his extraordinary ability to learn the trade were evidenced by his next assignment, Paris correspondent, and subsequently he became editor-in-chief of the European edition of the *Herald Tribune*.

The networks were notorious for failing to send fully qualified correspondents to Moscow. With rare exceptions such as Marvin Kalb of CBS, Ann Garrels of ABC, and Stuart Loory of CNN, they did not assign reporters who could speak Russian fluently, forcing them to rely on official interpreters. News directors plucked correspondents from London, New York, Saigon, Cairo, or Chicago, sometimes providing a modicum of language training before sending them on their way.

The correspondents themselves hold differing views on the skills and qualities that the ideal Moscow correspondent should possess. Is fluent Russian at the top of the list? Craig Whitney of the *Times* has called it "criminal for editors to send anyone to Moscow without knowledge of the Russian language. A reporter needs all the help he can get in Moscow, and one of the things that helps the most is the knowledge of language." But Robert Korengold of UPI and *Newsweek*, whose Russian was fluent, did not think language ability was essential.

"Given someone who is a good correspondent with the many other qualities that are necessary and doesn't have the language and someone who has the language but doesn't have journalistic smarts, then I would opt for the journalist first on the assumption that he will pick up the language."

Over the years, a number of reporters have performed well without the language: William R. Stoneman in the mid-1930s, Daniel Schorr and Max Frankel in the 1950s. Clifton Daniel, with a few words of Russian, established himself as one of the finest reporters on postwar Russia during the fourteen months he was the *Times* correspondent there. Robert Toth, despite his minimal Russian, opened up new fields for reporting with his coverage of science, but he strongly believed that a correspondent should have at least a year to study the Soviet Union and particularly the Russian language. The reality is that, except for the *Times*, the *Washington Post*, and the *Los Angeles Times*, few newspapers will invest the time and the money to provide a reporter with language training and education in Soviet affairs. They are willing to have a reporter read a few books, perhaps take a month-long intensive course in Russian at a nearby university or a Berlitz school, and then start packing. They even urge the correspondent to study Russian in Moscow in nonexistent spare time, a totally unrealistic expectation. As a result, although not entirely crippled by the handicap, reporters without Russian are largely cut off from Soviet society and fail to achieve the full potential of the assignment.

Transcending the question of the correspondents' professional skills is a larger issue: Have the press and TV had any significant impact on American public opnion and understanding of the Soviet Union? In the 1920s and 1930s, when Walter Duranty enjoyed a unique position as the *Times* correspondent, his reporting on Stalin's rise to absolute power and the emergence of Russia as a modern industrial nation undoubtedly influenced not only American public opinion but also U.S. government policy. Historically, however, Americans' perceptions of the Soviets have been shaped more by what politicians tell them than by what they read and see. The bomb-throwing, bearded Bolsheviks of 1917; the "Communist conspiracy" to "take over" the rest of the world; the "Iron Curtain"; and Ronald Reagan's description of the Soviet Union as an "evil empire" stamped attitudes toward the Kremlin far more firmly than Russia's sacrifices in World War II and military triumph over Nazi Germany or Moscow dispatches on the government's recent interest in restoring churches and landmark buildings. The Soviet Union has become such a villain in the American psyche that most of us carry a profoundly negative image of the Russians: bad, threatening, mysterious, powerful, anti-American. Although much of this image is rooted in reality, it means that no matter what the media report from Moscow, the fundamental "bad guy" image will not be affected. As Robert B. Cullen of *Newsweek* has put it:

"There's a lot of information that we convey that has a negative character, and that is partly because, by the nature of the business, we are much more interested when they shoot down an airliner than when they produce an interesting new play that criticizes the established way of doing things. I'd like to put more emphasis on the play than the airliner, but that's not the way the news industry operates."

The special status of the Soviets, oddly enough, has made it easier for the Moscow correspondents to get into print or on the air than for their colleagues in other capitals because of the public's hunger for information about the "enemy." A story on bathrooms, diapering babies, gas stations, or buying a suit, if datelined Vienna, Caracas, Sydney, or New Delhi, would end up in the editor's wastebasket. Under a Moscow dateline, it gets featured play.

Thirty years ago as a UP correspondent, I met a middle-aged Florida couple in the Metropole dining room who were astonished that the average Russian seemed so well dressed. "Why," exclaimed the woman, "they even wear fur hats!" The Americans scolded me for not reporting such important news. I countered that I frequently wrote features on women's styles, clothes, and shopping in Moscow but that not a single editor on the thousands of newspapers served by the agency would print a story, if I did write one, that a quarter of a million Russians walked down Gorky Street today wearing shoes. Americans, I said, should have learned in high school, not from the pages of their local newspaper, that Russians wear coats and hats.

Little has changed since then. Many correspondents feel that they are not getting the message across to the American public. They are concerned that despite their collective efforts over the decades, their hard work and voluminous reporting, Americans still do not, and have no desire to, understand the Soviet Union. Perceptions and stereotypes are so ingrained that most Americans will not permit the facts to undermine their prejudices or tightly held opinions. Perhaps Americans do not read what correspondents report, or they have a short attention span, or they scan the story and then go on to the sports pages. Whatever the reasons, correspondents believe that Americans have little comprehension of why the Russians behave the way they do. Without this understanding, they believe, there can be no successful efforts to influence Soviet conduct in world affairs. As an example, President Reagan conceded he was "baffled," as were many other Americans, when the recent KGB defector Vitaly Yurchenko, who had a choice between living in the United States and living in Russia, chose to return to Moscow. But as Craig Whitney saw it, Americans fail to understand the powerful attraction of the homeland, of its culture, of the sound of the Russian language.

"All those things that mean home to a Russian are in Russia, and the attraction of freedom, as great as it is for us, is one they don't know. . . . Russians are people, too, they have the same weaknesses and desires and hopes that we have. . . . That's the kind of thing we have failed to get across."

Craig Whitney's appraisal is shared by many other correspondents. Peter Osnos of the *Washington Post* has said that the reporting from Moscow "doesn't penetrate . . . fundamentally. Our readers do not understand that country. . . . It's a terrible fact of life that our people don't know very much about the Soviet Union. It's convenient to say it's because it's a closed society, but it isn't that closed, and we've been writing about it, and working hard at it, and there are people who did some of their best journalistic work there. And yet Americans do not absorb. They are still puzzled."

Coping with ignorance, indifference, and entrenched stereotypes about the Soviet Union may be beyond the capability of the American news media. The correspondents themselves are pessimistic about the impact of their efforts, and yet they still feel that on the whole a reader/viewer who is interested, who pays attention, and who digests information from different sources—magazines, newspapers, television, books—can obtain a fairly comprehensive and realistic view of life in the Soviet Union, the diversity of its peoples, the richness of its culture, the turbulence, the conflicts, the texture of daily living, and, most of all, the nonmonolithic nature of Soviet society. But only a specialist in Soviet affairs has the interest and the time to cover all available information. The average American will not.

Television could play a much more important role in informing the public, but so far it has not met the challenge. Except for CNN and the knowledgeable reporting of Stuart Loory, TV has by and large failed to convey the flavor of life in the USSR in a systematic way. In addition to the limitations imposed by the Soviets themselves, some networks, fearful of losing their bureaus, are careful not to produce unfavorable stories. When Soviet authorities began screening videotapes shipped by air freight in 1983, both CBS News and the U.S. embassy protested the policy as a violation of the Helsinki Accords, but NBC News President Reuven Frank announced that his company would not make "too big a fuss about it because we want to keep reporting from Moscow." Nor do the networks always provide airtime when a correspondent files a particularly interesting story. For example, when Murray Fromson spent five days on a Ukrainian collective farm, filming peasant life, sharing a farmer's quarters and food, showing harvesters mowing grain, interviewing the dynamic young party secretary, and playing billiards with tractor drivers—a fascinating and exclusive story—CBS News did not use a single foot of the three thousand shipped to New York.

"I was really sick when the logs came in," said Fromson, but this treatment was not unusual. The CBS correspondent has calculated that during his thirty-two months in Moscow, other than with summit meeting footage, his reports were shown on the evening news, anchored by former Moscow correspondent Walter Cronkite, for a grand total of three minutes.

Totally dependent on visual reporting for effective communication, the networks operate at an awesome disadvantage in Moscow. The cost of maintaining a bureau is high, but it can be justified if the usage is also high. When stories do not get on the air, the unit cost per minute can be mind-boggling, encouraging network accountants to ask why the bureau is kept open to produce such meager results. Then a political decision is made in favor of retaining the bureau because the prestige is greater than the financial burden. For economic and other reasons, all three networks at various times over the past thirty years have failed to maintain their bureaus, but at mid-1987, NBC, ABC, and CBS had fully staffed operations in Moscow.

American correspondents are their own severest critics, recognizing that for the most part they could be better prepared for the assignment. Those who went to Moscow without speaking more than a few words of Russian realized their handicap and strove to learn the language while on the job. They tried to catch up on Soviet history, culture, economics, and geography by reading some of the basic texts. Few were psychologically prepared, however, for the isolation, especially in the postwar years; for ghetto life in the tiny foreign colony; for the travel restrictions; for the endless and wearying battles with censorship and the bureaucracy; for official hostility; and for the pervasive tension between a foreigner and a suspicious, xenophobic society. Some correspondents conceded that their personal loathing for the totalitarian system and for the brutality and injustice they witnessed gave their reporting an anti-Soviet bias, a stance that ill served the American public.

Although some reporters were arbitrarily assigned to Moscow by their editors, the vast majority eagerly sought the post, many for the single reason that, like Mount Everest, it was there: the most challenging and important foreign story for an American correspondent, the other superpower, the ideological enemy, the great unknown, described by Winston Churchill as a riddle wrapped in a mystery inside an enigma.

Unsurprisingly, many found the Moscow assignment the high point of their journalistic careers. For Marvin Kalb it "was a dream come true. It was unbelievably exciting." Aline Mosby thought it was "like going to the moon." Robert Kaiser looks back at his three-year tour as "an enormous, consuming adventure." Inspired by his Moscow experience of almost eight years, Robert Korengold even half seriously considered writing a book called *Famous Historical Figures I Have Been in the Same Room With.* As it did for me, the Moscow assignment marked many reporters for the rest of their lives. From a privileged position they watched a great nation in travail, emerging from a world war, revolution, and civil war, and brutally transforming itself from a peasant society to a major industrial power as capable of repulsing and defeating a determined and resourceful foe as of developing nuclear weapons and sending men into space. The USSR offered a journalistic menu unparalleled in modern history. What reporter could resist a Moscow assignment?

During the first three decades of American reporting from the Soviet Union, there was occasional and sometimes harsh criticism of individual correspondents who were accused of being Kremlin propagandists for writing about the "achievements" of the Communist regime. After Stalin's death in 1953 and the rapid increase in the number of reporters, allegations concerning the professional behavior of the Western press corps did not arise until the mid-1980s. Andrew Nagorski, one of my successors in the *Newsweek* bureau, in a book describing his fourteen months in Moscow, accused some of his colleagues of serious transgressions. He charged that they were overly reliant on TASS and the Soviet press, deriving up to 90 percent of their stories from these official "handouts" and transmitting this information as "news" to an unsuspecting American public. Correspondents, he said, fearing that extensive ties with Russians and covering "unofficial" news could provoke retaliation from the Soviet authorities, restrained their normal reporting instincts. They wanted to remain in Moscow to enjoy such perquisites as apartments provided by employers, usually with a maid, and frequent paid vacations outside the Soviet Union. Furthermore, some correspondents were content to remain in their Moscow ghetto, avoiding the discomforts of travel and the risk of writing stories about real people, Nagorski said.

Based on my own experience and as a victim of expulsion, I disagree with the charges. For one thing, TASS, as the official news agency of the Soviet Union, speaks with the authoritative voice of the Kremlin. A correspondent would be derelict in his or her duty to ignore its dispatches and communiqués. Just as the White House press corps reports the official pronouncements of the president's press secretary, the Moscow press corps reports what TASS has transmitted. Nor do the correspondents simply rewrite TASS or what appears in the Soviet press. They analyze, interpret, and expand official statements and published articles, often utilizing information from other sources such as diplomats, dissidents, and other Soviet contacts. Because they go beyond TASS and *Pravda*, American correspondents are frequently attacked by the official newspapers, scolded by the Press Department, and occasionally expelled.

Eight four-drawer filing cabinets in the UPI Moscow bureau, the repository of almost thirty years of newspaper and magazine clippings, are proof of the value of the Soviet press to the reporters. In my time, the agency subscribed to more than twenty-five daily and weekly newspapers and perhaps ten journals and magazines. The bureau currently receives almost twice that number, an invaluable reference source for the correspondents. For example, Joseph Galloway, UPI bureau manager from 1976 to 1979, found the clippings particularly useful. A specialist in Soviet space programs, he diligently read through previous files and detected a pattern of ground launchings and orbital dockings that permitted him to predict what the Russians were planning next. His predictions were usually confirmed by a Soviet friend whose neighbor, an engineer, always participated in launchings. Before a launch, the engineer asked Galloway's acquaintance to pick up his mail for the next few days while he was absent. That was the immediate tip-off to the launch, but the massive clipping file provided the further clues.

"We used every tool available to us to find out what was going on in that country, and the techniques that were developed over the years worked well, a damn sight better than maybe the Russians wanted them to," Galloway told me.

The allegation that American correspondents softened critical stories, or refrained from filing "unfavorable" stories to avoid expulsion is, in my experience, generally untrue. Over the decades there may have been a few in that category, but not in numbers sufficient to affect the overall quality of the reporting. As for the perquisites such as rent-free apartments and frequent vacations, they were hardly so attractive as to seduce reporters into compromises with the Soviets. Many of the apartments, especially those of the agency correspondents, were small and shabbily furnished with what Joseph Galloway has described as "Salvation Army" castoffs. For example, Nick and Ruth Daniloff's creaky bed, a UPI perquisite left behind when he departed from Moscow in 1965, was still offering comfort to one of his successors thirteen years later. To accuse correspondents of ingratiating themselves with the Soviets because of the fringe benefits "is extraordinarily fatuous and self-righteous," said Craig Whitney of the *Times*. "Nagorski is being highly unfair to imply that he was one of the few persons in Moscow who conducted himself in a moral and professional fashion and everyone else is a sort of a whore who compromised his principles to get along with the Soviets. I think he has no right to make such a judgment."

"A cheap shot!" commented Stuart Loory.

As for perquisites, one AP correspondent, after four years in Moscow and three years in Warsaw, declined an assignment to Beijing, saying that he wanted to prove to his young daughter that "there was real toilet paper out there in the rest of the world."

*   *   *

Seven decades of American reporting from the Soviet Union reflect a gradual, sometimes erratic, but striking improvement in the working conditions of the correspondents and in the range and depth of their stories. While the freedom to wander around the Soviet Union enjoyed by William Henry Chamberlin in the 1920s, *New Republic* writer Louis Fischer's remarkable access to official archives, and the unimpeded contacts of Eugene Lyons with the Moscow intelligentsia were not matched by later generations of reporters, those earlier correspondents worked under the heavy hand of censorship. To sit down at a telex and transmit a story directly to New York, Washington, or London without thinking of repercussions from the Press Department was inconceivable to me or to my colleagues of the postwar years.

Despite the continuing barriers to reporting inherent in the system, I am convinced that the opportunities for covering all aspects of Soviet life—economic, political, and cultural—are better now than at any time since the Bolshevik Revolution. The challenge to American journalism—indeed, to Western coverage of Soviet affairs—is to raise the quality of the reporting to the level of the story's significance. The place to start is with the correspondents assigned to Moscow, for without a serious effort on the part of editors and publishers to increase reportorial competence, the opportunity will be missed and the victim will be the American public.

Herewith is my checklist for editors responsible for selecting a Moscow correspondent:

• Knowledge of Russian is indispensable. Acquiring it is expensive, but newspapers and TV networks should regard language training as an investment to be amortized over time, possibly by reassigning reporters for more than one tour in Moscow.

• A correspondent should have experience in Washington covering the White House or the State Department, where the issues that concern the USSR are also dealt with: arms control, Afghanistan, NATO, relations with

Eastern Europe, the Mideast, human rights, China, and bilateral issues.

- Background in Soviet and Russian affairs is essential to provide perspective. Muscovy has over a thousand years of history, of which the Soviet era is only a tiny part.
- The reporter should be a tireless, persistent worker ready to spend a hundred hours a week on the job, not so much writing, as observing, experiencing, and remembering. John Chancellor has said that Moscow was his only foreign assignment where 95 percent of his waking time produced story material.
- The correspondent must understand that the Moscow assignment is different from working anywhere else in the world and be prepared to operate as part detective and part diplomat.
- On the personal side, the correspondent should be a mature, stable individual who can represent his or her news organization with dignity and pride.

A considerable number of correspondents did possess many of these qualities, which may explain why, on the whole, the Moscow assignment produced an unusually distinguished corps of reporters. The roster of Moscow "graduates" is studded with the names of men and women who went on to some of the most prominent positions in American journalism. At the *Times*, the Moscow experience seemed to be a prerequisite for promotion. Harrison Salisbury served as national editor, while both Clifton Daniel and Seymour Topping held the post of managing editor; and Max Frankel, who was a Moscow correspondent at age twenty-seven, was named executive editor of the newspaper in 1986. Charlotte Saikowski is Washington bureau chief for *The Christian Science Monitor,* while Ann Garrels covers the White House for NBC. Robert G. Kaiser has moved up to assistant managing editor of the *Washington Post.* CBS anchorman Walter Cronkite endured the grim days of the Cold War for the United Press. John Chancellor and Marvin Kalb earned their TV spurs in Moscow. Robert Gibson went on to become foreign editor of the

Los Angeles Times, and James Jackson held the same title at the *Chicago Tribune.* At ABC, George Watson moved up to vice president for news.

But even a totally competent correspondent can be undermined by an ignoramus on the desk back home. Working with editors who know something about the Soviet Union can make a critical difference. *The New York Times,* for example, has a backup editor for its foreign correspondents, and for Moscow, that person, until his death in 1987, was Theodore Shabad, a walking encyclopedia on the USSR. When Serge Schmemann filed a story on the military budget submitted to the Supreme Soviet in November 1984, Shabad on the foreign desk in New York checked the files and found that this was the highest published level for military expenditures since the end of World War II. The new angle was significant enough to be worked into the lead. On the other hand, when Tom Lambert of the *New York Herald Tribune* phoned a story to New York in 1961 reporting another belligerent statement by Nikita Khrushchev, the deskman asked, "Who?" and "How do you spell it?"

Many correspondents are concerned about editors' preference for the superficial offbeat story showing the Soviets in an unfavorable light over the serious, thoughtful dispatch that was often buried in the back of the newspaper. Such features as the perennial shortage of toilet paper, how drivers make U-turns on Gorky Street, and long lines in food stores, the correspondents called "dumb Russian pieces." Such cliché stories, though, are what some editors think their readers want, and they reinforce the popular image of the Soviet Union. And even the Moscow dateline is often obliged to yield to an editor's other priorities. When, despite UPI's strict orders to use only cable communications instead of the more expensive telephone, Robert Korengold decided to call London about Nikita Khrushchev's latest nuclear threat, the editor at the other end was curt:

"Keep it short, Bud. Elizabeth Taylor is getting a divorce."

An editor who sends a correspondent to Moscow must have full confidence in that individual and provide total support vis-à-vis the Soviets and the story itself. No second-guessing should be permitted. Subject to space and time limitations, publications and networks should use what the correspondent produces based on firsthand information and observation. Anything less can produce embarrassment if not disaster. Time and again I have seen copy in print that was not written by correspondents in Moscow but by editors back home who hadn't the foggiest notion about the true story. Especially susceptible to this treatment were the newsmagazines, with their special format. One of the bad experiences I had as *Newsweek* bureau chief occurred when an item appeared in the "Periscope" column reporting that tanks had been deployed on Moscow streets, presaging ominous developments. Without checking with its Moscow correspondent, *Newsweek* published the item. The tanks and missiles parked on the embankments were, of course, rehearsing for the annual Revolution Day parade—and reported by an American tourist who did not understand what was happening. When the issue arrived in Moscow, the item caused me much embarrassment both with the Soviets, who were angry, and with Western diplomats, who teased me. The other correspondents were appropriately sympathetic.

Over the years, editors have become more sophisticated about reporting from Moscow. No longer are correspondents ordered to "charter a plane" to accompany a visiting dignitary or to obtain the Kremlin's reaction at 4:00 A.M. to a statement by President Reagan. One reason for this gradual growth of awareness is that many former Moscow correspondents have moved up to executive positions at newspapers, networks, and magazines. In addition, many editors have visited the Soviet Union and seen firsthand the working conditions under which their reporters labor. The Moscow visit is especially effective treatment for network executives and publishers accustomed to luxury hotels, super service, and fawning natives. The reality of a stay at the Hotel National or the Metropole, the inaccessibility of Soviet officials, their hostility, and their pervasive rudeness are jolting experiences that allow the editors to return to the

United States with a clearer idea of what correspondents must cope with daily.

Just as editors are important to the Moscow correspondent, so is the government of the United States. Ever since the Harding administration insisted in 1921 that the American people must be informed about the food distribution in famine-stricken Russia and thus pried open the doors for American reporters, Washington has played an important role in establishing the ground rules for working in Moscow. The U.S. government's official position has been, and still is, to use all diplomatic means to buttress the efforts of American news media to report on every facet of life in the USSR. That attitude is not likely to change in the foreseeable future. The government will continue to press the Soviets to improve conditions for correspondents, to institutionalize increased access to news sources, to provide unimpeded travel, and especially to protect correspondents from harassment in the exercise of their professional responsibilities. Only unremitting efforts to enforce the Helsinki Accords, which provide the legal basis for pressure on the Soviets, can achieve these goals. Although the Kremlin will attempt to undercut the Helsinki Accords, especially by delaying or withholding visas for Americans regarded with disfavor, the United States can be expected to retaliate, the only language the Russians understand. In fact, the State Department has already established a policy that extends beyond journalists. When visa applications of American reporters are held up, the United States will delay approval of visas for other Soviets, including officials assigned to the USSR mission to the United Nations.

Arthur A. Hartman, U.S. envoy to Moscow from 1981 to 1987, told me that the embassy had frequently warned the Foreign Ministry that the United States was prepared to increase the stakes and might expel two Soviets for one American, and not necessarily journalists.

"If we let the Soviets pick our correspondents," he said, "we are in serious trouble."

*   *   *

In 1948, one of the most trying years of the Cold War, Reuters correspondent Don Dallas wrote his London editor that "Moscow needs strong nerves and patience." His admonition will continue to hold true as American journalists report on a society that, if it does change under Mikhail Gorbachev's prodding, will change slowly. Confrontation between correspondent and Communist will remain a fundamental of political life in the USSR and be so recognized by Americans and Soviets. But since Dallas wrote those words, much has changed. The Cold War is history, although occasionally its atmosphere has been revived, and working and living conditions for reporters have vastly improved. What has not changed is the importance of Moscow, which together with Washington remains one of the two great news centers of the world.

With the Soviet Union possibly entering a new era, American correspondents face fresh challenges and opportunities as they witness Mikhail Gorbachev's attempts to carry out his ambitious reforms. At the beginning of the eighteenth century, Peter the Great had a similar "modernization" agenda; he secularized the Russian Orthodox Church and vanquished the powerful boyars to drag Old Russia into the mainstream of European politics and technology. With less power than the almighty tsar but able to communicate with his countrymen in ways that Peter could not even imagine, Gorbachev may succeed in launching a process that will, as he has admitted, take generations. In a tradition that now goes back almost seventy years, American correspondents in Moscow will be there to watch, interpret, and report on that turbulent, fascinating, and complex country.

If the general secretary can carry out his *glasnost* policy, open up Soviet society and restructure the economy, the Kremlin beat, as Robert Toth has put it, "is going to be one helluva story."

Bibliography

(Books followed by an asterisk are recommended for future Moscow correspondents.)

Atkinson, Oriana. *Over at Uncle Joe's.* Indianapolis, Ind.: Bobbs-Merrill Company, 1947.

Bohlen, Charles E. *Witness to History: 1929–1969.** New York: W. W. Norton & Company, 1973.

Bourke-White, Margaret. *Shooting the Russian War.* New York: Simon & Schuster, 1943.

Cassidy, Henry C. *Moscow Dateline.** Boston: Houghton Mifflin Company, 1943.

Davies, Joseph E. *Mission to Moscow.* New York: Pocket Books, 1943.

Deane, John R. *The Strange Alliance.* New York: Viking Press, 1947.

Doder, Dusko. *Shadows and Whispers: Power Politics Inside the Kremlin from Brezhnev to Gorbachev.** New York: Random House, 1986.

Duranty, Walter. *I Write as I Please.** New York: Simon & Schuster, 1935.

Gelb, Barbara. *So Short a Time.* New York: W. W. Norton & Company, 1973.

Gibbons, Edward. *Floyd Gibbons: Your Headline Hunter.* New York: Exposition Press, 1953.

Gilmore, Eddy. *Me and My Russian Wife.* Garden City, N.Y: Doubleday & Company, 1954.

Gramling, Oliver. *AP—The Story of the News.* New York: Farrar & Rinehart, 1940.

Hart, B. H. Liddell. *History of the Second World War.* New York: G. P. Putnam's Sons, 1971.

Kaiser, Robert G. *Russia: The People and the Power.** New York: Atheneum, 1976.

Kennan, George F. *Memoirs, 1925–1950.** Boston: Little, Brown & Company, 1967.

————. *Russia and the West.** Boston: Little, Brown & Company, 1961.

Khrushchev, Nikita S. *Khrushchev Remembers** (translated and edited by Strobe Talbot). Boston: Little, Brown & Company, 1970.

Kirk, Lydia. *Postmarked Moscow.* New York: Charles Scribner's Sons, 1952.

Knightley, Phillip. *The First Casualty.* New York: Harcourt Brace Jovanovich, 1975.

Lauterbach, Richard E. *These Are the Russians.* New York: Harper & Brothers, 1944.

Lesueur, Larry. *Twelve Months That Changed the World.* New York: Alfred A. Knopf, 1943.

Lyons, Eugene. *Assignment in Utopia.** New York: Harcourt, Brace & Company, 1937.

————. *Moscow Carrousel.* New York: Alfred A. Knopf, 1935.

Magidoff, Robert. *In Anger and Pity.* Garden City, N.Y.: Doubleday & Company, 1949.

Moats, Alice-Leone. *Blind Date with Mars.* Garden City, N.Y.: Doubleday, Doran & Company, 1943.

Morehead, Alan. *The Russian Revolution.* New York: Harper & Brothers, 1958.

Morris, Joe Alex. *Deadline Every Minute.* Garden City, N.Y.: Doubleday & Company, 1957.

Muggeridge, Malcolm. *Chronicles of Wasted Time.* Vol. 1, *The Green Stick.* New York: William Morrow & Company, 1973.

Nagorski, Andrew. *Reluctant Farewell.* New York: Holt, Rinehart & Winston, 1985.

Pares, Sir Bernard. *A History of Russia.** New York: Alfred A. Knopf, 1944.

Rauch, Georg von. *A History of Soviet Russia.* New York: Praeger Publishers, 1972.

Reed, John. *Ten Days That Shook the World.** New York: Modern Library, 1935.

Salisbury, Harrison E. *Journey for Our Times.* New York: Harper & Row, 1983.

————. *Without Fear or Favor.* New York: Times Books, 1980.

Schapiro, Leonard. *The Communist Party of the Soviet Union.** New York: Random House, 1960.

Schechter, Leona P. *An American Family in Moscow.* Boston: Little, Brown & Company, 1975.

Seldes, George. *Tell the Truth and Run.* New York: Greenberg: Publisher, 1953.

Shipler, David K. *Russia: Broken Idols, Solemn Dreams.** New York: Times Books, 1983.

Simon, Sascha. *Moscou.* Paris: Fayard, 1964.

Smith, Hedrick. *The Russians.** New York: Quadrangle/*The New York Times* Book Company, 1976.

Smith, Homer. *Black Man in Red Russia.* Chicago: Johnson Publishing Company, 1964.

Smith, Walter Bedell. *My Three Years in Moscow.* Philadelphia: J. B. Lippincott Company, 1950.

Steel, Ronald. *Walter Lippmann and the American Century.* Boston: Little, Brown & Company, 1980.

Stevens, Edmund. *This Is Russia—Un-Censored.* New York: Eton Books, 1951.

Stone, Melville E. *Fifty Years a Journalist.* Garden City, N.Y.: Doubleday, Page & Company, 1921.

Wells, Linton. *Blood on the Moon.* Boston: Houghton Mifflin Company, 1937.

Werth, Alexander. *Russia at War: 1941–1945.** New York: E. P. Dutton & Company, 1964.

———. *Russia: The Post-War Years.* New York: Taplinger Publishing Company, 1971.

White, William L. *Report on the Russians.* New York: Harcourt Brace & Company, 1945.

Whitney, Thomas P. *Russia in My Life.** New York: Reynal & Company, 1962.

Williams, Albert Rhys. *Journey into Revolution: Petrograd, 1917–1919.* Chicago: Quadrangle Books, 1969.

INDEX